TEACHER'S MANUAL

4

FOCUS
ON
GRAMMAR

AN INTEGRATED SKILLS APPROACH

THIRD EDITION

JEAN ZUKOWSKI/FAUST

PEARSON
Longman

Focus on Grammar 4: An Integrated Skills Approach, Teacher's Manual

Pearson Education, 10 Bank Street, White Plains, NY 10606

Staff credits: The people who made up the *Focus on Grammar 4 Teacher's Manual* team,
   representing editorial, production, design, and manufacturing, are: Rhea Banker,
   Christine Edmonds, Nancy Flaggman, Ann France, Laura Le Dréan, Martha
   McGaughey, and Kathleen Silloway.
Cover images: Large shell, background, Nick Koudis, RF; large shell, center image,
   Kaz Chiba; background, Comstock Images, RF
Text design: Quorum Creative Services, Rhea Banker
Text composition: ElectraGraphics, Inc.
Text font: 10/12 New Aster, 10/13 Myriad Roman

ISBN: 0-13-191234-8

LONGMAN ON THE **WEB**

Longman.com offers online resources for
teachers and students. Access our Companion
Websites, our online catalog, and our local
offices around the world.

Visit us at **longman.com**.

Printed in the United States of America
   5 6 7 8 9 10—BAH—12 11 10 09 08 07

Contents

Introduction

The *Focus on Grammar* series

Written by ESL/EFL professionals, *Focus on Grammar: An Integrated Skills Approach* helps students to understand and practice English grammar. The primary aim of the course is for students to gain confidence in their ability to speak and write English accurately and fluently.

The **third edition** retains this popular series' focus on English grammar through lively listening, speaking, reading, and writing activities. The new *Focus on Grammar* also maintains the same five-level progression as the second edition:

- Level 1 (Beginning, formerly Introductory)
- Level 2 (High-Beginning, formerly Basic)
- Level 3 (Intermediate)
- Level 4 (High-Intermediate)
- Level 5 (Advanced)

What is the *Focus on Grammar* methodology?

Both controlled and communicative practice

While students expect and need to learn the formal rules of a language, it is crucial that they also practice new structures in a variety of contexts in order to internalize and master them. To this end, *Focus on Grammar* provides an abundance of both controlled and communicative exercises so that students can bridge the gap between knowing grammatical structures and using them. The many communicative activities in each Student Book unit provide opportunities for critical thinking while enabling students to personalize what they have learned.

A unique four-step approach

The series follows a four-step approach:

Step 1: Grammar in Context shows the new structures in natural contexts, such as articles and conversations.

Step 2: Grammar Presentation presents the structures in clear and accessible grammar charts, notes, and examples.

Step 3: Focused Practice of both form and meaning of the new structures is provided in numerous and varied controlled exercises.

Step 4: Communication Practice allows students to use the new structures freely and creatively in motivating, open-ended activities.

Thorough recycling

Underpinning the scope and sequence of the *Focus on Grammar* series is the belief that students need to use target structures many times, in different contexts, and at increasing levels of difficulty. For this reason, new grammar is constantly recycled throughout the book so that students have maximum exposure to the target forms and become comfortable using them in speech and in writing.

A complete classroom text and reference guide

A major goal in the development of *Focus on Grammar* has been to provide students with books that serve not only as vehicles for classroom instruction but also as resources for reference and self-study. In each Student Book, the combination of grammar charts, grammar notes, a glossary of grammar terms, and extensive appendices provides a complete and invaluable reference guide for students.

Ongoing assessment

Review Tests at the end of each part of the Student Book allow for self-assessment. In addition, the tests in the new *Focus on Grammar* Assessment Package provide teachers with a valid, reliable, and practical means of determining students' appropriate levels of placement in the course and of assessing students' achievement throughout the course. At Levels 4 (High-Intermediate) and 5 (Advanced), Proficiency Tests give teachers an overview of their students' general grammar knowledge.

What are the components of each level of *Focus on Grammar*?

Student Book

The Student Book is divided into eight or more parts, depending on the level. Each part contains grammatically related units, with each unit focusing on specific grammatical structures; where appropriate, units present contrasting forms. The exercises in each unit are thematically related to one another, and all units have the same clear, easy-to-follow format.

Teacher's Manual

The Teacher's Manual contains a variety of suggestions and information to enrich the material in the Student Book. It includes general teaching suggestions for each section of a typical unit, answers to frequently asked questions, unit-by-unit teaching tips with ideas for further communicative practice, and a supplementary activity section. Answers to the Student Book exercises and audioscripts of the listening activities are found at the back of the Teacher's Manual. Also included in the Teacher's Manual is a CD-ROM that includes PowerPoint® presentations that offer alternative ways of presenting selected grammar structures.

Workbook

The Workbook accompanying each level of *Focus on Grammar* provides additional exercises for self-study of the target grammar for each unit. Tests included in each Workbook provide students with additional opportunities for self-assessment.

Audio Programs

The Student Book Class Audio Program includes the listening activities, the Grammar in Context passages, and various other exercises. The symbol ∩ identifies audio for the listening exercises. The symbol ∩ next to the Grammar in Context passages and other exercises indicates that the listening is optional. Audioscripts for the listening exercises are located in the back of the Teacher's Manual.

Some Student Books are packaged with a Student Audio CD. This CD includes the listening exercise from each unit.

CD-ROM

The *Focus on Grammar* CD-ROM provides students with individualized practice and immediate feedback. Fully contextualized and interactive, the activities extend practice of the grammatical structures in the reading, writing, speaking, and listening skills areas. The CD-ROM includes grammar review, review tests, score-based remedial practice, games, and all relevant reference material from the Student Book. It can also be used in conjunction with the *Longman Interactive American Dictionary* CD-ROM.

Assessment Package (NEW)

A comprehensive Assessment Package has been developed for each level of the third edition of *Focus on Grammar*. The components of the Assessment Package are:

1. Placement, Diagnostic, and Achievement Tests

- a Placement Test to screen students and place them into the correct level
- Diagnostic Tests for each part of the Student Book
- Unit Achievement Tests for each unit of the Student Book
- Part Achievement Tests for each part of the Student Book

2. General Proficiency Tests

- two Proficiency Tests at Level 4 (High-Intermediate)
- two Proficiency Tests at Level 5 (Advanced)

These tests can be administered at any point in the course.

3. Audio CD

- Audio CDs include the listening portions of the Placement, Diagnostic, and Achievement Tests.
- The audioscripts for the tests are located in the Assessment Package.

4. Test-Generating Software

The test-bank software provides thousands of questions from which teachers can create class-appropriate tests. All items are labeled according to the grammar structure they are testing, so teachers can easily select relevant items; they can also design their own items to add to their tests.

Transparencies (NEW)

Transparencies of all the grammar charts in the Student Book are also available. These transparencies are classroom visual aids that help instructors point out and explain important patterns and structures of grammar.

Companion Website

The *Focus on Grammar* companion website (www. longman.com/focusongrammar) contains a wealth of information and activities for both teachers and students. In addition to general information about the course pedagogy, the website provides extensive practice exercises for the classroom, a language lab, or at home.

What's new in the third edition of the Student Book?

In response to users' requests, this edition has:

- a new four-color design
- easy-to-read color coding for the four steps
- new and updated reading texts for Grammar in Context
- post-reading activities (in addition to the pre-reading questions)
- more exercise items
- an editing (error analysis) exercise in each unit
- an Internet activity in each unit
- a Glossary of Grammar Terms
- expanded Appendices

References

Alexander, L. G. (1988). *Longman English Grammar.* White Plains: Longman.

Biber, D., S. Conrad, E. Finegan, S. Johansson, and G. Leech (1999). *Longman Grammar of Spoken and Written English.* White Plains: Longman.

Celce-Murcia, M., and D. Freeman (1999). *The Grammar Book.* Boston: Heinle and Heinle.

Celce-Murcia, M., and S. Hilles (1988). *Techniques and Resources in Teaching Grammar.* New York: Oxford University Press.

Firsten, R. (2002). *The ELT Grammar Book.* Burlingame, CA: Alta Book Center Publishers.

Garner, B. (2003). *Garner's Modern American Usage.* New York: Oxford University Press.

Greenbaum, S. (1996). *The Oxford English Grammar.* New York: Oxford University Press.

Leech, G. (2004). *Meaning and the English Verb.* Harlow, UK: Pearson.

Lewis, M. (1997). *Implementing the Lexical Approach.* Hove, East Sussex, UK: Language Teaching Publications.

Longman (2002). *Longman Dictionary of English Language and Culture.* Harlow, UK: Longman.

Willis, D. (2003). *Rules, Patterns and Words.* New York: Cambridge University Press.

About the *Focus on Grammar* Teacher's Manual

This Teacher's Manual offers a multitude of ideas for working with the material in *Focus on Grammar 4: An Integrated Skills Approach,* third edition. In this manual, you will find the following information:

- **General Teaching Tips** (pages 1–14) describe the principles underlying the course and give suggestions for teaching the activities in the Student Book. A Strategies for Teaching Grammar page offers a quick reference for some of the most common and useful grammar teaching techniques. A Frequently Asked Questions section answers some of the most common issues encountered by teachers.
- **Unit-by-Unit Teaching Tips** (pages 15–90) give you additional ideas for completing the activities unique to each unit.
- **Supplementary Activities** (pages 91–99) provide extra practice exercises for use during your presentation of a grammar point.
- **Scoring Rubrics for Speaking and Writing** are provided on pages 100 and 101 of the Teacher's Manual. You can use the rubrics to assess various speaking and writing tasks throughout the Student Book.
- **Audioscripts** and the **Student Book Answer Key** are included at the back of the Teacher's Manual for easy reference.

The **PowerPoint® presentations CD-ROM** bound into this Teacher's Manual includes additional teaching tools and resources:

- **PowerPoint® presentations** for selected units in the Student Book offer an innovative method for the contextualized instruction of grammar. These theme-based, user-friendly presentations contain a variety of colorful graphics and animations to engage a wide range of learning styles. In addition to providing a stimulating visual reinforcement of the Grammar Notes, these presentations also include interactive practice activities.
- A **PowerPoint® presentation guide,** included on the CD-ROM in PDF format, offers guidelines for using the **PowerPoint® presentations.** It contains a variety of suggestions for getting the most out of the presentations in terms of both instructional benefit and learner participation.
- **Transparencies** of all Grammar Charts in the Student Book offer an additional teaching tool for presenting the target grammar points in the classroom.
- **Graphic Organizers** can be printed out and used in the classroom or assigned as homework. The graphic organizers provide support through the steps of pre-writing and writing a first draft.
- **Rubrics for assessing speaking and writing tasks** help teachers provide helpful feedback to students. Teachers are encouraged to use the scoring system provided, as well as write specific notes based on each student's performance.

General Teaching Tips

These tips are designed to guide you in teaching the recurring sections of the Teacher's Manual and Student Book. Experimenting with the various options will enliven your classroom and appeal to students' different learning styles.

In the following section and in the Unit-by-Unit Teaching Tips, the icon ⊕ indicates an optional step you may wish to include if time permits.

Unit Overview

The Unit Overview (offered in the Teacher's Manual) highlights the most important grammar points of each unit. It also points out common grammar trouble spots for students. You may also find it helpful to review the Grammar Charts and Grammar Notes in the Student Book before teaching each unit.

Grammar in Context

Each unit of the Student Book begins with a reading selection designed to raise students' interest and expose them to the target grammar in a realistic, natural context. The selections include newspaper and magazine excerpts, websites, newsletters, advertisements, conversations, and other formats that students may encounter in their day-to-day lives. All of the texts are also available on the Audio Program.

Background Notes

Where appropriate, background notes are provided in the Teacher's Manual to explain cultural and historical terms or concepts that appear in a reading selection. You can introduce these terms and concepts to students during a warm-up discussion, or you can use the notes as a reference if questions come up as students are reading.

Following the Background Notes is a list of vocabulary words and expressions that may be unfamiliar to students. Rather than pre-teaching these terms, you may wish to wait until students have finished reading. This allows students to focus on reading for general comprehension, building their reading fluency. See the section on vocabulary below for some ideas on how to respond to students' vocabulary questions.

Before You Read (5 minutes)

This pre-reading activity creates interest, elicits students' knowledge about the topic, and encourages students to make predictions about the reading.

Suggested Procedure for Before You Read
1. Have the class cover up the text and look at the illustrations.
2. Ask students to respond to the questions. Ask these questions in a conversational way, instead of reading them from the book.

Option A
- Have students work in pairs to read the questions and discuss their answers.
- Call on pairs to share their ideas with the class.

Option B
- Ask pairs of students to think about what they want to know about the topic and/or to prepare some questions they have about the topic.
- Call on pairs to share some of their questions and write them on the board.
- Have students try to find the information as they read.

Option C
- Have students work in groups of three.
- Each student chooses a question to memorize and, with books closed, ask their partners.
- Call on various groups to share their answers with the class.

Reading (15–25 minutes)

Depending on the needs of your class, have students complete the reading in class or at home (procedures for both options are given below). Whichever option you choose, encourage students (1) to read with a purpose; (2) to read the passage through once or twice without stopping for unknown words; and (3) to identify and deal with new vocabulary.

Comprehension questions and discussion topics are offered in the Unit-by-Unit Teaching Tips to supplement the grammar-focused activities of the Student Book.

Suggested Procedure for Reading

1. Play the audio and have students follow along in their books.
2. Write the comprehension questions from the Unit-by-Unit Teaching Tips on the board.
3. Have students read the passage again silently, looking for answers to the questions.
4. ⏱ Have students discuss their answers with a partner or in small groups.
5. Call on individuals to share their answers with the class.
6. Spend a few minutes going over any unfamiliar vocabulary terms. (See suggested procedures for Vocabulary.)
7. ⏱ Put students in pairs or small groups to discuss the reading. Invite them to respond to the reading in a way that is meaningful to them: What was most interesting? What did they learn? Refer to the Discussion Topics in the Unit-by-Unit Teaching Tips to help generate ideas for discussion.

Option A (At Home/In Class)

- Write the comprehension questions on the board for students to copy, or prepare them as a handout for students to take home.
- Have students read the passage and answer the questions at home.
- ⏱ Have students write a few additional questions about the reading.
- In class, have students work in pairs or small groups to discuss their answers.
- ⏱ Have students take turns asking and answering questions they prepared at home.
- Follow steps 5–7 in the Suggested Procedure for Reading above.

Option B (In Class)

- Have students work in pairs. Divide the reading in half, and have each student in the pair read one half.
- Have students summarize the information in their half of the reading for their partner.
- Follow steps 5–6 in the previous notes for Suggested Procedure for Reading.

Vocabulary

After students have read the passage and answered the comprehension questions, spend a few minutes going over any unfamiliar vocabulary terms. In addition to using the definitions provided in the Unit-by-Unit Teaching Tips, you may wish to use illustrations in the Student Book or pictures that you supply to illustrate the meaning of new words.

Suggested Procedure for Vocabulary

1. Have students make lists of the words in the reading they need help with.
2. Allow them to use their dictionaries or to work with other students to discuss, search for and find the meanings, or ask you for assistance.
3. ⏱ Write the new vocabulary items on the board, or have students write them, and provide definitions.
4. Encourage students to keep a record of vocabulary items by using a notebook or by making vocabulary cards. The entries should include a definition and an example sentence. Suggest that they be on the lookout for other examples of these items and add any new examples they find to their notebooks or cards.

Where appropriate, encourage students to draw pictures on the card or to record any information that helps them remember the vocabulary item. It may be helpful for students to include a translation of the new term in their own language.

Here's one way to do a vocabulary card:

```
                                    [front]
_____


               thrill (n., v., adj.)

_____

_____

_____

_____
```

```
                                     [back]
(n) + (adj) a strong feeling of excitement

and pleasure; (v) to feel or make someone

feel strong excitement or pleasure

(n) My grandmother always gets a thrill

when I call her.

(v) The skaters thrilled their fans with their

high jumps.

(adj) I was thrilled to hear the good news.
```

Option A
- Write new vocabulary and definitions on the board, but do not write the definitions next to the corresponding words.
- Ask students to find the appropriate match.

Option B
- If classroom time is limited, allow students to consult their dictionaries as they are reading.
- Remind them that they will not necessarily need to know the meaning of every word in order to understand the meaning of the passage.

After You Read (5 minutes)
These post-reading questions help students focus on the meaning of the target grammar without explicitly presenting the grammar point.

Suggested Procedure for After You Read
1. Have students work individually to answer the questions.
2. Tell students to compare answers with a partner.
3. Call on volunteers to read their answers aloud.

Grammar Presentation

There are many ways to teach the material in the Grammar Presentation. As a general rule, the more varied and lively the classroom activities, the more engaged students will be—and the more learning will occur! Approaching grammar from different angles and trying out different classroom management options can help increase student motivation.

The Strategies for Teaching Grammar on page 11 provides some guidelines to keep in mind when presenting a new grammar point. In addition to these strategies and the procedures outlined below, you can find specific suggestions for presenting the unit's grammar in the Unit-by-Unit Teaching Tips.

Identify the Grammar (5–10 minutes)
This section in the Teacher's Manual provides support for you to help students identify the target grammatical structures embedded in the reading. This helps students learn the usage of the target grammar point and helps you make a smooth transition from Grammar in Context to the Grammar Presentation.

Suggested Procedure for Identify the Grammar
1. Choose an example of the target grammar from the reading and write it on the board. The Unit-by-Unit Teaching Tips provide examples that focus on specific features of that grammar point.
2. Point out that the target grammar is presented in boldfaced type in the reading for easy identification. Elicit more examples from students and write them on the board.
3. Find out what your students may already know about that grammar point. List the information you have elicited on the board. As students continue with the Grammar Presentation, encourage them to compare these notes with the information presented in the Grammar Charts and Grammar Notes.

After studying the target grammar in context, students should be ready to study the isolated forms, meanings, and usage. You can use the charts, notes, and examples to present and review the grammatical structures in a straightforward and comprehensive way.

Note that common grammatical terms are used throughout the Grammar Presentations because they help make the explanations clearer and because students often have learned them in their own language. If students are having trouble understanding the grammatical terms, encourage them to use the Glossary provided in the back of the Student Book.

Grammar Charts (5–10 minutes)

The Grammar Charts provide a clear reference of all the forms of the target grammar. Students also become familiar with grammatical terminology. The charts also enable you to pre-teach some of the Grammar Notes that follow. In addition to the charts in the Student Book, you may want to use the Focus on Grammar Transparencies (on the CD-ROM in the back of this Teacher's Manual) to help direct all of your students' attention to the same focus point.

Suggested Procedure for Grammar Charts

1. Using the examples you wrote on the board (see Identify the Grammar above) and/or Focus on Grammar Transparencies, draw students' attention to important features in the models by asking them questions or by pointing out the key features.
2. Confirm students' understanding by engaging them in some recognition activities. Try one or two activities from Strategies 3, 4, 5, or 6 (page 11).
3. Get students to manipulate the new structures through substitution or transformation drills. See Strategy 7 (page 11) for an example of a transformation drill.
4. Encourage students to make sentences that are personally meaningful using the new grammar.

Option A

- Have students study the Grammar Charts at home.
- In class, follow step 1 in the suggested procedure above.
- Move directly to the Grammar Notes section. Carry out steps 2, 3, and 4 in the suggested procedure above using the notes together with the charts.

Option B

- Assign individual students responsibility for presenting a topic to the class by combining the information in the charts and the relevant notes. Give them newsprint and a marker to prepare a display in class or at home.
- ⏱ Meet with students individually. Allow them to rehearse their presentations and provide any coaching needed.
- Call on students to present their topics to the class. Encourage class questions.
- Choose appropriate practice activities from Strategies 4–8 (page 11) OR move directly to the Grammar Notes section.

Grammar Notes (10–30 minutes)

These notes provide helpful information about meaning, use, and form of the grammatical structures that students have encountered in the introductory reading selection and Grammar Charts. They include the following features to help students understand and use the forms.

- Where appropriate, time lines illustrate the meaning of verb forms and their relationship to one another.
- *Be careful!* notes alert students to common errors among English language learners.
- *Usage Notes* provide guidelines for using and understanding different levels of formality and correctness.
- *Pronunciation Notes* are provided when appropriate.
- Below the notes and examples, references to related structures are provided.

The Grammar Notes section includes cross-references to the Focused Practice exercises in the Student Book and to the Supplementary Activities in this Teacher's Manual. Have students complete the appropriate exercises after you present each note. This breaks up the grammar presentation into manageable chunks and allows students to check their understanding of the note.

Suggested Procedure for Grammar Notes

1. Have students read each note at home and/or in class.
2. For each note, write examples on the board and elicit from students the important features of the form (see Strategy 1, page 11, for suggestions) or point out the key features yourself.
3. If possible, demonstrate the meaning of the grammatical form(s) by performing actions (see Strategy 6, page 11).

4. Model the examples and have students repeat after you so that they become comfortable with the appropriate stress, intonation, and rhythm.

5. Engage students with the grammar point by choosing appropriate activities, for example:
- Elicit examples of the target structure.
- Confirm students' understanding by having them categorize examples or perform actions that illustrate structure. See Strategies 5 and 6 (page 11) for examples.
- Provide controlled practice with quick substitution or transformation drills.
- Encourage students to make personally meaningful sentences using the new grammatical forms.
- Use the Focused Practice exercises in the Student Book and/or the Supplementary Activities starting on page 91 of this Teacher's Manual.

6. You may want to repeat steps 2–5 for each Grammar Note. Where appropriate, the Unit-by-Unit Teaching Tips give suggestions for presenting two or more notes simultaneously.

Option
- Photocopy one set of Grammar Notes for each group of three or four students in your class. Cut them up so that the notes and their corresponding examples are not attached.
- Divide the class into groups of three or four students and give a set of cut-up notes to each group.
- Give students their task:
  1. Match the examples with the correct notes.
  2. Attach the notes and corresponding examples to a sheet of newsprint (a large piece of paper).
  3. Have students create more examples for each note.
- Circulate to ensure that students are on the right track, and provide help as needed.
- Have students post their results around the room, and invite groups to look at each other's work.
- Regroup as a whole class to answer questions.

Focused Practice

The exercises in this section provide practice for the structures in the Grammar Presentation. You may wish to have students complete the corresponding exercise immediately after you have presented the relevant Grammar Note. Another option is for students to complete one or more of the exercises at home, using the cross-references to the Grammar Note(s) for support.

If you decide to have students complete the exercises in class, you can keep them motivated by varying the order of the exercises and/or the way you conduct them. Following are various ways of conducting the exercises. In the Unit-by-Unit Teaching Tips, you will find definitions for potentially unfamiliar words and phrases that appear in the Focused Practice exercises.

Discover the Grammar (5–10 minutes)
This opening activity gets students to identify the target grammar structures in a realistic context. This recognition-only activity raises awareness of the structures as it builds confidence.

Suggested Procedure for Discover the Grammar
1. Go over the example with the class.
2. Have students complete the exercise individually or in pairs.
3. Elicit the correct answers from students.

Controlled Practice Exercises (5–10 minutes each)
Following the Discover the Grammar activity are exercises that provide practice in a controlled, but still contextualized, environment. The exercises proceed from simpler to more complex and include a variety of exercise types such as fill-in-the-blanks, matching, and multiple-choice. Exercises are cross-referenced to the appropriate Grammar Notes so that students can review as necessary. Students are exposed to many different written formats, including letters, electronic bulletin boards, résumés, charts, and graphs. Many exercises are art-based, providing a rich context for meaningful practice.

Options
- Have students work in pairs to complete the exercises.
- If the exercise is in the form of a conversation, have students complete the exercise and then work in pairs to practice and perform the conversation for the class.
- When going over answers with students, have them explain why each answer is correct.
- Whenever possible, relate exercises to students' own lives. For example, if an exercise includes a time line, elicit from

students some important events that have happened in their own lives.

Editing (10 minutes)

All units include an editing exercise to build students' awareness of incorrect usage of the target grammar structures. Students identify and correct errors in a contextualized passage such as a student's composition, a journal entry, or an online message-board posting. The direction line indicates the number of errors in the passage.

Suggested Procedure for Editing

1. Have students read through the passage quickly to understand its context and meaning.
2. Tell students to read the passage line by line, circling incorrect structures and writing in the corrections.
3. Have students take turns reading the passage line by line, saying the structures correctly. Alternatively, read the passage aloud to the class and have students interrupt you with their corrections.
4. There are also usually examples of the correct usage of the structures in each editing exercise. After students have identified the errors, point out the correct usages and ask why they are not errors.

Communication Practice

These in-class exercises give students the opportunity to use the target structure in communicative activities. These activities help develop listening and speaking fluency and critical thinking skills, as well as provide opportunities for students to "own" the structures. As with the Focused Practice exercises, you may wish to vary the order of these activities to keep student motivation high.

Since there are many different exercise types in the Communication Practice section, specific ideas and guidelines are provided in the Unit-by-Unit Teaching Tips. Following are general suggestions for the three main types of exercises. (Note: See the FAQ on pages 12–14 for more information about setting up pair work and group work.)

Listening (10 minutes)

Each Communication Practice section begins with a listening and a comprehension exercise. Students hear a variety of listening formats, including conversations, television scripts,

weather forecasts, and interviews. After listening, students complete a task that focuses on the form or meaning of the target grammar structure. The listening exercises are included on the Student CD so that students may also complete these exercises outside of class.

Suggested Procedure for Listening

Before students listen
1. Explain the situation or context of the listening passage. Provide any necessary cultural information, and pre-teach any vocabulary students may need to know. Definitions are provided in the Unit-by-Unit Teaching Tips for words and phrases that may be unfamiliar to students. (Note that some of these words and phrases may appear in the listening, not in the exercise itself.)
2. Ask students to read the exercise questions first so that they know what to listen for.

Listening
1. Play the audio or read the audioscript aloud. If you choose to read:
   • Speak with a lot of expression and at a natural pace.
   • Change positions and tone of voice to indicate who the speaker is. Another method is to draw stick figures on the board and label them with the characters' names so that you can point to the appropriate character as you change roles.
2. Have students listen the first time with their pencils down.
3. Have students listen again and complete the task.
4. You may want to let students listen as many times as necessary to complete the task.

After students listen
1. Elicit answers for the exercise items and write them on the board. Answer any questions the students may have.
2. ⏱ Students listen a final time and review the passage.

Option A
• Make photocopies of the audioscript and hand it out to students.
• Play the audio recording and have students read along with it in chorus. Explain that this exercise will help them to hear and practice the rhythms, stresses, and clusters of English sounds.

Option B
Have students listen and complete the exercise at home or in a language lab.

Role Plays (10–20 minutes)

In these classroom speaking activities, students role-play a real-life encounter, such as a business meeting or an interview.

Advantages of Role Plays
• They are fun and motivating for most students.
• Role-playing characters often allows the more hesitant students to be more outgoing than if they are speaking as themselves.
• By broadening the world of the classroom to the world outside, role playing allows students to use a wider range of language than less open-ended activities.

Suggested Procedure for Role Plays
1. When possible, bring in props or costumes to add drama and fun.
2. Review the task so students understand what is required.
3. Perform a sample role play with a volunteer in front of the class.
4. Divide the class into the suggested groupings and give them a fixed time limit for completing the task.
5. Have students write a script for the role play. Then have them write key words on cards and perform the role play using the cards as prompts. OR Have students plan the action without a script and present it extemporaneously.
6. While students are working, circulate among the pairs or groups to answer students' questions and help them with the activity.
7. Have various pairs or groups perform their role plays in front of the class. If possible, tape-record or videotape the role plays for students' own listening or viewing. You may want to use the Speaking Rubric on page 100.

Information Gaps (10–20 minutes)

These games are designed to encourage communication between students. In these activities, each student has a different set of information. Students have to talk to their partners to solve a puzzle, draw a picture (describe and draw), put things in the right order (describe and arrange), or find similarities and differences between pictures.

Advantages of Information Gaps
• Like role plays, information gaps are motivating and fun.
• Information gaps are additionally motivating because there is a real need for communication in order to combine the information to solve a problem and complete the task.
• Information sharing allows students to extend and personalize what they have learned in the unit.

Suggested Procedure for Information Gaps
1. Explain how the Student A and Student B pages relate to each other (how they are different or similar).
2. Refer students to the examples and to any language provided.
3. Divide the class into pairs (Student A and Student B) and have them position themselves so that they cannot see the contents of each other's books.
4. Tell the Student Bs what page to turn to, and circulate to check that they are looking at the correct page.
5. Have students read their separate instructions. Check comprehension of the task by asking each group, "What are you going to do?"
6. Remind students not to show each other the contents of their pages.
7. As students are working, circulate to answer individual questions and to help students with the activity.

Writing (15–25 minutes in-class time)

These activities give students the opportunity to develop their writing skills and provide additional practice using the target grammatical structures. There is a variety of realistic formats, including paragraphs, essays, letters, and journal entries. The themes are related to material covered in the unit so that students already have some preparation for the writing task.

A Scoring Rubric for Writing is included on page 101 so that you can assess students' general writing skills as well as their ability to apply the target grammar point within a written context. This rubric allows you to give students a holistic score from 1 to 5 that reflects how well students have responded to the topic, organized their ideas, and incorporated the new grammar points from the unit. It is best to hand out copies to students before they begin working on the assignment, so that they understand what competencies are required.

The rubric provided in this book is for classroom use. To see an example of a rubric used to evaluate writing in a formal assessment situation, you can look at the one used by raters of the writing section on the TOEFL® iBT. This is available to download at http://ftp.ets.org/pub/toefl/Writing_Rubrics.pdf.

Suggested Procedure for Writing
Pre-writing
1. Go over the requirements of the assignment to make sure students understand what they are expected to do.
2. Write some questions on the board, and have students work in pairs or small groups to brainstorm ideas for the writing assignment. The Unit-by-Unit Teaching Tips provide suggestions for questions you might write on the board.
3. Call on volunteers to answer the questions as you write key words and phrases on the board.
4. Remind students to include the grammar studied in the unit as they complete the assignment.

Composing and correcting
1. Have students compose a draft of the writing assignment at home and then submit it to you or share it with a partner in class.
2. Give students feedback on the following features:
   • Content: Has the student responded appropriately to the task? Are the main points well supported?
   • Organization: Is the flow of ideas logical and effective?
   • Accuracy: Are there any major errors in the grammar points taught in the unit? (At this stage, you may want to focus your comments on errors related to the target grammar point. Circle the errors, but let students make the corrections. If students are providing feedback to each other, encourage them to focus on content and organization.)
3. ⏱ For longer assignments, have students complete a second draft. When you check these drafts, point out any further areas needing correction, concentrating especially on errors in the target grammar point or grammar points from a previous unit.
4. Have students prepare their final draft at home.

Presentation
1. In class, have students share their final drafts. There are a variety of ways to do this:
   • Post students' work on the class bulletin board.

   • Publish it in a website or a magazine that the class creates.
   • Exchange papers with others in the class.
   • Read papers aloud.
2. ⏱ Have your students put all their corrected written work into a folder, or portfolio, which you can review at the end of the course. This will allow your students and you to see the progress they have made.

Internet Activity (20 minutes in-class time)
This activity gives students an opportunity to do research related to the content of the unit and to discuss or present their findings in class. The activity varies from unit to unit. In some cases students are given very specific questions to research, and the reporting task is brief. In other cases, the investigation is more open-ended, and there is potential for a more extensive presentation.

Suggested Procedure for Internet Activity
Before class
Try the activity yourself, and prepare a list of appropriate key words or specific websites. Note: some suggested website addresses are listed on the *Focus on Grammar* Companion Website (www.longman.com/focusongrammar).

In class: preparation
1. Go over the directions to be sure students understand them. Have students work in small groups to brainstorm ideas for their research.
2. For some projects, you may want to have students work in small groups to divide up the research tasks.
3. Ask students to think about how they would search for their topics. Discuss useful key words and/or write some suggested websites on the board. Remind students that they can find websites on the *Focus on Grammar* Companion Website (www.longman.com/focusongrammar).
4. Elicit language that students are likely to use when discussing their research results. Remind them to review language they have studied in the unit.

At home / language lab
1. Students research their topics and take notes.
2. Ask students to review the notes they made on each website and summarize the most important information.

In class: wrap-up

1. During the next class session, put students into small groups to discuss their research findings.
2. Call upon a spokesperson for each group to report what the group discussed and, if appropriate, what conclusions they came to.

Option (40–60 minutes in-class time)

- Follow the above procedure, but instead of having small group discussions, have students deliver more formal spoken presentations. You may wish to use the Speaking Rubric on page 100.
- When going over the directions to the activity, tell students that they should take notes as they do their research and prepare a short (5-minute) presentation.
- Talk with students about elements of successful spoken presentations, including the importance of making eye contact and using body language. Encourage them to practice at home and to bring in visuals if possible.
- Coach students as they present and provide feedback on their presentations. You may wish to have students complete feedback forms for other students' presentations.

Further Practice

One or more Further Practice activities (in the Teacher's Manual only) can be found at the end of every unit in the Unit-by-Unit Teaching Tips. These exercises offer additional communicative practice with the target structure of the unit. Most can be done in class with no before-class preparation.

GRAMMAR OUT OF THE BOX ......

This activity (in the Teacher's Manual only) offers ideas for how to bring "real life" into your grammar classroom. Using video, pictures, news articles, or other realia, these activities help students make the connection between the structures they learn in the classroom and their application in the real world.

From Grammar to Writing

The From Grammar to Writing section at the end of each Part of the Student Book includes a grammar point and relates this grammar point to the writing focus. Students first practice the teaching point in a controlled exercise such as fill in the blanks, identification, or editing. Following these exercises, students practice pre-writing strategies such as making charts, time lines, schedules, story maps, Venn diagrams, notes, and outlines. Finally, students apply the teaching point in a writing task. Text types include both formal and informal writing, such as personal letters, business letters, essays, summaries, and reports. The section concludes with peer review and editing.

Suggested Procedure for From Grammar to Writing

Pre-writing

1. Have students work individually to complete the controlled practice exercises. Then have them exchange books and compare answers.
2. Go over the answers as a class and answer any questions that students have at this point.
3. Explain the pre-writing task. Where appropriate, provide a model for students on the board or on an overhead.
4. Have students work in pairs or small groups to complete the pre-writing task. Circulate while they are working to answer any questions and to help them with the activity.

Composing and correcting

1. Go over the requirements of the assignment to make sure students understand what they are expected to do.
2. Have students complete the writing assignment at home.
3. In class, complete the peer review portion of the task. Circulate while students are working together to make sure they are on task and to provide appropriate feedback. (See Suggested Procedure for Writing on page 8 for examples of what kind of feedback to provide.)
4. ⏱ Have students revise their writing and turn in the second draft to you. You may wish to use the Scoring Rubric for Writing on page 101 to correct these drafts and to include the drafts as part of the students' writing portfolios.

Option

- Have students complete the controlled practice exercise(s) at home.
- In class, have students work in pairs to compare answers.
- Follow the suggested procedure, starting from step 4 in the pre-writing phase.

Review Test

The last section of each Part of the Student Book is a review feature that can be used as a self-test. These exercises test the form and use of the grammar content presented and practiced in that Part. They give students a chance to check their knowledge and to review any problematic areas before moving on to the next part. An Answer Key is provided at the back of the Student Book, with cross-references to units for easy review.

Suggested Procedure for Review Test

1. Have students complete the exercises at home and check their answers in the Answer Key.
2. During the next class, go over any remaining questions students may have.

Option

- Have students complete the exercises in class. Give them a time limit of 20–30 minutes and circulate as they work.
- Have students use the Answer Key to check and correct their answers in pairs. Or you can go over the answers as a class.

Strategies for Teaching Grammar

1. Develop awareness
- Ask questions that help students become aware of the form of the structure. For example, for the contrast between the simple past and past progressive (FOG 4, page 12, Grammar Note 3), ask, "What was he doing?" *(He was skating.)* Ask what verb form is used in that question and answer *(past progressive)*. Then ask, "What happened to him when he was skating?" *(He collapsed.)* Ask what verb form is used in this question and answer *(past)*. Ask for the difference between the verb forms used for *skate* and *collapse. (One happened over a period of time; the second took only an instant.)* The collapsing interrupted the skating; so the simple past is used with *collapse.* How do we decide which verb should be in the past progressive? *(We determine which action is interrupted by the other.)*
- Compare information in the Grammar Charts. For example, the comparison of the past with the present perfect and the present perfect progressive (FOG 4, page 20) shows a difference in the use of auxiliary verbs in questions (both *wh-* and *yes/no*) and in the short answer form. Ask, "What do we need to add to the simple past in order to make a *wh-* and *yes/no* question or a short answer?" *(did/didn't)* "What do both present perfect and present perfect progressive take to form a *wh-* and *yes/no* question or short answer?" *(has/have or hasn't/haven't, which are already in the verb)*

2. Present meaning
Show the meaning of a grammatical form through a classroom demonstration. For example, to illustrate the use of present perfect progressive, you could show a picture of a person carrying grocery bags full of food *(He/She has been shopping.)*.

3. Identify examples
Ask students to go back to the Grammar in Context section and label examples in the reading passage with the grammatical terms in the Grammar Charts.

4. Generate examples
Find examples from the reading or elsewhere that could fit into the Grammar Charts. An interesting way to do this is to photocopy and enlarge the Grammar Chart. White out the targeted structures and replace them with blank lines for each missing word. Make copies and distribute them to students in pairs or small groups. Have students fill in the blanks, using examples from the reading. Then generate more examples. Books can be open or closed, depending on the level of challenge desired.

5. Show understanding by categorizing
Check comprehension of a grammatical principle by asking students to label multiple examples appropriately. For example, students can label verbs "present" or "future" or they can label examples "correct" or "incorrect."

6. Show understanding by performing actions
Check comprehension of the meaning of a grammatical form by having students follow instructions. Ask students, for example, to think of and perform a set of actions that they could describe using the past progressive and the simple past. (Note that some grammatical forms lend themselves better than others to this strategy.)

7. Manipulate forms
Have students manipulate the examples in the Grammar Charts to practice the form. Drills such as substitution or transformation help students to build fluency. For example, in Unit 6 (FOG 4, pages 68–69), you might have students transform future perfect statements into future perfect questions and then provide short affirmative answers, followed by negative answers:

A: *I'll have earned interest by then.* →

B: *Will you have earned interest by then?*

A: *Yes, I will.*

B: *No, you won't!*

Similar drills can be done with the future perfect progressive on page 69.

8. Personalize
Ask students to provide personal examples. For example, on page 78 in Exercise 10, students are asked about their goals. Have two or three students, in turn, share a personal goal with the rest of the class:

A: I want to finish my thesis by next June.

B: I want to buy a car by the end of the summer.

Have other students paraphrase these goals, using the target verb form:

C: By next June, [A] will have finished his thesis.

D: By the end of the summer, [B] will have bought a car.

9. Repeat, reinforce
Students need to be exposed to new grammar many times in order to internalize it completely. You can first present a new structure on the board, then point it out in the book, then have students use it in an informal oral exercise, then do a written exercise in pairs, and finally review the same structure in homework. Varying the content and focus of these activities will keep students interested, and the grammar will be reinforced almost automatically.

Frequently Asked Questions (FAQ)

1. When should I have students work in pairs or groups rather than individually or as a whole class?

Varying your classroom organization to suit particular activity types will result in more effective and more interesting classes. Many students are not accustomed to working in pairs or groups, so it is important to use these groupings only when they are most beneficial.

- **Whole-class teaching** maximizes teacher control and is especially good for:
  —presenting information, giving explanations and instructions
  —showing material in texts and pictures or on audio or videotape
  —teacher-led drills (such as substitution or transformation) or dictations
  —reviewing answers or sharing ideas after students have completed an activity
  —enabling the whole class to benefit from teacher feedback to individuals
- **Students working individually** allows quiet, concentrated attention and is most effective for:
  —processing information or completing a task at students' own pace
  —performing writing tasks

For objective exercises such as fill-in-the-blank, matching, multiple choice, and editing, vary your class organization to keep student motivation high. Students can sometimes complete these exercises individually, and sometimes they can work with a partner.

- **Students working in pairs** maximizes student speaking time, breaks up the routine and "teacher talk," and is ideal for:
  —information-gap activities
  —role plays
  —writing and/or reading dialogues
  —predicting the content of reading and listening texts
  —comparing notes on what students listen to or see
  —checking answers
  —peer assessment

Pair work can also be very effective for completing objective exercises such as fill-in-the-blank, matching, multiple-choice, and editing.

- **Students working in groups** creates ideal conditions for students to learn from each other and works well for:
  —generating ideas
  —pooling knowledge
  —writing group stories
  —preparing presentations
  —discussing an issue and reaching a group decision

2. How should I set up pair work and group work?

- **Streaming:** Grouping students according to ability or participation has certain advantages.
  —**ability:** Grouping weaker and stronger students together allows more able students to help their less fluent classmates.
  —**participation:** If you see that some students participate less than others, you could make a pair or group of weak participators. By the same token, you can also put especially talkative students together.
- **Chance:** Grouping students by chance has many benefits, especially if it results in students working with varied partners. You can group students by chance according to:
  —**where they sit:** Students sitting next to or near one another work in pairs or groups. This is the easiest option, but if students always sit in the same place, you will want to find other ways of grouping them.
  —**the "wheels" system:** Half the class stands in a circle facing outwards, and the other half stands in an outer circle facing inwards. The outer circle revolves in a clockwise direction, and the inner circle revolves in a counterclockwise direction. When you tell them to stop, students work with the person facing them. This is a very effective way to have students engage in meaningful repetition, such as asking the same question of many different partners.
  —**assigned letters:** Assign each student a letter from *A* to *E*. Then ask all the As to form a group, all the Bs to form a group, and so on.
  —**birthdays:** Students stand in a line in the order of their birthdays (with January at one end and December at the other). The first five students form one group; the second five students another group, and so on.

—**native language:** If possible, put students in groups or pairs with others who don't share a native language. This helps create an "English-only" classroom.

3. How can I make activities more successful?

Before the activity:

- **Motivate students and explain the purpose.** Make it clear that something enjoyable or interesting is going to happen. Explain the rationale for the activity. Making sure students understand the purpose of the activity is to practice what they learned and encourage them to participate.
- **Provide clear directions.** Explain what students should do in every step of the activity. Have students paraphrase or demonstrate the task to be sure they understand it.
- **Demonstrate.** Show the class what is supposed to happen in an activity. This might involve asking a student to demonstrate the activity with you or having two students role-play in the front of the room.
- **Provide a time frame.** It is helpful for students to know how much time they have and exactly when they should stop. Approximate times are given for all the activities in this Teacher's Manual.

For open-ended activities, such as the Internet Activity or writing exercises, you will also want to:

- **Stimulate thinking.** When there are choices for students to make, it is often helpful to set up small-group and/or whole-class brainstorming sessions to define the focus and/or content of their task.
- **Prepare language.** Review grammar and vocabulary that students may need to complete the task. This can be done as a follow-up to a brainstorming activity where you elicit ideas and write key language on the board.

During the activity:

- **Observe students.** Walk around the room watching and listening to pairs or groups.
- **Provide assistance as needed.** (See FAQ #5 for suggestions on giving feedback and correcting errors.)

After the activity:

- **Elicit student responses.** For some activities, you may ask for volunteers or call on students to share some of their ideas with the class. For other types of activities, a few pairs or groups can be asked to role-play

their discussions to demonstrate the language they have been using.

- **Provide feedback.** In many cases, this is most conveniently done in a whole-class setting. It may be preferable, however, for you to meet with individuals, pairs, or groups. While the principal focus in a grammar class is language use, it is also important to acknowledge the value of students' ideas. See FAQ #5 below for suggestions on feedback and error correction.

4. What can I do to encourage students to use more English in the classroom?

It is perfectly natural for students to feel the need to use their first language in an English class. There are a number of actions that teachers can take to promote the use of English.

- **Set clear guidelines:** Some teachers in monolingual classes find that activities such as providing vocabulary definitions, presenting a grammar point, checking comprehension, giving instructions, and discussing classroom methodology are best done in the students' native language.
- **Use persuasion:** Walking among the students during speaking activities and saying things like "Please speak English!" or "Try to use English as much as possible." helps to ensure that students will speak English most of the time.

5. What's the best approach to giving feedback and correcting errors?

Be selective in offering correction. Students can't focus on everything at once, so concentrate first on errors relating to the target grammar point and grammar points from units previously studied, as well as any errors that interfere with communication. Whether you respond to other errors depends on your judgment of students' readiness to take in the information. If you see a teachable moment, seize it! Rather than correct every error individual students make in the course of activities, it is generally preferable to note commonly occurring mistakes and give a short presentation for the whole class at the end of the activity.

- **Recasting.** If a student makes an error—for example, "I *didn't came* to class yesterday because I was sick."—you can recast it as, "You *didn't come* to class yesterday because you were sick?" The student ideally notices the difference and restates the original sentence: "Right. I didn't come to class yesterday because I was sick." This process can be effective because the student has the opportunity to self-correct an error that is still in short-term memory. As a variation, you can restate but stop, with rising intonation, right before the potential error: "You didn't . . . ?"

6. What can I do to accommodate different learning styles?

Focus on Grammar recognizes different styles of learning and provides a variety of activities to accommodate these different styles. Some learners prefer an analytical, or rule-learning (deductive) approach. Others, especially younger learners, respond best to an inductive approach, or exposure to the language in meaningful contexts. Indeed, the same students may adopt different styles as they learn, or they may use different styles at different times.

As teachers, we want to help the students in our classes who prefer to follow rules become more able to take risks and to plunge into communicative activities. We also want to encourage the risk-takers to focus on accuracy. *Focus on Grammar* provides the variety to ensure that students achieve their goal: to learn to use the language confidently and appropriately.

Unit-by-Unit Teaching Tips

UNIT 1 Simple Present and Present Progressive

Unit Overview

Unit 1 contrasts simple present and present progressive.
- The simple present describes events, situations, or activities not connected to time restrictions; it is also used for general statements of truth or fact.
- The present progressive describes what is happening right now or in the extended present (these days, this month, this year) with action verbs.
- In sentences with both simple present and present progressive, the present describes the situation and the present progressive describes the continuing action.

Grammar in Context (pages 2–3)

Background Notes

- Nicknames are sometimes a short version of a full name (*Tom* for *Thomas*, *Liz* for *Elizabeth*). They can also describe a personality trait (*Tiger, Sassy*) or a physical trait (*Red, Tiny, Curly*). Sometimes they are a combination (*Big Bill, Mama Sue*).
- A *mouthful* is something that is not easy to pronounce.

Vocabulary

come back: to become fashionable or popular again

get used to: to become comfortable with

identity: sense of who a person really is

Comprehension Questions

- Why does Dusya use her nickname? (*Her friends find her full name difficult to pronounce.*)
- *Mr., Ms.,* and *Professor* are _____. (*titles*)
- Why didn't Dusya want to call her teachers by their first names at first? (*It seemed disrespectful.*)

- What is Jorge's middle name? (*Santiago*)
- In Spanish-speaking cultures, does the father's or mother's family name come first? (*father's*)

Discussion Topics

- Many families and cultures have naming traditions, such as naming a child after a grandparent or using a part of a parent's name. Ask students to explain their families' traditions.
- Why do some people change their names? Ask students how they feel about their names as part of their identities. Or have students ask one another, "Do you like your name?"

Grammar Presentation (pages 3–4)

Identify the Grammar

SIMPLE PRESENT
It still seems a little disrespectful . . .
We don't use titles like "Mr."

PRESENT PROGRESSIVE
This year I'm living and working . . .
. . . but it's coming back.
. . . but I'm getting used to it.

Grammar Charts

- Select one example from the target grammar points. Discuss whether both verb forms will work in this example.
- Take a simple verb (not necessarily from the reading) and put it on the board in both forms. *Speak* works well. Discuss the difference in meaning. (*I speak Spanish at home; I'm speaking English now.*) Now add more sentences from the reading.
- Quick pairwork: Students ask each other: "What language do you speak at home/are you speaking now?" "What language does [a famous person] speak at home? What language is he or she speaking now?"

Grammar Notes

Note 1 *(Exercise 2)*
- Have students find examples of the simple present in the reading, then have them close their books and make up their own simple present sentences using the same verbs or different ones. Try to elicit contractions as opposed to long forms. *(He doesn't live in Texas.)*
- To review the present progressive, have students find sentences in the reading that express continuing action. *(My name is coming back into style. / Some friends are trying to convince me to call myself "George.")* Have students make up more examples.
- Have students generate examples which show contrast. *(I wear slippers at home, but I'm wearing shoes now. What do you wear at home/are you wearing now? He smokes, but he's not smoking now.)*
- Point out the pitfalls of both verb forms *(forgetting the "s" in third-person present, neglecting to pronounce the "m" in "I'm speaking English now").*
- Stress contractions, and mention that there is no difference in meaning between "You aren't speaking Spanish" and "You're not speaking Spanish." You can mention that "you're" rhymes with "her."

→ For additional practice, see the Supplementary Activities on page 91.

Note 2 *(Exercise 2)*
- Use the list of non-action verbs in Appendix 2, page A-2. Ask the students to choose some verbs that they use frequently. Write these verbs (not generally used in progressive forms) in a column on the board. Have students come to the board and write sentences using these verbs.
- Write the column heads *Emotions, Mental States, Perceptions, Appearance,* and *Possession* on the board. Then ask the students to find three verbs for each heading. Have students make sentences with each verb.

Note 3 *(Exercise 2)*
- Make a list of topics that are unchanging over time (for example, *the Earth, the sun, the moon, the oceans, rivers, trees, animals, fish, the weather in each season*).
- Write a scientific fact and a physical fact on the board. Invite the students to use the unchanging topics to write more sentences using the simple present. *(The Earth moves around the sun. Ice floats on water.)*

- Point out that general statements and specific statements can use simple present and present progressive to show a contrast between what usually happens and what is happening now. *(It doesn't rain much in the desert, but it's raining in Phoenix today.)*

Note 4 *(Exercise 1)*
- Have students make one-line statements in the simple present about recent movies they have seen. *(The main actor plays the part of an unusual doctor.)*
- Quick pairwork: Have the students ask their partners, "Have you seen any good movies lately? Which one? Who was in it? What's it about?"
- Have students comment on books or stories they have read. *(In the film* Titanic, *a luxury ship hits an iceberg in the Atlantic Ocean.)*

Note 5 *(Exercise 2)*
Have students think of both positive and annoying habits of people they know and write examples of things "they are always doing." *(Carolina is always smiling. / My brother is always talking in class. / The teacher is always correcting my spelling.)*

Focused Practice (pages 5–6)

Exercise 1
vary: to be different
tend to: to be likely to do a particular thing
shrinking: becoming smaller
record numbers: larger numbers

Exercise 2
violet: light purple
expect a baby: to be pregnant

Exercise 3
profile: general description (of a person)
initials: first letters of a person's first and last names

Communication Practice (pages 7–8)

Exercise 4
- Before students listen, have them talk about each of the photographs in pairs or small groups. Ask what they notice about each person, and if any of the names fit the pictures—even before they hear the descriptions. Have students guess the names and then check out their guesses as they listen.

- Quick pairwork before listening: Have the students match names to pictures. Ask: "Which one do you think is named Red? Why? Which one is named Sunshine? Why?"

Exercise 5
- Prepare the class for this exercise by eliciting possible get-to-know-you questions on the board: *What kind of movies do you like? Where is your family living now? Are you reading a good book?*
- Write the exercise on the board with student names and blanks for the verbs and some of the subjects, followed by cue words. *Hi, _____ Susan. (I, be). _____ Eddy. (I, look for)*

Exercise 6
Questions to generate ideas and elicit vocabulary:

- What are your interests?
- What are your hobbies?
- What are your plans for the future?

Further Practice
1. Have students use the information they gathered about one another in "Getting to Know You" to write a few lines about the person they "found."
2. Have small groups of students create a "profile" of a famous person and present it to the rest of the class, who are asked to guess the identity of the famous person.

GRAMMAR OUT OF THE BOX ......

What is that person doing? Have students bring in family (or other) photos, or have them take a video of the class and use the freeze-frame feature to get a still picture. Write these questions on the board: *What is the background for the picture? What do you see in the picture? What is happening in the picture?* For example, if the picture shows a boy skiing down a mountain slope, the students might write these sentences: *The picture shows a snowy mountain and a boy. There are many trees, a blue sky, and sunshine. The boy is skiing fast down the mountain.*

Simple Past and Past Progressive

Unit Overview

Unit 2 focuses on the meanings of the simple past and the past progressive—specifically when these verb forms appear in sentences with two clauses.
- The simple past describes an action that was completed at a specific time in the past.
- The past progressive describes an action that was in progress at a specific time in the past.
- In sentences with both the simple past and the past progressive, the past progressive describes an action that was interrupted by another action; the simple past describes the interrupting action.

Grammar in Context (pages 9–11)

Background Notes
- The *Sorbonne* is part of the University of Paris.
- *Nobel Prizes* are granted every year for extraordinary work in the fields of medicine, science, literature, economics, and peace.
- The *conga* is a type of fast dance music that originated on the island of Cuba.

Vocabulary
mild-mannered: gentle in behavior

cover stories: to research and write news articles

"The Man of Steel": nickname for Superman, because of his strength

propose: to ask someone to marry

accomplish: to do something important; achieve

physicist: scientist who studies matter and energy

radioactivity: quality of substances having radiation

recover: to get better

thrill: to make someone feel strong excitement and pleasure

collapse: to fall down and become unconscious

solo: alone

Comprehension Questions
- Why are these super couples special? *(They accomplish/accomplished great things together.)*
- Why wasn't Lois interested in Clark Kent at first? *(She was more interested in "The Man of Steel.")*
- What were the Curies researching? *(radioactivity)*

- What was Gloria doing when she met Emilio Estefan? *(going to high school)*
- What was Sergei Grinkov doing when he collapsed? *(practicing)*
- Which couple isn't real? *(Lois and Clark)*

Discussion Topics

- All four couples described in the readings overcame great obstacles to find success. Ask students to think of other people they know who faced similar difficulties on the way to achieving their life goals.
- Ask students to talk about their personal or public heroes. Here is an example to use as a model:

  "Christopher Reeve, who played Superman in the movies, was famous for his strength and grace. One day while riding his horse, Reeve fell and became paralyzed from the neck down. Although he no longer looked like a hero in the physical sense, he became a Superman in a different way: He spoke for paralyzed people everywhere who didn't have a voice. When Christopher Reeve died in 2004, he was mourned by all as a true American hero."

Grammar Presentation (pages 11–13)

Identify the Grammar

SIMPLE PAST
. . . , *this world-famous character met Lois* . . .
When Kent proposed, Lois accepted.

PAST PROGRESSIVE
. . . *the two were working as newspaper reporters* . . .
While she was studying at the Sorbonne, . . .

Grammar Charts

- Choose one of the examples on the board and write two contrasting sentences:

  SIMPLE PAST
  Marie studied at the Sorbonne.

  PAST PROGRESSIVE
  Marie was studying at the Sorbonne.

- Erase the verbs in the examples and replace them with blanks.
- Point to the tense names and ask:
  —How many words are needed for the simple past? *(one)*
  —How many words are needed for the past progressive? *(two)*

- Ask a student to write the missing words in the blanks *(studied, was studying)*.
- Ask another student to make the sentences negative *(didn't study, wasn't studying)*. Then ask the class:
  —How do you form the negative simple past? *(didn't + base form of verb)*
  —How do you form the negative past progressive? *(wasn't + -ing form of verb)*
- Continue in the same way with *yes/no* questions, short answers, and *wh-* questions.

Grammar Notes

Note 1   *(Exercises 2, 3)*
- To review simple past questions and statements, have students make *What time* questions about common daily activities to ask a partner *(What time did you get up yesterday? What time did you leave the house?)*. Have several students write their partner's responses on the board:

Kim got up at 5:30.
Kim left the house at 6:30.
Abdul got up at 7:00.
Abdul left the house at 8:00.

- Drill the class on some of the more common irregular simple past verbs (listed in Appendix 1, pages A-1–A-2), giving a base form and quickly eliciting the past: e.g., *begin/began, buy/bought, drink/drank.*
- Draw attention to the REMEMBER! note. Ask students if they know which example sentence it refers to. *(Marie had a degree in physics.)* Elicit additional examples of non-action verbs not usually used in the progressive *(love, remember, want, see, seem)*. You can refer students to Appendix 2, page A-2 for a list of non-action verbs.

Note 2   *(Exercises 2, 3)*
- To review past progressive questions and statements, ask several students, "What were you doing last night at 8:30?" Ask students to respond with complete sentences, and have other students stand at the board and write them down:

At 8:30 last night,
Ines was eating dinner.
Carlos was working.
Jonah and Yuri were watching TV.
Susan was doing homework.

- Have students use the information you wrote on the board to make comparison statements using the past progressive: ("When Kim was getting up, Abdul was sleeping." "Jonah and Yuri were watching TV when Ines was eating dinner.")

- To clarify the difference in meaning between the simple past and past progressive, pantomime a set of actions and then ask students to describe what happened (for example, *You were sleeping when the phone rang.*).

Note 3 *(Exercises 2, 3, 4)*

- Point out that *when* is usually used with a specific time or date, and *while* is usually used with a duration of time.
- Have students work in small groups to think up actions they can demonstrate for the class to describe using the two tenses (for example, *While Tim was writing a letter, his cell phone rang.*).

Note 4 *(Exercises 2, 3, 4)*

- Draw the time line from the Student Book on the board. Point to the word *now* and say, "Right now I'm talking and you're listening." Then point to the word *past* and say, "A minute ago, you were talking and I was writing on the board."
- Have pairs think up and act out simultaneous actions for the class to describe after the fact (for example, *While Alicia was reading a book, Natasha was polishing her nails.*).

→ For additional practice, see the Supplementary Activities on page 91.

Note 5 *(Exercises 2, 3, 4)*

- Write an example sentence on the board with one clause in the simple past and the other in the past progressive. Number the clauses to illustrate the order of the actions. For example:

2
When my roommate called his parents,

1
I was making breakfast.

Point out that here, *when* means "at the time."

- Write an example sentence on the board with both clauses in the simple past. Again, number the clauses to illustrate the order of the actions. For example:

1
When my roommate called his parents,

2
I left the house.

Explain that here, *when* means "after."

- Ask pairs of students to create additional examples and write them on the board,

numbering the clauses to show the order of the actions.

Focused Practice (pages 13–16)

Exercise 1
wrong number: not the telephone number you wanted

kind of: in some ways

blind date: an occasion when someone arranges for two people who have not met before to go out together

Exercise 2
autograph: a famous person's name, written in his/her own writing

pretend: to behave as if something is true when you know it isn't

drop: to accidentally let go of something you're holding or carrying so that it falls

Exercise 3
The rest is history: "We all know what happens next."

graphic: related to drawing or printing

Exercise 5
aisle: (in this situation) the long passage between seats in a church

rash: a lot of red spots on someone's skin caused by an illness or a reaction to food, plants, or medicine

poison ivy: a bush with an oily substance on its leaves that makes your skin itch after you touch it

Communication Practice (pages 17–18)

Exercise 6
Before students listen, have them describe what is happening in each series of pictures. Then have them list the differences between the pictures. *(Series a starts and ends when it's sunny; series b starts and ends during a storm; series c starts during a storm and ends when it's sunny.)*

Exercise 7
- Point out the contrast between simple past and past progressive in the example, asking, "What was the person doing?" and "What happened while she was doing that?"
- Give or elicit additional examples of short anecdotes using simple past and past progressive. *(I was waiting for the elevator last night when a young woman and her little boy came down the hall. She was pushing him in his stroller, and they were singing. When the*

little boy saw me, he stopped singing and said, "Hi. My name's Toby and this is my mommy, Lauren.")

- Circulate as students work in their groups. Encourage students to make their stories more interesting by varying clause order and sentence length.
- Choose a few students to report on what others in their groups said.

Exercise 8

- Before students begin their time lines, elicit examples of important life events *(moving to a new place, getting married, going on a trip)*. Students may refer to the time line on page 16 for ideas.
- Tell students to ask at least three questions about their partner's time line.
- Call on several volunteers to tell the class what they learned about their partners.

Exercise 9

Questions to generate ideas and elicit vocabulary:
- Who is an important person to you?
- When did you meet this person? How did you meet?
- What were you doing (or thinking about) when you first met?
- Why is this person important to you?

Further Practice

Elicit names of famous couples (for example, *Romeo and Juliet, Victoria and Albert, Tristan and Isolde, Antony and Cleopatra, Bonnie and Clyde*). Create a role-play card for each person named. Write the name of the person and information about that person on the card. Then distribute one card to each student. Each student takes on the role of the person on the card. They take turns giving clues about themselves to find their partners. The other students guess who they are. For example:

A: I was working on radioactivity, and you were working with me.

B: That's right! We won a Nobel Prize.

C: They're Pierre and Marie Curie.

Current events. Bring in some newspaper or magazine pictures of events that happened in the recent past (for example, a weather

disaster, a blackout, a sports event). Give pairs of students one picture and ask them to write three sentences about it, combining the simple past and past progressive. Call on students to read their sentences to the class. Alternatively, have pairs or groups create a news story about their picture and present it to the class. Videotape "the news" with the class!

UNIT 3 — Simple Past, Present Perfect, and Present Perfect Progressive

Unit Overview

Students will learn the meanings and uses of the simple past, present perfect, and present perfect progressive—specifically when more than one of these verb forms appears in a single sentence or situation.

- The simple past describes an action that occurred in the past or was completed at a specific time in the past.
- The present perfect and present perfect progressive describe an action that began in the past and is just ending or might continue into the future.
- Note that these differences in verb forms do not exist in other languages, and therefore students will not find equivalents in their native languages.

Grammar in Context (pages 19–20)

Background Notes

Point out that this reading is from a personal website. If possible, show students other examples of personal websites, and ask whether any students already have their own.

Vocabulary

extreme sports: sports that are done in a way that is more dangerous than usual

take time out: to use some time for a special purpose

skydive: to jump from an airplane with a parachute for fun

social life: activities with one's friends

get engaged: to agree to marry

engagement: agreement to marry

Comprehension Questions

- Where is Jason from? *(Australia)*
- How did Jason learn to love adventure sports? *(from his family)*
- What kind of person has Jason always been? *(a work-hard, play-hard kind of guy)*
- Where has Jason been studying? *(in Sydney)*
- Why did Joy want to go skydiving? *(to celebrate their engagement)*

Discussion Topics

- What kind of sports do you like? What kind of sports did you like when you were a child? What kind of sports did you like 10 years ago?
- Have you ever gone skydiving or sailing? Have you ever been to Australia? Have you traveled anywhere else?
- Would you like to go skydiving, bungee-jumping, or motorcycle riding? Why or why not?

Grammar Presentation (pages 20–22)

Identify the Grammar

SIMPLE PAST
I grew up in Perth . . .
. . . my family did adventure sports . . .

PRESENT PERFECT
I've written this page . . .
Lately, people have named these activities extreme sports, . . .

PRESENT PERFECT PROGRESSIVE
I've been building this site for a while, . . .
Joy hasn't been skydiving . . .

Grammar Charts

- Write one example sentence at a time on the board. Have the students change the verb form. Note that to change the verbs to other forms, the time context often requires adding time expressions. For example, *My family has been doing adventure sports since 1985.*
- Write the names of the three verb forms on the board. Also write more sentences from the reading on the board. Erase the verbs and replace them with blanks. If you have colored chalk, use it to underline the main part of the verb and/or the helping (auxiliary) verbs *(have, has, -ing)*.

Grammar Notes

Note 1 *(Exercises 1, 2, 3)*
- Write an example sentence from your own life on the board: *Ten years ago I lived in Toronto. I didn't live here.*
- On the board, draw a time line that corresponds to the example sentence. Point to "now" and draw a dot at "Ten years ago," and write "Toronto" under the dot to show that the time is finished. Note: Leave the time line on the board to use when reviewing grammar notes 2–4.
- Do a quick teacher-directed oral review of the principal parts of common irregular verbs such as *choose, wear, drive, read, grow, fly, see, buy, give, shake, speak.* (See Appendix 1, pages A-1–A-2.) You can model this by saying, "drink, drank, drunk" as you count off the three parts on your fingers, then prompting a student with "choose . . . ?" and holding up one and then two and three fingers until the student responds with "choose, chose, chosen."

Note 2 *(Exercises 1, 2, 3)*
- On the same time line on the board, draw a dot and say, "I came here in [year]" and label the dot with the year. Then draw a line from the dot to "now," and say, "I've lived here for five years. I've been living here for five years."
- Point out that present perfect and present perfect progressive are connected to the present and can mean the same thing with certain verbs like *live, work,* and *teach:* "I've lived here for five years. I've been living here for five years."
- Quick pairwork: Have students work with partners to ask each other, "How long have you lived here? How long has your family lived in their house?"

Notes 3 and 4 *(Exercises 1, 2, 3)*
- Use the time line on the board to review the difference between a point in time with *since (January 1, 2006, yesterday, a month ago, 4:00)* and a length of time with *for (a year, a month).*
- Emphasize that expressions with *ago* are specific points in time and are used with *since* if the situation requires the present perfect or with the simple past.
- Be sure that your students understand that the same situation can be described with different verbs <u>and</u> different tenses: *I came here five years ago. I've been here for five years.*
- Quick pairwork: Have students ask each other questions about the same situation, using both tenses:

A: When did you come here?

B: I came here three years ago.

A: So you've been here for three years.

A: When did you buy that jacket?

B: I bought it last year.

A: So you've had it for a year.

→ For additional practice, see the Supplementary Activities on page 91.

Note 5   *(Exercises 1, 2, 3)*

• Point out that actions expressed in the present perfect can continue or affect the present. Say, "She's eaten lunch (so she's not hungry now). I've been to Mexico (and I might go again). He's worked on his project (and he needs to work on it some more)."

• Point out that often present perfect shows that something is finished, either recently or at some unspecified time in the past, while present perfect progressive shows that something is still going on.

• Quick pairwork to practice this difference:

A: What's your favorite book?

B: My favorite book is _____.

A: How many times have you read it?

B: I've read it _____ times.

A: And what have you been reading lately?

B: Lately I've been reading _____.

Note 6   *(Exercises 1, 2, 3)*

Point out that the time of day sometimes determines whether simple past tense or present perfect is appropriate; we use the present perfect to ask about breakfast before noon: *Have you eaten breakfast?* After noon (lunchtime), we would ask in the past tense: *Did you eat breakfast this morning?*

Focused Practice (pages 23–25)

Exercise 1

natural choice: easy decision

ceremony: formal ritual

run into: to meet by chance

psychotherapist: mental health professional, counselor

leadership skills: ways to influence and help other people

Exercise 2

sell out: to sell all of something, to have nothing left to sell

fad: popular interest

craze: (same as *fad*)

trade: exchange

Exercise 3

snapshot: informal photograph

amateur: not professional

Exercise 4

communicate: to exchange information

Communication Practice (pages 26–27)

Exercise 5

• Before students listen, review the meanings of each of the items on the list. Have them expand the phrases into sentence contexts. For example, *renew passports* means "Send our passports to the Passport Office with a filled out application form, a money order, and new photographs."

• Quick pairwork: Have students practice new vocabulary by asking partners, "Have you ever renewed your passport?" "When did you renew your passport?" "How long does it take to renew a passport?" "Have you traveled often?"

Exercise 6

• Tell your students about your own plans for the week: "Last week I had so many plans. I wanted to clean my desk, to write to my grandmother, to pay my bills, and to go shopping. But I didn't do anything."

• Point to a student and ask, "How about you? What plans did you have for last week?"

• After a few students have answered, expand to the present perfect; "And this week? What have you done this week?"

• Have students write a few ideas on the board ("clean my room") and then have them expand them orally to include the past and either the present perfect or present perfect progressive. Give students time cues such as "last week" and "this week." For example:

—*clean my room:* "Last week I <u>wanted</u> to clean my room. I <u>have been cleaning</u> it a little each day this week."

—*take my coat to the cleaners* "Last week I <u>planned</u> to take my coat to the cleaners, but I <u>haven't done</u> it yet."

Exercise 7

• Ask your students to name their hobbies, and make a vertical list on the board.

• After each hobby, write some vocabulary items that will help them in asking and answering

questions about the hobby *(sewing: shirt, skirt, pattern, zipper, thread, sewing machine)*.
- Quick pairwork: Have students discuss their hobbies. Provide some sentence cues on the board: *Have you ever _____? I have _____ since I was (age)*. Encourage students who have easily portable hobbies (knitting or stamp-collecting, not motorcycle repair) to bring examples of their hobbies to class.

Exercise 8
- Generate ideas and elicit vocabulary with these and other questions:
  —What is your name?
  —Where do you live? How long have you lived there? Where else have you lived?
  —What kind of person are you?
  —What have you done that other people might be interested in?
  —What have you been doing recently?
  —What are your plans for the next few years?
- ⏱ Students can write about someone else (a classmate, a famous person, or even a cartoon character).

Further Practice
Make a list of time expressions and write them on the board: *last week, since I was born, for 10 years, that long, last month, since last month, for two weeks*. Use the sentences from the reading to get started and then have the students create sentences of their own. Or make a simple board game with the time expressions in numbered boxes on a sheet of paper. You will need a distinctive button for each student and a die. Students throw the die, advance to a box, and make up an original sentence with the time expression specified in that box and appropriate grammar. Give a prize for originality or outrageousness.

What's the story? Have students bring in a video cued to a scene. They play the scene, then ask other students to guess what the history of the character is, up to right before the scene. *(He's only been living in New York for a short time. He just came home from a party. He just got some bad news.)* Alternatively, you could bring in the video and ask students to guess. Or have students bring in pictures of a famous person who's been in the news lately and give a short report about what the person has done, been doing, just did, and/or has never done.

Unit Overview
Students will learn the meanings and uses of the past perfect and the past perfect progressive verb forms in comparison with the simple past; the contractions involved in conversational use; and the uses of *yes/no* questions, *wh-* questions, and positive and negative short answers for both verb forms.
- The past perfect is used in contrast with the simple past; the past perfect action happened before the past action.
- The past perfect progressive is also used in contrast with the simple past, but it describes continuing action before (or by) a specific point of time in the past.

Grammar in Context (pages 28–29)

Background Notes
- An *Oscar* is an award given every year by the motion picture industry to the best actors, directors, and technicians in a variety of categories. Getting an Oscar is an enormous help to the winner's career. Every movie is based on a story (the script). The script must be accurate, so many people do research on facts, customs, and background.
- Martial arts include many Asian forms of self-defense such as karate, judo, kung fu, and tae kwon do.

Vocabulary
nomination: act of being chosen for a competition
brilliant: extremely intelligent
transfer: to move to a new place
desperate: willing to do anything to change a bad situation
researcher: person who looks up information for a project

Comprehension Questions
- What had Ang Lee been doing before 1985? *(He had been going to college in the United States, making a student film, and preparing to return to Taiwan.)*
- How had the family been making money? *(His wife had been working as a researcher, and Lee had been writing scripts.)*

- What happened to the two scripts he entered in a competition in 1991? *(They both won.)*
- What film-making dream had Lee always had? *(of making a martial arts movie)*

Discussion Topics

- Ang Lee is now successful in a difficult field: film-making. Why is the movie business so competitive? What other businesses are risky? Are the rewards great? Are the suffering and the worrying worth it?
- "Hitting bottom" or "the low point in one's life" are ways of describing a common phenomenon: that many people experience hard times just before success. Ang Lee's story is one example. Other stories often involve people overcoming health or personal problems. Have students, in pairs, tell stories about hitting bottom and also about being successful, thinking either of celebrities or of people they know.

Grammar Presentation (pages 29–32)

Identify the Grammar

PAST PERFECT
By the end of the evening, it <u>had won</u> four Oscars.
. . . (more than any foreign language film <u>had</u> ever <u>gotten</u>).
Before this, Lee <u>had made</u> big, successful English language movies . . .

PAST PERFECT PROGRESSIVE
For six years, his wife <u>had been working</u> as a researcher, . . .
. . . he <u>had been writing</u> scripts . . .

Grammar Charts

- Choose one of the examples in the book, and write two contrasting sentences:

PAST PERFECT
He'd written scripts.

PAST PERFECT PROGRESSIVE
He'd been writing scripts.

- Erase parts of the verbs, replacing them with blanks. Have students write the missing parts in the blanks, noting how many words the past perfect and past perfect progressive require.
- Ask individual students to make the sentences negative and to form *yes/no* questions, short answers, and *wh-* questions from the examples.

Grammar Notes

Note 1 *(Exercises 2, 3, 6, 7)*
- Write a date on the board, like 2000. Elicit some examples of past perfect from students' lives and put them on the board: *By 2000, I had left my hometown / had studied English for five years, but I hadn't found a job / had started school here / hadn't met you.*
- Quick pairwork: Have students make up statements about themselves using the past perfect and the date, writing their sentences down for expansion in work with Note 2.

Note 2 *(Exercises 4, 5, 6, 7)*
- If possible, use the situations that the students created for Note 1 to expand into the past perfect progressive, and put the sentence on the board. *Before I came here, I had studied English for five years. → Before I came here, I had already been studying English for five years.*
- Point out that in the first example *(had studied)* the emphasis is on the amount of time (five years), whereas in the second *(had been studying)* the emphasis is on the process (so long in school, so many tests, so much instruction!).
- Remind your students that the past perfect progressive is not usually used with stative verbs. For example: *I had always wanted to succeed.* (NOT: *I had always ~~been wanting~~ to succeed.*)

Note 3 *(Exercises 4, 5, 6, 7)*
- Give students several other examples of evidence sentences, and ask them to draw conclusions, such as:
  —The road was wet. *(It had been raining.)*
  —My computer was on. *(Someone else had been using it.)*
  —Her eyes were red. *(She had been crying.)*
  Point out that the use of past perfect, in many cases, makes it unnecessary to use such expressions as *It was clear that/I realized that . . .*
- Ask students to draw conclusions based on other evidence situations: *The candy dish was empty. There was no gas in the car. The kitchen sink was full of dirty dishes. The refrigerator was empty.*
- ⏱ Quick pairwork: Prepare slips of paper with these situations written on them. One student reads the situation, the other gives the conclusion using past perfect progressive.

Note 4 *(Exercises 2, 4, 7)*

- Have one student draw a time line on the board, noting today's date and dates one year ago, five years ago, and ten years ago.
- Have the other students draw their own time lines on paper.
- Then have them work in pairs creating sentences comparing a past and a "more past" or past perfect or past perfect progressive situation. They can contrast their experiences or time frames. *(One year ago, I hadn't learned to drive, but I had learned to ski. Five years ago, I'd already met my wife, but you hadn't met your husband.)* You can circulate to check pronunciation and encourage the use of contractions.
- Ask students to generate sentences, using real-life situations, which show the contrast between simple past and past perfect. *(When you came, I left. / When you came, I had left.)*

Note 5 *(Exercises 2, 3, 7)*

- Have students work in pairs to write down three things they have done since the school year started.
- Have each pair create three sentences comparing this year with last: *Before classes started, I had never _____ .* Then have them write three sentences about things they had been doing <u>before</u> the beginning of the school year: *I had been _____ before this school year started.* Have them keep these sentences for the pairwork done for Note 6.

Note 6 *(Exercise 7)*

Have the students rephrase the sentences from Note 5 using both simple past and past perfect: *After classes started, I _____ . After classes had started, I _____ . Before classes started, I _____ . Before classes started, I had been _____ .*

Note 7 *(Exercises 2, 5, 7)*

- Have students, working with partners, change the sentences from notes 5 and 6 by beginning with these expressions: *By the time classes started, I had been _____ . By September, I had _____ .*
- Point out that in many contexts, past perfect is not really necessary if the difference between the two events is clear, and that past perfect becomes necessary only when one past time needs to be clarified as more past than the other. *(Before I met Pat and fell in love, I had dated two other people.)*

→ For additional practice, see the Supplementary Activities on pages 91–92.

Focused Practice *(pages 33–39)*

Exercise 1
break: period of time when something stops for a while

guest: someone famous who is invited to take part in a performance

Exercise 3
an "extra" actor, an extra: actor with a small, unimportant part in a movie

journal: written record that you make of the things that happen to you each day

film location: place where a movie is filmed

Exercise 4
bandit: someone who robs travelers

tragic: very sad and shocking

Exercise 5
talk-show host: interviewer in a television show in which famous people answer questions about themselves

kung fu: ancient Chinese fighting art in which you attack people with your hands and feet

Exercise 6
depressed: very sad

arrest: (for the police to) take a person away because he or she is thought to be guilty

Exercise 7
make up one's mind: to decide

hang up: to replace the phone receiver and stop the conversation

Exercise 8
design: to make a plan for something that will be made or built

Communication Practice *(pages 40–42)*

Exercise 9
Before they listen, ask students to think about the possible order for these events. Which events cannot happen before another? *(They can't talk about moving back until they have moved the first time.)*

Exercise 10
- Have students compare their answers to the exercise.

- Partners of very busy people can nominate their partners for the "Busy Bee Award."
- Have nominees read their answers aloud, and then have classmates vote.
- ⏱ Another possibility is to vote for the least busy person for the Couch Potato Award.

Exercise 11

Have pairs of students write one sentence on the board using the frame, *Before this year, I had never. . . .* Encourage the use of high-frequency verbs: *eaten, seen, tasted, attended, played with, visited, tried, considered,* and the like.

Exercise 13

Use these questions to generate ideas and elicit vocabulary:

- What had you worried about before you tried to achieve this goal?
- Who had you asked for help?
- Why had you been thinking that you might not succeed?

Further Practice

On the board, brainstorm a list of five to seven questions to use in an interview with a famous sports figure, movie star, writer, or singer about his or her childhood and entrance into the world of sports or entertainment. Start out with a question about the star's first success. Then ask about previous experiences (which led to stardom). Use this question form: *Before your big break, what / how / when had you . . . ?* Then select one member of the class to role-play the famous person. Record the answers so that class members can answer questions about the famous person.

GRAMMAR OUT OF THE BOX . . . . . .

Talk show. Have a student record a talk show with an interview of a famous person, or record one yourself. Select a five-minute segment during which the famous person is talking about his or her past. Pause the video after each piece of information about the famous person's past and have the students write a sentence about it, using past perfect or past perfect progressive. Have students work in small groups to write paragraphs from their sentences.

Unit Overview

Students will learn the meanings and uses of the future and the future progressive—specifically how different tenses are used to show future meaning.
- The simple present, the present progressive, the auxiliary *will* + verb, and *be going to* + verb base form all show future meaning with a future time adverb.
- The future progressive uses either *will* or *be going to* + *be* + base verb form + *-ing*.

Grammar in Context (pages 52–53)

Background Notes

- A *millennium* is a thousand years. The new millennium began—technically—with the year 2001 and will continue until the year 3000.
- A *shuttle* is regularly scheduled to-and-from transportation, for example from the airport to your hotel, for which advance tickets are often not required.

Vocabulary

millennium: period of 1,000 years

century: 100-year period

era: long period of time beginning on a specific date

relate to: to be directly connected

bother: to make the effort to do something

high-tech: the most modern

robot: machine that can move and do some of the work of a person

Comprehension Questions

- When does the story take place? *(2115)*
- What hasn't changed in education? *(University teachers still teach in classrooms.)*
- Who cooks? *(a robot)*
- Why isn't Rocky's father at home? *(He flies to Mars on a regular schedule.)*
- Why are the freeways safer? *(There's a freeway guidance system so people don't have to "drive" anymore.)*

Discussion Topics

- Your new robot will do any part of your daily work. What will your robot do?

- Discuss the concept of a GPD for everyone. Is this a good or a bad idea?

Grammar Presentation (pages 54–57)

Identify the Grammar

FUTURE
. . . her clothing <u>will keep</u> her comfortably warm . . .

SIMPLE PRESENT
The shuttle <u>leaves</u> Mars at 6:00 P.M. today . . .

PRESENT PROGRESSIVE
Rocky's class <u>is going</u> on a field trip today . . .

<u>GOING TO</u>
Instead, she<u>'s going to listen</u> to music . . .

FUTURE PROGRESSIVE
Her son <u>will be waking up</u> soon . . .

Grammar Charts

- Write the four forms (simple present, present progressive, going to, and future) as column heads on the board.
- Have students find more examples in the reading of the four types and write the verb phrases for them on the board under the appropriate column heads.
- Do the same for the two forms of future progressive.
- Have students change the sentences on the board into yes/no questions and give the answers. Then make the statements negative.

Grammar Notes

Note 1 (Exercise 2)
- Point out that some of the differences among the four ways of giving future meaning are related to the situations: simple present is used for scheduled events (events planned now for later) so simple present makes sense: My train leaves at three.
- Will is used when a sudden decision or definite plans are made and when a prediction is made that the speaker is fairly sure of. Will may be the easiest to learn, but it is not used as frequently as the other forms are by native speakers. It tends to be over-used by nonnative speakers.
- Point out that be going to is much more common. It is used for less certain predictions, when a situation in the present leads to the prediction, and when one is

discussing intentions or plans. The present progressive is used for intentions, plans, and arrangements with not much difference between present progressive and be going to: I'm going home at three. / I'm going to go home at three.
- Encourage your students to use contractions and reductions so that it is easier for native speakers to understand them: I'll do it instead of I will do it.
- Quick pairwork: Have the students ask their partners: "What are you going to do this weekend? / What are you doing this weekend?" Emphasize that there is almost no difference between these two forms, but that pronunciation (contraction, reduction) is very important: Try to get students to say "Whadderya" and "gonna" or at least to expect to hear these from native speakers.
- To cover the difference between will and be going to, say, "I've just decided that I'm going to give a test tomorrow. What will you do tonight?" (We'll study.) (Future action decided at the moment of speaking.) Say, "It's going to rain tomorrow. What will you take when you leave your house tomorrow morning? (I'll take an umbrella.) (Certain or predicted event in the future influences present action.)
- Write on the board: There's a party tomorrow night. / There's going to be a party tomorrow night. (Remind students again that these forms are interchangeable.) Ask one student: "You got an invitation a week ago, and you've already bought new shoes just for the party, so . . ." (Student 1) I'm going to go. (It's sure.) Ask another student, "You just heard about the party today, and you're not really busy, so maybe . . ." (Student 2) Maybe I'll go.

Note 2 (Exercises 3, 4, 5)
- Quick pairwork: Students ask each other, "What will you be doing at this time tomorrow?" "On Saturday or Sunday at this time?" "Next month?" "In three months?"
- For students who need more challenge, insist on the reduction in the question: "What'll you be doing . . . ?"

Note 3 (Exercises 4, 5)
- Point out that when indicates a point in time (simple tense) and while denotes a length of time (progressive). In either case, one half of the sentence is some form of present even though the idea is future.
- Quick pairwork: Say, "I'll have dinner when I get home tonight." (Indicate a point in time

on the board.) "I'm going to clean my house on Saturday." (Indicate a length of time.) Students ask their partners, "What will you do when you get home tonight?" "What will you be doing while [teacher's name] is cleaning her/his house on Saturday?"

→ For additional practice, see the Supplementary Activities on page 92.

Focused Practice (pages 57–61)

Exercise 1
present: to give a performance in front of an audience

stay in: to live in a place for a while as a guest

conference: large formal meeting for members of a profession

hold (a news conference): to invite reporters to come at a particular time to ask questions

Exercise 2
for sure: certainly

Exercise 3
vacuum: to clean using a vacuum cleaner

massage: action of pressing and rubbing someone's body with your hands to reduce pain or help him/her relax

Exercise 4
telemarketer: salesperson who sells through telephone calls

Exercise 5
earthly: relating to life on Earth

defy: to refuse to obey

gravity: force that makes objects fall to the ground

compartment: smaller enclosed space inside another enclosed space

complimentary: given free to someone

swaying: moving gently from side to side

delay: to wait until a later time

Exercise 6
planet: (Mars, Venus, Saturn) very large round object that moves around the sun

Communication Practice (pages 62–65)

Exercise 7
• Before students listen, review the meaning of the concept of *being available.* Say, "I'm available at three o'clock. I can see you then. I'm not available at four; I can't see you then."
• Quick pairwork: "Let's plan a class picnic. Ask your partner: 'When are you available?'"

Exercise 8
Before students begin the exercise as indicated in the book, have them work with a partner to decide which things they enjoy doing and which are drudgery—not fun. Note that for some people, gardening might be fun and for others it is drudgery.

Exercise 9
Make sure students understand that neither calendar is complete.

Exercise 10
Repeat the concept of being available by asking questions such as "What will you be doing at (time and day)? Are you available for a meeting at (time and day)?" Stress that three forms are possible and equally correct here.

Exercise 11
• Make a list of questions to generate ideas and vocabulary. Write *NOW* and *10 YEARS FROM NOW* on the board and then these questions under the headings.

NOW
What are you doing now?
What are your plans for today?
What hobbies do you have now?
How are you preparing for the future?

10 YEARS FROM NOW
What will you be doing in 10 years?
What do you plan to be doing in 10 years?
What are you going to be doing for relaxation?
How are you going to be using your education?

• Quick pairwork: Have students work with partners to rehearse their answers orally before they write.

Further Practice
Students work with partners to answer one or more of the following questions in the most outrageous way they can. That is, they want to think of something bigger, better, funnier, more unusual than anyone else.

• Your country's ruler is coming to dinner at your house. What are you going to serve?
• You have been invited to a costume party. What will you wear?
• A television crew is coming to your house to interview you. What are you going to be doing when they arrive?
• You have been asked to give a speech on any topic. What do you plan to say?

Interview. Brainstorm ideas about interviewing people your students know outside of class, preferably people who are not students or teachers. Students will ask about typical days at work. You can use questions like these to get students started:

• Where do you work? (They might not have to ask this one.)
• What time do you get to work?
• By (two hours later), what work will you be doing? What will you still have to do?
• By the time your work day is half over, what are you probably doing?
• An hour before you finish your work for the day, what are you going to be doing?

Then have students report on what a working person's life is like.

(Suggestions of people to ask: people who work at fast-food restaurants and have to follow strict schedules, people who work in bookstores, office assistants, people who work in supermarkets, and professionals such as nurses, doctors, lawyers, or artists.)

UNIT 6 Future Perfect and Future Perfect Progressive

Unit Overview

Students will learn and practice the meanings and uses of the future perfect and the future perfect progressive.
• The future perfect, like one of the future forms, uses *will*, and like present perfect, it also uses *have*. It is used for action that will be completed by a specific time in the future (for example, by this time next week).
• The future perfect progressive uses *been* + base verb form + *-ing* in addition to *will* and *have*. Like all progressive forms, this tense is used to talk about action in progress at a certain time (in the future).

Grammar in Context (pages 66–67)

Background Notes

• Taking a show on the road (traveling to different cities and broadcasting from different cities) increases its popularity because people enjoy watching shows being made and participating in them.
• A good credit history is important for nearly everyone. Most people, for example, need to borrow money in order to buy a car.

Vocabulary

panel: a group of people who are chosen to discuss something

statistics: [plural] collection of numbers which represents facts or measurements

triple: to increase by three times

interest (on a loan): money that you must pay for borrowing money

essentials: things that are important and necessary

credit history: listing of all the recent money transactions like borrowing from and paying back a person or company

credit rating: composite number comparing a person's or company's credit history to a standard

Comprehension Questions

• Who are the panel members? *(Debbie, Sung, and Jeff)*
• How do college freshmen get credit cards? *(Credit card companies send them offers.)*
• What two mistakes do many college students make with their credit cards? *(They use them for things they want, not things they need. They pay only the minimum payment and thus have to pay a great deal of interest later.)*
• Why should a college student get at least one credit card and use it? *(to build up a credit history)*

Discussion Topics

• What are the advantages of using a credit card? What are the disadvantages?
• Do people who use cash (and not credit cards) really buy less?
• ⏱ Have students ask each other, in turn, how many credit cards they have. Keep a running tally of the numbers on the board as each student answers. When every student has answered, add up the numbers and divide by the number of students in the class to determine the average number of credit cards. Have the students, in small groups, discuss what they use the credit cards for, and whether they think they have more cards than they need.

Grammar Presentation (pages 68–71)

Identify the Grammar

FUTURE PERFECT

A typical college freshman will have gotten eight credit card offers by the end of the first semester.

Everything you bought on that card will have cost twice as much as the actual price.

FUTURE PERFECT PROGRESSIVE

. . . By the end of tonight's Money Talks, we'll have been traveling for a month, . . .

. . . I'll have been paying interest for nine months on pizzas I ate last September!

Grammar Charts

- Point out that the future perfect examples focus on a number or an amount (eight cards, twice as much) while the future perfect progressive examples focus on a length of time (for a month, for nine months).
- Write a sentence that can work in either tense on the board, for example (future perfect), *By 2010, I'll have lived here for six years.*
- Have the students change the sentence to future perfect progressive. Remind them that, as with present perfect and present perfect progressive, some verbs *(live, work, teach)* can be used in either form with little or no difference in meaning.
- Have students, working in pairs, find three time expressions for future perfect and future perfect progressive in the reading. Ask them to find differences between the forms *(future perfect: point in time; future perfect progressive: action in progress; also that future perfect is used with* yet, already, *and amounts or quantities, and future perfect progressive with duration of time).*

Grammar Notes

Note 1 *(Exercises 2, 3, 4)*
- Ask your students, "By this time next week, what will we have finished in class?" *(We will have finished Unit 6. We will have started Unit 7.)*
- Quick pairwork: Have partners ask each other, "What will you have done by this time next week?"

Notes 2–3
- Quick pairwork: Write the following sentence on the board and ask students to create two

sentences (one each in future perfect and future perfect progressive) from the information: *Mariana and Jim moved into their apartment on December 20, 2004.* If necessary, give them the hint that they'll need to use the verb *live.*
- Write *Mariana and Jim were married in December 2004.* Ask students if both forms are possible here. *(No, only future perfect, because no progressive form is possible with* be.)
- Brainstorm with students to make a list of five personal goals for next year. Then, working with partners, have them ask each other *yes/no* questions about these goals.

   A: Will you have learned to drive a stick shift car by next year?

   B: Yes, I will. / No, I won't.

- Use the list of goals on the board and establish a particular date (maybe two years from now). Quick pairwork: Have student pairs ask each other future perfect progressive questions with the goals and a length of time.

   A: By _____, how long will you have been volunteering at the hospital?

   B: I'll have been volunteering for five years by then.

- To contrast the two tenses, say, "I'm running a race on Saturday at two o'clock." Ask students to come up with sentences in both tenses to describe your situation at 2:30 on Saturday. *(You will have run three miles. You will have been running for 30 minutes.)* Stress pronunciation, especially because there are so many auxiliaries here which are not emphasized in normal native speaker English: *You will've been running for 30 **minutes**.*

→ For additional practice, see the Supplementary Activities on page 92.

Note 4 *(Exercise 3)*
Repeat the information that *yet* plus negative means we expect the action to happen—soon. *Already* indicates that the action happened before we expected it to happen.

Focused Practice (pages 71–76)

Exercise 1
anniversary: date on which something important or special happened in an earlier year

newsletter: short written report of news about a club, organization, or particular subject that is sent regularly to people

Exercise 5

resolution: a formal or official decision agreed on by a group, especially after a vote

Communication Practice (pages 77–78)

Exercise 6

- After students have heard the conversation, write five column heads on the board: *present progressive, future perfect, future progressive, future, future perfect progressive.*
- Have students write sentences from the listening in the appropriate columns: Thea and Don are contrasting *what they are spending* (present progressive) with *what they will have saved by next summer* (future perfect). They also realize how much less *they will be spending* (future progressive) this year as they plan for their trip. By two years from now they *will be* used to saving (future tense). They *will have been saving* money without thinking about it (future perfect progressive). If necessary, play the conversation again, stopping to let students fill in the information in each column.

Exercise 7

- Prepare students for this exercise by writing several categories on the board: *food and snacks, coffee or tea, transportation (bus, subway, gasoline and parking), school supplies, entertainment.*
- Quick pairwork: Have students work in pairs to figure out how much they spend in each of these categories and how they might save.

Exercise 8

- Ask the students how they will ask the questions. Write the questions on the board, working with the students to correct any errors in the grammar.
- Quick pairwork: Have student partners practice the questions before they gather into small groups for the survey.

Exercise 10

Help students think of reasonable goals by brainstorming ideas as a class. Write them on the board: *learn to play tennis, get fit by exercising and improving diet, learn to drive, train a dog to behave well, climb a mountain, redecorate my living space, take the TOEFL.*

Further Practice

"Ten years from now, I will be a successful _____. I will own my own home. This is

what I will have done to make it my dream house. . . ." Have students, working in pairs, discuss their dream homes, adding more sentences in the future perfect about making their houses into dream houses.

OUT OF THE BOX ● ● ● ● ● ●

Let me be your tourist guide. Team up students from the same area for this activity. Ask them to prepare a one-minute presentation on visiting their home regions. If many of your students are from the same area, have them choose another area that they would like to visit or present to the rest of the class. Have them bring in maps and pictures (perhaps get them from the Internet). Encourage the use of future perfect and future perfect progressive tenses: *By the time you get to Phoenix, you will have experienced a five-hour airplane ride. You will probably have been wondering how hot it will be. You will have seen many brown and gray mountains from the plane. By the time we arrive at the hotel, you will have passed . . .*

UNIT 7
Negative Yes/No Questions and Tag Questions

Unit Overview

Students will learn and practice making negative *yes/no* questions and tag questions.

- *Yes/no* questions can begin with a form of *be* or an auxiliary like *do/did* or *doesn't/didn't, has/have, can,* or *will.*
- Tag questions use the appropriate form (number and tense) of *be* or the auxiliary (the appropriate form of *do* or a modal) and the pronoun that matches the subject.

Grammar in Context (pages 88–90)

Background Notes

To help students activate their passive tourism vocabulary, have them gather tourist brochures, travel magazines, and Internet information sites about cities of the world and post them on the bulletin board.

Vocabulary

conduct a survey: to ask a large number of people a set of questions in order to find out about their opinions and behavior

adjustment: small change made to a machine, system, or calculation

endless: continuing for a very long time, especially in a way that is annoying

pond: small area of fresh water that is smaller than a lake

Comprehension Questions

• How does the reporter know Sousa is not a native of Rio? *(her accent)*
• What makes Rio a marvelous city? *(the bay, the beach, the mountains, and the places for entertainment)*
• Where are Kada and the reporter? *(Seoul, South Korea)*
• According to Okaya, where does it almost never rain? *(Cairo)*
• Where is Okaya from? *(Nairobi, Kenya)*
• According to Tessa Bradley, what is the most important difference between England and Canada? *(size)*

Discussion Topics

• What attracts you most about a big city? Why do you want to visit it?
• What kind of tourist are you? Do you like to see the "tourist places," or do you prefer to get to know about the daily lives of the native people? Do you like to visit many places or spend a long time in one or two? What do these preferences tell about you?

Grammar Presentation (pages 90–94)

Identify the Grammar

TAG QUESTIONS
That's not in Seoul, is it?
You're not from Rio, are you?
It gets awfully hot here in the summer, doesn't it?
You could tell right away by my accent, couldn't you?

NEGATIVE *YES/NO* QUESTIONS
Don't you miss your family . . . ?
Hey, didn't you buy anything?

Grammar Charts

• Write some example sentences with tag questions on the board. Have students change the verb forms.

• Have the students change the sentences with tag questions into negative *yes/no* questions.
• Try this drill to practice tag questions: Teacher offers rapid oral statements, students supply only the tags. Try to go in an order of progressive difficulty: "He's Japanese," *(isn't he?)* "She's not French," *(is she?)* "He doesn't speak French," *(does he?)* "She speaks English," *(doesn't she?)* "He was here yesterday," *(wasn't he?)* "She wasn't here Sunday," *(was she?)* (This is easier if you stay away from "I" and "you.") You can add humor as well as do a brief review if you work your way up to more complicated verb forms: "By 2010, he will have been studying English for many many years," *(won't he?)*. This will also show the students that even if the question is very long, the tag is still short and simple.

Grammar Notes

Note 1 *(Exercises 4, 5)*
Try this exercise to help students practice the subtle difference between a negative *yes/no* question and a statement with a negative tag question.
• Write some simple information statements on the board: *It's raining. She has a dog. We always come to school on time. They like apples.*
• Write *Check information* and *Get information.*
• Point first at one of your sample statements, then at either *Check information* or *Get information,* and then at a student, who should then say, "Doesn't she have a dog?" (for *Get information*) or "She has a dog, doesn't she?" (for *Check information*).

Note 2 *(Exercises 4, 5)*
Remind students that people who ask negative questions usually expect positive answers. You can do a quick drill of this by asking students questions to which they know you know the answers *(Isn't your name Pablo? Don't you usually write with a green pen?)* and then having them ask you similar questions, which you can prompt by giving just one information word *(teacher/far from the school/English).*

Note 3 *(Exercises 2, 3, 5)*
• Point out that positive statements have negative tag questions and negative statements have positive tag questions.

→ For additional practice, see the Supplementary Activities on pages 92–93.

Notes 4–5 *(Exercises 3, 5)*
To practice commenting/checking information with question tags, prepare two sets of cards,

using a different color for each set. One set has simple statements: *Today is Tuesday. It rained yesterday. We're having a test tomorrow. You've been working really hard lately.* Each card in the other set (an equal number of cards, in a different color) says either *Get information* with an arrow that indicates rising intonation or *Check/Comment* with an arrow that indicates falling intonation. Students work in pairs: One draws a statement card, the other an intonation card, then together they create the tag question with the appropriate intonation.

Note 6   *(Exercises 4, 5)*
• Rapid oral drill: Ask students simple but fast-paced negative *yes/no* questions and tag questions: "You're from Argentina, aren't you?" "You're not a musician, are you?" and insist on fast short answers. Many students have difficulty with the negative answer to a negative question. ("Didn't you come here on Sunday?" *No, I didn't.*) This rapid drill can be a good warm-up exercise even after you finish this unit.

Focused Practice (pages 94–98)

General note: Because intonation is so important to this structure, students can really benefit from listening to all of these exercises with a pencil to mark rising and falling intonation in the tags.

Exercise 1
vacant: empty and available for someone to use

Exercise 2
movers: people whose job it is to move furniture and personal items from one house or apartment to another

disconnect: to separate something from the thing it is connected to, or to become separated

Exercise 3
not have a cent: to be without even the smallest amount of money

work out: to gradually stop being a problem

Exercise 5
compose: to write a letter, poem, piece of music, etc. thinking very carefully about it as you write it

art installation: plan for using design and art in a project

Exercise 6
show one's face: to come and be seen; to appear

be wanted: to be looked for by the police

turn to someone: to try to get help, advice, or sympathy from someone

plenty: large amount that is enough or more than enough

Communication Practice (pages 98–101)

Exercise 7
Model rising and falling intonation using a sentence from grammar note 4 or 5. Remind students that a speaker asking a negative question with a rising intonation expects an answer. If the negative question form is being used as a comment, the intonation falls.

Further Practice
The police are looking for someone who has been stealing bicycles on campus. They know that the bicycle thief always wears black clothes and gloves, that the person uses a black van, that the stealing happens only at night, and that the thief must be aware of the campus police patrol schedule (because the police can never catch the thief). They also know that the thief is very strong (able to cut through bicycle security chains) and can ride any bicycle fast. Have students make up questions for suspects. To role-play, assign four to six people to be the police. Then secretly select a "thief" by passing (to the rest of the class) a cap with folded pieces of paper, one of which has the word *thief* on it. Only the student who draws the "thief" slip knows that he or she is "guilty." Encourage the use of negative questions *(Don't you have a black van?)* or statements with tag questions *(You can ride bicycles well, can't you?)*, and then let the interrogation begin!

Not yet? For this activity, have your students do some outside-of-class research. Have them ask at a tourism office, check on the Internet, or ask at an automobile club what is necessary to prepare for a road trip. Have them generate a list of questions related to planning a car trip. In class you can collect the results of their research and brainstorm ideas with your students. Write only the verb phrases on the board: *get maps, gather information from the Internet on places to see, make motel reservations, check the tires, fill*

the gas tank, pack the suitcases, go to the bank for traveler's checks, stop mail delivery, arrange for someone to take care of the pets, and so on. Pair students, give them 5–8 slips of paper on which to write their questions using the negative *yes/no* question form: *Haven't you . . . ? Didn't you . . . ?* These slips can be put into a bag to be chosen by the person who will answer. Then have students change partners and interview their new partners, taking slips out of the bag and alternating *yes* and *no* answers. *(Yes, I already have/did.* OR *No, I haven't done that yet.)*

UNIT 8 *So, Too, Neither, Not Either,* and *But*

Unit Overview

Students will learn and practice the use of *so, too, neither, not either,* and *but* for additions to sentences.

Grammar in Context (pages 102–104)

Background Notes

Identical twins look alike and, in fact, are physically identical because they come from the same egg. Fraternal twins come from two eggs; therefore, they do not usually look alike. In fact, one can be female and the other male.

Vocabulary

environmental: relating to situations, things, and people around us

factor: one of several things that influence a cause or situation

genetic: relating to genes or genetics

coincidence: situation in which two things happen together by chance, in a surprising way

turn up: to appear

astonishing: very surprising

govern: control the way a system or situation works

Comprehension Questions

• What are identical twins? *(two babies born from the same mother at the same time who look the same)*
• What is special about identical twins? *(They are exactly the same, physically.)*
• What is heredity? *(what we get genetically from our parents)*

• What is surprising about Mark and Gerald? *(Their lives have been very similar, but they grew up in different families and different places.)*
• Where do social influences on our lives come from? *(the environment)*
• How are Andrea and Barbara different? *(Andrea is outgoing, but Barbara isn't.)*

Discussion Topics

• If twins are separated at birth, and if the parents know, should they tell a child that he or she has a twin somewhere?
• Which do you think is more important in forming a personality, heredity (nature) or environment (nurture)?

Grammar Presentation (pages 104–107)

Identify the Grammar

SO AND *BUT*
Mark is a firefighter, and <u>so</u> is Gerald.
Andrea stayed in Germany, <u>but</u> Barbara didn't.

TOO
Mark likes hunting. . . . Gerald does <u>too</u>.

NOT EITHER AND *NEITHER*
Clearly, heredity doesn't completely govern our lives. Our environment doesn't <u>either</u>.
Mark has never been married, and <u>neither</u> has Gerald.

Grammar Charts

• Write one example sentence at a time on the board. Have students rewrite the sentences, changing a sentence with *too* to one with *so,* a sentence with *not either* to one with *neither.* Use colored chalk to highlight the changes in word order.
• Write an example sentence with *but.* Highlight the negative with colored chalk. *Andrea stayed in Germany, but Barbara did<u>n't</u>.*

Grammar Notes

Note 1   *(Exercises 2, 4)*
• Start by pointing out the need for these forms; show how awkward language becomes when we don't use them by writing this sentence on the board: *Heredity doesn't completely govern our lives, and our environment doesn't completely govern our lives.*
• Have the students look for similarities among their classmates so they can make comparisons. Suggested categories include

color of hair, color of eyes, style of clothing, type of backpacks, height, and ways of walking, laughing, speaking, smiling, and carrying books.

- Write the sentences on the board, for example:

    Greta has blue eyes, and so does Theo.

    Greta and Theo have blue eyes, but Paulo and Elsa don't.

    Alma smiles a lot, and so does Enrique.

- Quick pairwork: Have your students, working in partners, make up five sentences about themselves. (*I don't have red hair, and neither does Tam. Tam has black eyes, but I don't. I don't have any sisters, and Tam doesn't either.*) Encourage both partners to start with "I" so as to avoid sentences such as "We both have brown eyes."

Note 2   *(Exercises 2, 4, 6)*

Use the ideas from the Note 1 activities to form sentences with *too, neither,* and *not either.* Examples:

- Paulo doesn't have blue eyes, and neither does Elsa.
- Paulo doesn't have blue eyes, and Elsa doesn't either.
- Paulo has brown eyes, and Elsa does too.
- Ado talks loudly, and Ali does too.
- Fatma doesn't laugh loudly, and neither does Maya.

Notes 3 and 4   *(Exercises 2, 4, 6)*

- Remind students that *so* and *too* are used to show <u>similar</u> views or opinions.
- Note also that there is a change in word order if the speaker uses *too* and *so.* (*I enjoy mystery movies, and <u>Lee does too</u>. = I enjoy mystery movies, and <u>so does Lee</u>.*)
- Point out that *but* is used to show how two people or two things are <u>different</u>. (*Lee and I love mysteries, but Chou doesn't.*)

→ For additional practice, see the Supplementary Activities on page 93.

Note 5   *(Exercises 2, 4, 6)*

- Point out the rules about verbs for tag questions:
  1. *be* verb in main statement means *be* verb in the tag question
  2. modal in main statement means modal in the tag question
  3. neither *be* nor a modal in main statement means a form of *do* in the tag
- Mention that these rules hold true in additions with *so, neither, not either,* and *but.*

Notes 6 and 7   *(Exercise 3)*

- Brainstorm a list of modals and modal-like verbs and write them on the board (for example: *can, won't, should, want to, have to, had better, like to*).
- Have the students call out things they can do (for example: *speak English, ride a bicycle, swim, play a musical instrument, skydive, drive a car, sing well, hike*).
- Have students write sentences about themselves using the modal and the verb phrases. (*I can't skydive. I can sing well. I like to drive a car.*) Then have them work with a partner, alternately reading a sentence and responding to it with true personal information. (*You can't skydive, and I can't either.*)

Focused Practice (pages 108–111)

Exercise 2

innocence: state of not being guilty of a crime

be astounded: to be very surprised

Exercise 3

double: someone who acts and looks very similar to someone else

detest: to hate something or someone very much

Exercise 5

have in common: to have the same interests, attitudes, etc., as someone else

easygoing: not easily worried or annoyed

Communication Practice (pages 112–115)

Exercise 7

Before students listen to the recording, review how the expressions with *so, too, neither,* and *not either* show that two people agree about things. Only *but* is used to show differences, and *but* can be left out.

A: I never eat fast food.

B: I do. Sometimes I'm really in a hurry. (*A doesn't eat fast food, <u>but</u> B does sometimes.*)

Exercise 8

- Have students start at the top of Luigi's advertisement and make as many comments about it as they can.
- Have them expand their statements to compare Luigi's and Antonio's.
  (*Luigi's Italian Restaurant is named after a man, and so is Antonio's. The name of Luigi's Italian Restaurant uses English only, but Antonio's doesn't.*)

- Ask students which restaurant is probably more expensive, and why they think so. *(Antonio's: the Italian language used in the name, reservations suggested . . .)*

Exercise 9
Ask students what the man and woman disagree on (only sports).

Exercise 10
Use the last two items on the survey (numbers 11 and 12, which students make up themselves) to find out opinions on a hot topic at school. How compatible are the members of the class with one another?

Exercise 11
To help students get started with this exercise, brainstorm what the students notice in the two pictures, for example: the shelves and what is on them, the hairstyles, the glasses, the mustaches, the kind of clothing, the fact that they fold their arms left over right, tidiness, . . .

Exercise 12
Encourage students to use examples from the main reading and from Exercise 5.

Exercise 13
Review Exercise 5 before students start to write.

Further Practice
In small groups, have your students discuss growing up. What do they remember learning? How did they have fun? Give each student a slip of paper to write a statement about his or her childhood years. (Examples: *I learned to swim in a river. I couldn't have a part-time job. I had a pet monkey. I didn't have a bicycle. I learned to ski downhill.*) Then have the students pair up and find out whether their partner had a similar experience or not. They should create sentences like these:

I had a pet monkey, but Yuko had a kitten. Ahmet learned to swim in a river, and so did I. I didn't have any brothers, and neither did Maria/Maria didn't either.

GRAMMAR OUT OF THE BOX . . . . . .

And what do you think? Have your students interview someone or several people outside of class. Prepare for the interviewing by

brainstorming a list of topics about which people are likely to have opinions: *sports, food, a law about wearing helmets while bicycling, littering laws (what people should have to clean up if they litter), vegetarianism, high-risk sports.* Then students can come up with reports on their interview findings. *(Mary liked football, and so did Linda. Bob doesn't eat meat, and neither does Michael. Joan and Carlos think bicycle helmets are a good idea, but Karam doesn't and neither does Jaime.)*

UNIT 9 | Gerunds and Infinitives: Review and Expansion

Unit Overview

Students will learn and practice the meaning and use of gerunds and infinitives.
- Gerunds are base verbs + *-ing* used as nouns. *(I like hiking.)*
- Infinitives are *to* + base verb in form. *(I like to hike.)*
- Often the gerund and the infinitive have essentially the same meaning, so there is a lot of rote memorization involved in learning to use them correctly.

Grammar in Context (pages 124–125)

Background Notes
Because most fast foods are made with taste and not nutrition in mind, they are not necessarily healthy.

Vocabulary

synonymous: having a strong association with another quality, idea, situation

on the run: being very busy doing a lot of different things and going to different places

hectic: very busy, hurried, and slightly exciting

apart from: except for

be fed up with: to be annoyed with and want to change

in a word: introduces a simple answer

quality time: time that you spend giving someone your full attention, especially time you spend with your children

condemn: to say very strongly that you do not approve of something

Comprehension Questions

• Why is this reading named "McWorld"?
(There are McDonald's restaurants on almost every continent.)
• Why do people like fast foods? *(convenience, price, taste)*
• What food that is popular in your region could be sold at a fast-food restaurant? *(Students' answers will vary.)*
• Why does McDonald's sell vegetable burgers in some parts of the world? *(There are vegetarians everywhere, but in some places most people— potential customers—don't eat meat.)*
• What are the "golden arches"? *(the two sides of the deep gold-colored M of the McDonald's sign)*

Discussion Topics

• Why do you think so many fast foods are high in sugar, salt, and fat?
• How does the fast-food industry affect the environment?

Grammar Presentation (pages 126–128)

Identify the Grammar

GERUNDS
Dining on fast food has become a way of life . . .
But apart from the speed of ordering and getting served, . . . customers talk about . . .
. . . fast-food restaurants may prevent families from spending quality time together . . .

INFINITIVES
. . . it's easy to see that fast-food restaurants . . . aren't going away.
It's a high price to pay for convenience.
. . . people don't want to waste time.

Grammar Charts

• Use the example sentences to show the functions of the gerunds and infinitives:
Dining on fast food . . . is a gerund followed by a prepositional phrase as the subject.
. . . the speed of ordering and getting served . . . The two gerunds are objects of the preposition *of.*
. . . it's easy to see that . . . The adjective *easy* is followed by the infinitive, telling what action is easy.
. . . people don't want to waste time . . . The infinitive follows the verb *want.*

• Check that the students know the difference between an infinitive and a gerund by writing a pair of sentences and underlining the relevant parts: *Eating at McDonald's is easy. / It's easy to eat at McDonald's.*
• This could move into pairwork and a substitution drill. Ask, "What else is easy?" *(It's easy to drive in the country. It's hard to drive in the city. / Driving in the country is easy. Driving in the city is hard.)*
• Quick pairwork: Have students make up sentences parallel in structure to those in the charts. (From the chart: *They plan to reduce fats in the food.* Parallel to chart: *I plan to take a trip to South America.*)

Grammar Notes

Note 1 *(Exercises 2, 4)*
Quick pairwork: Put on the board a list of adjectives: *easy/difficult, fun/boring, cheap/ expensive.* Have students make up sentences with various activities plus the adjectives. *(Taking tests is boring. Shopping is fun.)*

Notes 2 and 3 *(Exercises 2, 3, 4)*
• Point out that there are four main patterns for these structures:
1. verb + gerund (+ object) *I enjoy eating (breakfast).*
2. verb + infinitive (+ object) *I want to eat (breakfast).*
3. verb + object + infinitive (+ object) *I want you to eat (breakfast).*
4. verb + preposition + gerund (+ object) *I look forward to eating (breakfast).*
• Re-emphasize that the preposition *to* in pattern 4 is not the same as the infinitive *to* in pattern 2. Use one colored chalk to underline the infinitive, *to,* and a different color for *to* before a gerund.
• Remind students that there are lists of verbs which follow these patterns in Appendices 3 and 4 (pages A-2–A-3), and that some of these just need to be memorized.
• Quick pairwork to practice the very high-frequency structures with *want*: Have students ask their partners (1) "What do you want to do this weekend?" (2) "What do you want your friend/husband/wife/sister/ roommate to do this weekend?" (3) "What does your friend/husband/wife/sister/ roommate want you to do this weekend?" Circulate and check grammar and pronunciation (reductions: *Whaddya* for *what do you, wantcha* for *want you*).

- Point out that gerund plus possessive is very formal written English (for example, *I dislike Jason's interrupting me.*).

→ For additional practice, see the Supplementary Activities on page 93.

Note 4 *(Exercises 3, 4)*
- Emphasize that some verbs can take either a gerund or an infinitive with little or no change in meaning. Examples include *begin, continue, hate, like, love, prefer, start.*
- Point out that some verbs can take either a gerund or an infinitive, but there is a difference in meaning. Examples include *forget, remember, try, stop . . . (from).*
- Quick pairwork: Have students make sentences with these verbs and add a second sentence to explain the difference in meaning for each example. *(I forgot to water the plants. [I didn't water them at all.] I forgot watering the plants. [Oh, yes, and I almost forgot to tell you: I also watered the plants.])* You might give the students the situation and have them create the sentences. Say, for example, "A man was working, using both hands, but he wanted a cigarette. He couldn't smoke and work at the same time, so . . ." *(He stopped to smoke.)* Then say, "A man smoked for years but then wanted to become healthier, so . . ." *(He stopped smoking.)*

Note 5 *(Exercises 2, 4)*
- Have students use the verb + preposition combinations in Appendix 7 (page A-3) to make true sentences about themselves and their friends.
- Remind students that *to* in these cases is a preposition, not an infinitive; hence the tricky *look forward to having.*
- Quick pairwork: Have students ask their partners "What are you looking forward to doing tomorrow/this weekend/next year?" Again, stress the reduction: *"Whadderya."*

Note 6 *(Exercises 2, 4)*
- Verbs that are commonly followed by an adjective and an infinitive are listed in Appendix 9, page A-4.
- Quick pairwork: Have student pairs practice asking and answering questions like these: "What are you afraid to do?" *(I'm afraid to try skydiving. I'm afraid to swim where there might be sharks.)* Note also that some people say, *"I'm afraid of swimming where there might be sharks."*
 "What foods are you reluctant to try?" *(I'm reluctant to try raw fish. I'm reluctant to try some tropical fruits.)*

Note 7 *(Exercise 4)*
- Point out that almost any noun can be followed by an infinitive phrase in order to provide additional information (for example, *a doll to play with, a day to remember/forget, paper to write on*).
- Have students ask each other, "What do you want to buy, and why?" *(I want to buy some new shoes to wear on Saturday.)*

Note 8 *(Exercise 4)*
- Remind students that this use of the infinitive is connected to the question *Why? (Why does Doug eat fast food? To save time.)*
- Point out that this also can be seen as an abbreviation of *in order to.* Put on the board, *Doug eats fast food in order to save time.* Then cross out *in order.*

Note 9 *(Exercise 4)*
As a class, have students do a substitution chain drill with these structures.

1. Student A creates a sentence with a **gerund** subject. *(Riding an exercycle is good exercise.)*
2. Student B changes the gerund subject to the it + noun phrase + **infinitive** structure. *(It's good exercise to ride an exercycle.)*
3. Student C changes the adjective. *(It's boring to ride an exercycle.)*
4. Student D changes it back to a **gerund** subject. *(Riding an exercycle is boring.)* Let students change any part of the sentence. If they get into a rut, you can offer a prompt: "It is . . ." or "Watching television every night . . ."

Focused Practice (pages 129–133)

Exercise 1
issue: subject or problem that people discuss

Exercise 2
nutritionist: specialist in knowing the right types of food for good health and growth

Exercise 3
mess: place or group of things that is not organized or arranged neatly

Exercise 4
sombrero: broad-brimmed, tall-crowned felt or straw hat of a kind worn in Mexico

fast-food court: central place in a shopping area where several fast-food outlets share a common table area

commuter: someone who travels to work or school every day

Exercise 5

vegetarian: someone who doesn't eat meat or fish

octopus: sea creature with a soft body and eight tentacles

tender (food): food easy to cut and eat

dumpling: small piece of dough, steamed or boiled and served with meat or soup

Communication Practice (pages 134–137)

Exercise 6

Victor and Lily have a discussion in which they talk about the school's food services. Quick pairwork: Have pairs of students discuss their ideas about a school's food services. *Should there be fast foods available? Who should decide what kinds of foods students can buy? What kinds of food services are common in other parts of the world? Why do fast-food franchises open restaurants on campuses?*

Exercise 7

Use the ideas from the pairwork in Exercise 6 for the questionnaire.

Exercise 8

Students can help one another learn about traditional foods from other places. Have students who have similar traditions work together to talk about particular foods.

Exercise 9

Make sure that the students understand that together they have all of the information. Suggest that pairs of students interview each other to see which interests they have in common.

Exercise 10

• Ask small groups of students to prioritize the four problems listed: *people being overweight, traffic, literacy problems,* and *homelessness.*

• Ask them to explain their reasons. Note that the priorities will vary in different regions.

Exercise 11

• Start with pairwork: Ask students, "What are some issues that people are discussing on television, in the newspapers, and around school?" Ask each pair to come up with three ideas.

• Open up the discussion to the whole class so that there are a number of topics in addition to the social problems in Exercise 10 for students to choose from. (Examples: *flooding on the streets after storms, violence in movies*

and on TV, people throwing trash out on the roads [littering].)

Further Practice

(This can be done as a five-minute per class activity over the course of an entire semester.) Use the lists from Appendices 3–5 and 7, pages A-2–A-3 (verbs followed by infinitive, gerund, or preposition + infinitive). Type them up in mixed order, and then photocopy so that each student has a list. Ask students, individually, to go over the list and mark *to* or *-ing* or *prep. + inf.* next to each verb. (You can suggest symbols or abbreviations.) When they've finished, you read out the correct answers and have students mark the verbs where they made a mistake.

You then generate a master list of the class's "problems" from these individual lists (total class time: about 10 minutes). Spend five minutes per class on three or four different verbs from this selective list by playing "Going to Jerusalem" in groups of three. Here's how it works: If the verbs for the day are *demand, promise, hesitate, mention,* students make a chain of sentences using these verbs.

A: I demand to go home.

B: She demands to go home, and I promise to take her home.

C: She demands to go home, she promises to take her home, but I hesitate to leave early.

A: I demand to go home, she promises to take me, he hesitates to leave early, and I mention being tired and hungry.

Sometimes this slips naturally into past tense, which is fine; just make sure the gerunds and infinitives don't change.

GRAMMAR OUT OF THE BOX . . . . . .

Tell me about the job. Have students bring the classified ads to class, and look at the Help Wanted or Job Openings section. As they read the ads, have them discuss the qualifications for the jobs using gerunds. *(A restaurant chef's job includes washing, peeling, and cutting up vegetables. A security officer's job is checking locks and watching for trouble.)* More directly, they could say, *I'm a chef. My job is cutting up vegetables. . . .* Have the students write the titles of the jobs they find on index cards with a list of responsibilities under it to post on the bulletin board.

UNIT 10 — Make, Have, Let, Help, and Get

Unit Overview

Students will learn the meanings and uses of *make, have, let, help,* and *get* as verbs used as auxiliaries to show that one person can <u>cause</u> (or <u>require</u>, <u>permit</u>, or <u>persuade</u>) another person to do something.

Grammar in Context (pages 138–139)

Background Notes

In general, people naturally seem to distrust animals just as animals distrust people. Perhaps that is why tamed animals are so dear to people who love their pets.

Vocabulary

orca: killer whale

collar: narrow band of leather or plastic put around the neck of an animal

leash: piece of rope or leather fastened to a dog's collar in order to control the dog

humane: treating people or animals in a way that is kind, not cruel

positive reinforcement: doing something pleasurable to make a behavior stronger

draw blood: to take blood from a person or animal for medical reasons

tests: medical examinations

abuse: cruel or violent treatment of someone or something

captive: kept in a prison or in a place that you are not allowed to leave

Comprehension Questions

- How much does an orca weigh? *(about nine tons)*
- What are the two ways to train animals? *(with cruel punishments or with positive reinforcement—a kind, humane way)*
- What is the difference between an elephant trained with punishment and an elephant trained with positive reinforcement? *(Punishment makes elephants angry so that they rebel and can become dangerous. Positively reinforced elephants are gentle animals that seem to understand that their trainers want to help them.)*
- What is an animal actor? *(an animal that has been trained to perform for audiences)*

- What is the opinion of some animal rights organizations? *(that animals should be allowed to live their natural lives)*

Discussion Topics

- What are some basic human rights? Do animals also have rights? What do you think their rights should be? How are animals and people different? The same?
- "Vote with your feet." People who work for the freedom of animals urge others to stay away from circuses and animal parks. Ask your students to explain why.
- Are wild animals always less happy in captivity? What are disadvantages to life in the wild?

Grammar Presentation (pages 140–141)

Identify the Grammar

But how do trainers . . . <u>make them "dance"</u>?
. . . a trainer <u>lets an animal act</u> freely.
. . . parks wanted to <u>have dolphins do tricks</u>.
Gary Priest . . . <u>helped the keepers train</u> the elephants . . .
But how do trainers <u>get a nine-ton whale to do acrobatic tricks</u> . . . ?

Grammar Charts

- Write *make, help, let,* and *have* on the board. After each one, write an example sentence from the reading. Erase the subject and have the students provide a new one. Next erase the phrase after *make, help, let,* or *have.* Have the students write a new sentence ending. Encourage them to find humorous ideas (for example, *The teacher lets the students sleep in class!*)
- Write the example sentence with *get . . . to do (something)* on the board. Erase different parts for students to supply new words (for example, *How could I . . . ?* in place of *How do trainers . . . ?*)

Grammar Notes

Note 1   *(Exercises 2, 3)*
- Emphasize the causative meanings of *make, let, have. Make* means "require" or "force" or "cause." *Have* means "cause" but in a neutral way. *Let* means "allow" or "permit."
- Point out that these causative verbs are very common and often sound more natural (to native speakers) than their non-causative equivalents: *permit, require, force.*

Note 2 *(Exercises 2, 3)*
Emphasize that *help* means "assist." Some people use *to* with *help: The medicine helped me (to) sleep.*

Note 3 *(Exercise 3)*
- Emphasize that *get . . . to do (something)* means "convince" or "persuade."
- Quick pairwork: Ask students to think of positive reinforcement ways to get students to do their best work, hand in assignments on time, and volunteer for class activities.
- Have each pair share their ideas with the rest of the class.
- Point out that *get . . . to do (something)* is more common in combination with another verb (for example, *try to get the kids to practice piano, can't get my husband to do the dishes*).

→ For additional practice, see the Supplementary Activities on page 93.

Focused Practice (pages 141–145)

Exercise 1
term paper: long paper or report assigned to be written by a student in a course during a school or college term

Exercise 2
authority figure: person seen or thought of as having power or status

overtime: time that you work on your job in addition to your usual working hours

physical: medical examination by a doctor to check that you are healthy

chore: job that you have to do

landlord: someone who owns a building or other property and rents it to other people

Exercise 3
context: situations, events, or information that are related to something, and that help you to understand it

flash: bright light on a camera that you use when taking photographs indoors or when there is not much light

Exercise 4
captivity: state of being kept as a prisoner or in a small space

embarrassing: making you feel ashamed, nervous, or uncomfortable

retrain: to teach someone or something to do something in a different way, in this case in the original way

Communication Practice (pages 146–148)

Exercise 5
- Simon needs some help with his essay. Review *wh-* question words (*who, what, when, where, why,* and *how*).
- Call students' attention to the fact that Mrs. Jacobson helps Simon help himself by giving him ways to think about details.

Exercise 6
Quick pairwork: Have students ask each other questions about a good class: "What does a good teacher do?" *(lets us answer slowly, helps us understand, gets us to use only English in class, makes us do the homework)* "How do good students act in class?" *(listen carefully, try to answer, think about other ways to say something)*

Exercise 7
- Have your students work in small groups to come up with one example each of what their parents *made them do, let them do, helped them learn to do, had them do around the house,* and *got them to do even if they were afraid.*
- Have the groups share their ideas with the rest of the class.

Exercise 8
- Quick pairwork for problem 1: Students ask each other: "What arguments does a parent have against buying a new dress?" "What arguments does a parent have against makeup for a 12-year-old girl?"
- Quick pairwork for problem 2: Students ask each other: "What are the arguments against animal acts?" "What arguments are there for animal acts?"

Exercise 9
- Isolate the expressions with *make, have, let, help,* and *get* from the paragraph in the book. Write them on the board.
- Review the sentences and then replace everything except the verbs with blanks.
- Have students supply examples from personal experience for each of the five verbs.

Further Practice
On the board, write the five causative verbs: *make, have, let, help,* and *get.* With the whole class, brainstorm figures of authority like *a police officer, the government, a good boss, a bad boss, my mother, the head of the school.* Encourage the use of all five verbs, and point out if one is not being used. Encourage

students, in any case, to make negative as well as positive sentences and to create humorous sentences. *(A police officer made me stop picking flowers in the park. The head of the school got me to try out for the lead in the school play.)*

GRAMMAR OUT OF THE BOX ......

Other people at work. Have students go back to the same working people they interviewed for Grammar out of the Box in Unit 5. This time they will ask them about their relationships with other people at work, either people they supervise or people who supervise them. What do they have people do, make people do, get people to do during their working day? Students then report back to the class. *(I spoke to a doctor. She tries to get patients to eat right. She has them take medicine when they need it. Her job makes her feel tired.)*

Phrasal Verbs: Review

Unit Overview

Students will learn the meanings and uses of phrasal verbs: transitive and intransitive, separable and inseparable.

- Phrasal verbs, also called two-word verbs, are made up of a verb and a particle (which "looks like" a preposition). Note that the particle often does not help make the meaning clear out of context.
- Most transitive phrasal verbs are separable (meaning that the object can go before or after the particle).
- Intransitive phrasal verbs cannot be separated.

Grammar in Context (pages 158–159)

Background Notes

There is a great deal that we do not know about the world and how things work. How energy flows may be one of those things. Feng shui is an old idea in China, but it is new in many other parts of the world. Write *feng shui* on the board. Ask whether any of your students know

how to pronounce the words. Ask whether any members of the class know what the term means. Ask if someone knows what *chi* is *(good energy)*. Tell the class that this reading is about adding good energy to your life.

Vocabulary

pay a fortune for: to give a very large amount of money for

prosperity: the condition of having money and being successful

lay out: to arrange

Comprehension Questions

- What was Ho Da-ming's problem with his restaurant? *(He was losing money.)*
- What are the two forces in all environments? *(good energy, or* chi, *and bad energy, or* sha*)*
- What is the Chinese belief about *chi* and *sha*? *(They can affect health, wealth, and happiness.)*
- What do the words *feng shui* mean? *(wind and water)*
- What, according to the feng shui consultant, was wrong with the restaurant? *(The entrance was letting the prosperity out.)* (Opportunity for review: Remind students about "let" in Unit 10.)

Discussion Topics

- Do you believe the arrangement of things in a house can affect people? Why or why not?
- Do you like to move things around in your room or your house? How do you feel after you do it?
- How does art affect you? Does a painting ever give you really good feelings? Do some paintings depress you? Why do you think you have these reactions?

Grammar Presentation (pages 159–161)

Identify the Grammar

TRANSITIVE PHRASAL VERBS
He had <u>set</u> it <u>up</u> on a busy street.
The desperate owner <u>tore down</u> the old entrance and <u>put up</u> a new one.

INTRANSITIVE PHRASAL VERBS
But customers rarely <u>came back</u>.
His action <u>paid off</u>.
Feng shui has <u>caught on</u> with homeowners and architects everywhere.

Grammar Charts

- Write one sentence with an intransitive phrasal verb on the board. *(His hard work paid off.)* Point out that the two-word verb really has one meaning (*come back* = return, *pay off* = succeed).
- Emphasize that phrasal verbs are less formal than single-word verbs and are used more frequently, and that often the single-word equivalent sounds "funny" or overly formal to native speakers, for example *fetch* or *collect* instead of *pick up*.
- Write a transitive sentence with a phrasal verb from the examples on the board. Show how the direct object can move before and after the particle:
  He had set his restaurant up on a busy street.
  He had set up his restaurant on a busy street.
- Point out that the pronoun *it* could take the place of *his restaurant*, but only if the verb *set up* is separated: *He set it up.* If the direct object is a pronoun, it has to go between the verb and the particle.

Grammar Notes

Note 1 *(Exercise 2)*
Use the examples of phrasal verb sentences on the board. Circle the particles, explaining that they might look like prepositions, but they act differently. Say and demonstrate, "I'm looking up at the ceiling." "I'm looking up the new word in my dictionary."

Note 2 *(Exercises 2, 3)*
- Point out that phrasal verbs can have more than one meaning. Students will be familiar with the concept of idioms, and they might have already noticed that phrasal verbs are much like idioms in that their meaning is greater than the sum of their parts.
- Quick pairwork: Have student pairs add to the sentences with the phrasal verbs in the chart: *come back, figure out, look into, pick out, put up, turn down. (Customers didn't come back after the first time they ate at the restaurant because of the entrance. We had to figure out the problem because no one else would do it. We looked into feng shui to find a reason for the problems with our health.)*

Notes 3 and 4 *(Exercise 4)*
- Point out that transitive phrasal verbs are separable: The direct object noun can go before or after the particle. If the direct object is a pronoun, it must go before the particle.

- Quick pairwork: Have student pairs make new, longer sentences with the phrasal verbs in the chart: *call off, pick out, take away, think up, work out.*
- Quick pairwork: Have students work in pairs (a) to change the noun direct objects into pronouns and (b) to state the sentences with the pronouns between the verb and the particle. For additional practice with transitive phrasal verbs, use the verbs in Appendix 17 (pages A-6–A-7).
- Suggest that your students try adding adjectives to direct objects so that there are more than three words in the direct object and the verb becomes inseparable. More than four words is too long to "fit" between a verb and a particle. Explain that *He looked the number up* or *He looked up the number* are both OK, but not *He **looked** the number of his new classmate with red hair and glasses **up**.* Encourage the students to have some fun with this idea: to try to make the sentence longer and longer (but still grammatically correct).

Note 5 *(Exercise 3)*
Quick pairwork: Give each pair of students four intransitive verbs to make sentences with. (Use the list of intransitive verbs in Appendix 18, page A-8, for more practice with your students; there are about 60 verbs in the list.) Have the students share their sentences with the class—one student reading the sentence and the other restating it with the meaning clarified. For example: *The news announcer went on for five more minutes. = The news announcer continued for five minutes. He talked five more minutes.*

→ For additional practice, see the Supplementary Activities on page 94.

Focused Practice (pages 162–166)

Exercise 1
phoenix (bird): bird in ancient times that burns itself up at the end of its life and is born again from the ashes

inspiration: something that encourages you to do or produce something good

tortoise: slow moving land animal that can put its legs inside the shell that covers its body

cubicle: small, partly enclosed part of a room

mobile: decoration made of small objects tied to string and hung up so that they move when air blows around them

overall (adj): including everything

promotion: a move to a better, more responsible position at work

Exercise 2

Q and A: questions and answers

scarf: piece of material that you wear around your neck, head, or shoulders to keep you warm or make you look attractive

Exercise 3

controversial: something that causes a lot of disagreement because many people have strong opinions about it

harsh: unkind, cruel, or strict

perfectionistic: striving for an extreme degree of excellence

press for something: to try very hard to persuade someone to accept something

Exercise 4

depressing: making you feel sad

cracked: having lines on the surface because it is damaged

Exercise 5

sunny: full of light from the sun

chipped (paint): broken on the surface

touch something up: to improve by making small changes

spacious: having lots of space or room for you to move around

end up: to be in a place, situation, or condition after a series of events, usually when you did not plan it

Communication Practice (pages 166–168)

Exercise 6

Be prepared to repeat the conversations, as the particles are not emphasized and your students might have difficulty hearing them. In some cases, it might be a good idea to follow the exercise with small group work during which the students read their completed conversations to one another.

Exercise 7

Discuss what things can be *covered up, done over, hung up,* etc.

Exercise 8

As an expansion activity, have students discuss in general what they have changed or would like to change in the appearance of their bedrooms.

Exercise 9

To help the class get started with this writing assignment (which could be done over several days as a journal writing project), begin with a whole class brainstorm. Make a list of decorating ideas that students like. Then brainstorm a list of decorating ideas (or bad housekeeping ideas) that they do not like. Have student pairs ask each other how a tidy environment or an attractive environment affects how they feel about working and living in that space. (Or is one partner someone who doesn't seem to notice a pleasant or unpleasant environment?)

Further Practice

Have students work with a partner. First, they should find 10 phrasal verbs in Appendices 17 and 18, pages A-6–A-8, that neither knows. Then they should write a dialogue using those verbs.

Home improvement interviews. Ask students to find at least two native speakers of English and interview them about improvements or changes they have made to their homes. Students then write down all the phrasal verbs that the native speakers have used (or as many as they can), and share them with the rest of the class, giving context and examples. Some phrasal verbs should come up in several student interviews (for example, *do over, fix up, take apart, put together, take down, put up*).

UNIT 12 — Phrasal Verbs: Separable and Inseparable

Unit Overview

Students will learn the meanings and uses of more separable and inseparable phrasal verbs.

Grammar in Context (pages 169–170)

Background Notes

Advertising can take many forms. In this reading, telephone sales, direct mail sales, and electronic sales techniques are explained. In particular, polite but firm ways to handle telemarketers are described.

Vocabulary

exhausted: extremely tired

case of the flu: example of a disease like a very serious cold

invasion: occasion when an army enters a country using military force

tactics: way in which soldiers, weapons, etc., are arranged in a battle

unfamiliar: not known to you

count on: to depend on someone or something

eliminate: to get rid of something completely

solicitation: act of asking someone for money or help

get to someone: to reach someone (note: *get someone to do something* (in Unit 10) means to persuade another person to do something)

Comprehension Questions

- What is telemarketing? *(the practice of selling products and services by phone)*
- Why is telemarketing becoming so widespread? *(The number of telephones has gone up and costs of telephones have come down.)*
- Why do people have Caller ID? *(You can see what number is calling you and answer only the calls you want to receive.)*
- What is junk mail? *(unwanted offers and requests)*
- What do we call advertising, free offers, and requests on e-mail? *(spam)*

Discussion Topics

- It costs a lot less to send many identical pieces of mail at one time. The rates are called bulk mail rates. Advertisers send out thousands of pieces of mail at one time. The people who get this mail call it junk mail. Most people throw away the paper (one problem). However, because of bulk mail income for postal services, the cost of ordinary personal and business letters can be lower (one benefit). Discuss whether bulk (junk) mail is good or bad.
- The job of telemarketer is a hard one because many people are rude to people who make unwelcome calls. However, telemarketing is a job that helps people support their families. Are the advantages or disadvantages for society greater?

Grammar Presentation (pages 171–172)

Identify the Grammar

INSEPARABLE TRANSITIVE
. . . *write down* the date and time of the call.
(Note: This direct object is too long to go before the particle.)
. . . *get off* the phone.

SEPARABLE TRANSITIVE
You hesitate to *pick* it *up*.
"Junk mail" *fills up* our mailboxes (and later our trash cans when we *throw* it *out*).

INTRANSITIVE (INSEPARABLE)
You just *got back* from a long, hard day at the office.
"I'm *hanging up* now."

Grammar Charts

- Choose an example sentence with a separable phrasal verb and write it on the board. Show students how the direct object can move. Then substitute a pronoun for the direct object and show how the phrasal verb must separate to allow the pronoun in.
  You hesitate to *pick up* the telephone.
  You hesitate to *pick* the telephone *up*.
  You hesitate to *pick* it *up*.
- Quick pairwork: Write these words on the board: *take away, the package, put away, their library books, take back, your promise.* Have students substitute one item at a time in a chain replacement drill.

Grammar Notes

Note 1 *(Exercises 2, 3)*
Go over the note in the student book with your class. Then ask these questions and ask students to answer them.

What did you take off when you came into the building? *(I took off my coat.)*
What did you write down in your notebook? *(I wrote down some answers/new words.)*
What forms have you filled out? *(I've filled out a scholarship application form, a driver's license application, and a survey.)*

Note 2 *(Exercises 2, 4)*
With your students, make up a few sentences using these inseparable verbs: *run into* (meet unexpectedly), *carry on* (continue), *stick with* (not quit), and *come off* (become loose or break

off) are the most common verbs in this small group. For example: *I ran into an old friend at the mall. His son will carry on the business. Pat decided to stick with the company for a few more years. The paint came off in a number of places.*

Note 3 *(Exercises 2, 4)*
- Point out that a few transitive phrasal verbs must be separated. Write ONLY the verbs on the board: *ask someone over* (invite someone to one's home), *bring someone down* (depress, cause to lower), *do something over* (redo, do again), *get something out of something* (benefit from), *keep something on* (not take something off), *see something through* (finish something), *start something over* (begin again), *talk someone into* (persuade), *turn someone or something into* (change from one form to another). Note that some of these verbs frequently occur with a gerund. They always require a gerund if the object of the preposition isn't a noun: *get something out of (doing something), talk someone into (doing something).*
- Have your students, working in small groups, make up sentences with these verbs (for example, three verbs per group). Stress that the sentence should be interesting AND show the meaning of the verb: *I wanted to ask my friends over, but I didn't have any food in the house, so we went out.*

Note 4 *(Exercises 2, 4)*
- Review a few of the common phrasal verb + preposition combinations: *put up with, get out of, look forward to, keep away from, keep up with, come up with, drop out of.*
- Quick pairwork: Write these phrasal verb + preposition combinations on the board and have students work with partners to practice them: *What do you look forward to doing this weekend? What do you always try to get out of doing? Have you ever had trouble keeping up with a class?* If they have trouble, put a few cue words on the board: *what, when, why, ever, this weekend, last year.* Circulate and check students' pronunciation and use of gerunds.

→ For additional practice, see the Supplementary Activities on page 94.

Focused Practice (pages 173–177)

Exercise 1
strategy: planned series of actions for achieving something
hold on: to wait

Exercise 2
return a favor: to give something back to a person who helped you
be obligated: to feel it is your duty to do something

Exercise 5
talk someone into something: to convince someone of something

Communication Practice (pages 178–180)

Exercise 6
Before students listen, make sure they are familiar with all of the terms in Mr. Chen's notes: *long-distance, a plan, phone service, included, monthly fee, activation fee.*

Exercise 7
On the board write your students' pros (arguments in favor of telemarketing) and cons (arguments against telemarketing). Ask two groups of students to debate the concept of telemarketing, using the ideas on the board.

Exercise 8
Have students practice their role plays. Ask for volunteers to perform for the class.

Exercise 9
Ask your students to look for junk mail to bring to class. Discuss concepts like intended audience (retired people, teenagers, young parents, grandparents), attractiveness of the junk mail (bright colors, photographs, shiny paper), misuse of the word "free."

Exercise 10
- Have students work in pairs to answer these questions:
  Who calls you on the telephone? *(family and friends, telemarketers, people confirming appointments, bill collectors)*
  What do you need to have a telephone for? *(to connect to the Internet, call friends, get information about movie times, order a pizza)*
  What problems have you had with the telephone? *(wrong numbers, telemarketers, bad connection, confusion over who is calling, confusion over why the person is calling)*

- Have students tell a story about a telephone experience using at least three phrasal verbs *(hang up, end up, pick up, write down, talk someone into).*

Further Practice

Have students try to work as many separable or inseparable phrasal verbs as they can into a five-sentence paragraph. Encourage them to use Appendices 17 and 18 (pages A-6–A-8) as sources for their phrasal verbs. Ask them to underline the phrasal verbs. Have a prize for the student with the highest number in five sentences. This assignment might be more fun if you have pairs or small groups of students work together.

GRAMMAR OUT OF THE BOX......

Tell me how you make it. Have students look for directions for how to make something simple (a candle out of ice using a piece of string, paraffin wax, and a quart milk container; a photo album using squares of cardboard, a hole punch, and ribbon; a special greeting card). Simple craft books available at public libraries have many ideas. Have the students work in pairs to write out directions (using phrasal verbs) for the projects. Supply some phrasal verbs from Appendix 17 (pages A-6–A-7) which might be useful: *cover up, cut off, cut out, do over, lay out, move around, pick out, pick up, put back, put together, take off, tear up, turn around, turn over.*

| UNIT 13 | **Adjective Clauses with Subject Relative Pronouns** |

Unit Overview

Students will learn the meanings and uses of adjective clauses in which the subject is a relative pronoun.
- The subject relative pronouns are *who, that,* and *whose* (with a noun).
- These subject relative pronouns are the subjects of clauses within a full sentence.

Grammar in Context (pages 190–191)

Background Notes

Margaret Mead is a famous name among anthropologists and social scientists who study people and their relationships. Dr. Mead studied and wrote about how culture affects personality. Among people in different parts of the world, she pointed out, there are different ideas about right and wrong. Through her work, social scientists have come to understand the importance of fieldwork.

Vocabulary

chat with: to have a friendly conversation with someone, especially on the Internet

acquaintance: someone you know, but not very well

vice versa: the opposite of the situation just described

innermost: most strongly and privately held (feelings)

notion: idea, belief, or opinion, especially one that you think is wrong

temperament: part of your character that makes you likely to be happy, angry, sad

mutuality: feeling of shared ideas and values

fade: to disappear gradually, to lose color

casual: not close

Comprehension Questions

- What is a friend to a Russian? *(someone who knows you "behind the soul")*
- What does a French person know about his or her friends? *(the others' intellect, temperament, interests)*
- What happens to two German friends who have a deep disagreement? *(Their friendship is probably, and sadly, over.)*
- What are British friendships based on? *(interests in common)*
- What is unusual about American friendships? *(Americans make friends fast and give them up fast. Americans tend to have friends in different categories: baseball or football friends, friends who share hobbies with them, shopping friends, church friends, school friends.)*

Discussion Topics

- Why do definitions of *friend* differ within a culture?
- What do you think of this definition of *friend?* "A friend is someone who has laughed with you and cried with you."
- What is your opinion of the following statement? "We are stuck with family, but we choose our friends."

Grammar Presentation (pages 192–195)

Identify the Grammar

ADJECTIVE CLAUSES AFTER THE MAIN CLAUSE
For some, a friend can be a person who chats with you on the Internet.
. . . friendship is a relationship that emphasizes sharing your innermost feelings . . .
We may not be able to select . . . the people that ride the bus with us . . .

ADJECTIVE CLAUSES INSIDE THE MAIN CLAUSE
For French friends, who enjoy arguing about intellectual issues, disagreement is "the breath of life."
. . . for Germans, whose friendships are based on mutuality of feeling, deep disagreement on any subject that matters to both is . . . a tragedy.

Grammar Charts

- Write an example sentence on the board.
  —Show that the subject relative pronoun refers to the preceding noun by writing the sentence like this:

  A friend is a person

        who chats with you.

  —Draw a circle around *person* and *who*.
  —Draw an arrow from one to the other, to show that one replaces the other.
- Follow the same procedure with another example sentence.

  . . . on any subject   is a tragedy.

        that matters to both

  —Draw a circle around *subject* and *that*.
  —Draw an arrow from one to the other, to show that one replaces the other.
- Do the same with any of the other example sentences.
- Quick pairwork: Have pairs of students choose two sentences from the reading and show how they are related in a similar way. (See Grammar Note 2.) Give the students an example:
  I know a man.   His house is big.
  I know a man WHOSE house is big.

Grammar Notes

Note 1
- Quick pairwork: Dictate these sentence starters to your students. Have pairs of students finish them. Encourage your students to be outrageous. (*I want a diamond ring that costs a lot.*)
  —I want a car that _____.
  —I'd like a new girlfriend/boyfriend who

      _____.
  —I know a clown whose _____.
  —I chose this tiny dog, which _____.
  —I prefer a box of chocolates that _____.
  —I love to eat something which _____.

Note 2
Have the students make the examples in Note 1 into two individual sentences. *I want a diamond ring that costs a lot. = I want a diamond ring. The ring has to cost a lot.*

Note 3   *(Exercise 2, 3)*
Quick pairwork: Ask the students to circle the subject relative pronouns in the reading and identify the noun each pronoun refers to.

Note 4   *(Exercises 3, 4)*
If helpful, provide two more example sentences: *We know a man who rides a unicycle.* (masculine, singular) *Our neighbors have two daughters who have long hair.* (feminine, plural)

Note 5   *(Exercise 3)*
If needed, provide additional examples of subject-verb agreement: *The chef who cooks at Antonio's comes from Italy. The subjects that are offered include the classics.*

→ For additional practice, see the Supplementary Activities on page 94.

Notes 6 and 7   *(Exercises 3, 4)*
- Write a simple sentence on the board: *Alberto is a good singer.*
- Ask a student to add some "unnecessary" or "extra" information about Alberto: *He likes football. He has a dog.* Write two or more of these sentences below the original sentence, and surround them with large and visible commas.
- Draw an arrow from the added sentences to the place in the original sentence where one of them will be inserted, and replace the capital letter with a lower case letter.
- Point out that, in some situations, this "extra" information might be important, but that it is still set off with commas: *Alberto, who studied piano for 10 years, is a good singer.*

  A: *I asked Alberto to sing.*

B: *I know two Albertos. Which one do you mean?*

A: *I mean the Alberto <u>who comes from Venezuela</u>.*

- Expand this into a pronunciation exercise. Have students, as a class, generate a few examples of sentences that can go either way: *The students, who studied, passed the test.* (All of them passed.) *The students who studied passed the test.* (Only those who studied passed.)
- List the sentences on opposite sides of the board (one with commas, labeled *A* or *"identifying"*; one without, labeled *B* or *nonidentifying*).
- Have the class generate more sentences that could be either identifying or nonidentifying, and put them on the board in a column between the *A* and *B* headers.
- Have students practice reading a sentence to their partner with one of the two possible intonations (with or without a pause).
- The other student then tells whether he or she heard sentence *A* or *B*.

Focused Practice (pages 196–200)

Exercise 1
wart: small, hard raised spot on your skin caused by a virus

intimate: having a very close relationship with someone

get together: to socialize with friends

carpool: to drive to work with other people in order to save cost

isolated: far away from other places, things, or people

recall: to remember something

shy: nervous and embarrassed about meeting and speaking with other people

Exercise 2
album: book in which you put photographs or stamps that you want to keep

confidant: someone to whom you tell personal or secret information

empathy: ability to understand someone else's feelings and problems

Exercise 3
loyalty: quality of always supporting a person, set of beliefs, or country

Exercise 4
loan: to lend

Exercise 5
love at first sight: immediate strong romantic feeling for someone

be compatible with someone: two people who are compatible are able to have a good relationship because they share interests, ideas

distracting: taking away one's attention

Communication Practice (pages 201–204)

Exercise 6
Prepare students for the listening exercise by having them describe each person, starting with the man who is standing. Encourage them to use adjective clauses with subject relative pronouns to make sentences like these: *The man <u>who is standing</u> is tall. He's talking to a woman <u>who is wearing glasses</u>. The man <u>that is on her right</u> is holding up a coffee pitcher. The woman <u>that's holding a photograph</u> is sitting next to him. At the end of the table a man is talking with a woman <u>who has a scarf around her shoulders</u>. A man <u>who isn't talking to anyone</u> is sitting next to her. The woman <u>who is reaching for the photograph</u> is wearing a lot of jewelry.*

Exercise 7
Quick pairwork: Have students tell their partners the name of a person or descriptive title of a person who. . . . Be sure to encourage them to use ". . . is someone who," in order to elicit adjective clauses. Students should make other internal changes as appropriate: *My friend Anna is someone who always tells me the truth. Our neighbor Mr. Mickels is someone who has known me for a long time.*

Exercise 8
This exercise will be easier if all the students have the same definitions for the terms. Review the differences before they attempt the exercise.

Exercise 9
Quotes, like proverbs and aphorisms, may not be easy to explain. Working in groups can make the task easier and more enjoyable. Make sure that every quote is addressed by at least one group. Use this discussion to bridge to the writing assignment in Exercise 10.

Exercise 10
Suggest that students consider one of the quotes as a beginning idea for the writing assignment. They can pick a favorite quote and discuss it in groups: "I like this one because . . ."

Further Practice

The class plays the game "I Spy." Each student looks around the classroom and finds something that the other students will have to guess.

A: (seeing the globe on a shelf) I spy something that is round.

B: Is it something that I could eat?

A: No, it's not.

C: Is it something that I could hold in my hand?

A: Yes, it is.

D: Is it something that is sitting on the shelf?

This continues until one student guesses what the object is.

GRAMMAR OUT OF THE BOX ......

Poem. Have students write poems about people who have been significant in their lives: mother, father, relative, friend, teacher. Encourage them to use the following form:

PERSON'S NAME OR RELATIONSHIP TITLE
Someone who is always . . .
Someone who is never . . .
Someone who has always been . . .
Someone who has never been . . .
Always (List three adjectives here that describe the person.)
Dear to me forever.

UNIT 14 — Adjective Clauses with Object Relative Pronouns or *When* and *Where*

Unit Overview

Students will learn the meanings and uses of adjective clauses with object relative pronouns or *when* and *where*.

- An adjective clause will use *that, who, whom, whose* + noun, *where,* or *when.*
- An adjective clause can modify the subject (and therefore comes before the verb) or the direct object (which typically comes after the main clause).

Grammar in Context (pages 205–207)

Background Notes

Many people look forward to a new life when they emigrate. Few think about what they left behind, because their new life means the hope of better jobs and more prosperity for their families. In *Lost in Translation,* Ewa Wydra (Eva Hoffman) thinks about the change in her life as she tells her story. Ben Fong-Torres, writer of *The Rice Room,* is a first-generation Chinese-American. The gap in his life is the difference between his parents' experience and his own. Emigrating from their home in China was his parents' dream; what was lost in this family is the connection within the family. *Lost in Translation* and *The Rice Room* are examples of autobiography, a person's story told in his or her own words.

Vocabulary

filled to the brim: completely full, emotionally

pore over: to read or look at very carefully for a long time

intensely: with strong feelings

emigrate: to leave your own country to live in another

language barrier: difficulty caused by differences in language

first-generation: member of the first generation to be born in a new country

Comprehension Questions

- What are the two worlds of Eva Hoffman? *(her native Poland and Canada)*
- What are the two worlds of Ben Fong-Torres? *(his parents' Chinese-American community and his mainstream society)*
- What does Eva Hoffman miss most about life in Cracow? *(the intense lifestyle, the human contact, the cultural values of the community)*
- What does Ben Fong-Torres see as the great sadness of his life? *(the language barrier between Chinese and English for his family)*
- Why can't Ben discuss family matters with his parents if he spoke Chinese as a child? *(His Chinese did not develop beyond the level of a child's language.)*

Discussion Topics

- How do people learn languages, either their first language or a second one? Why didn't Ben's Chinese language ability develop as he grew older?

- How does a difference in culture affect a person? Why did Eva Hoffman feel "lost" as she got used to her new country?
- Can you explain the two titles? (*Lost in Translation* and *The Rice Room*)

Grammar Presentation (pages 207–210)

Identify the Grammar

ADJECTIVE CLAUSES AFTER THE MAIN CLAUSE
It was a place where life was lived intensely.
. . . she feels no connection to the English name of anything that she feels is important.
. . . he only has the Chinese that he had learned as a child.

ADJECTIVE CLAUSES INSIDE THE MAIN CLAUSE
. . . her friendship with Marek, whose apartment she visited almost daily, deepened . . .
. . . many of the problems that he describes are . . . connected to language.

Grammar Charts

- Write one example sentence on the board: *It was a place where life was lived intensely.*
- Ask your students to break the sentence into the two clauses, the main clause and the adjective clause. Write *Main clause* and *Adjective clause* above the clauses.

> *Main clause   Adjective clause*
> *It was a place where life was lived intensely.*

- Point out that *place* and *where* both mean the same thing.
- Draw circles around *place* and *where*.
- Do the same for the second set of sentences:

> *Main clause   Adjective clause*
> *. . . many of the problems that he describes . . .*

- Draw circles around *problems* and *that*.

Grammar Notes

Note 1   *(Exercises 2, 3)*
- To show the difference between adjective clauses in units 13 and 14, ask your students whether the pronoun refers to the subject (Unit 13) or the object (Unit 14) of the clause within the main clause.
- Point out that in either case (subject or object relative pronoun) the relative pronoun starts the adjective clause.

Note 2   *(Exercises 2, 3)*
Review the concept of identifying and nonidentifying clauses. You might refer to Grammar Note 6 of Unit 13 and make up more examples.

Note 3   *(Exercises 2, 3)*
- Review how each sentence is made up of two sentences with one common element:
  Write on the board: *He's the star. I met the star.*
  Cross out the period and "the star."
  Students say: "He's the star who/whom/that I met."
  I read the book. She wrote the book. = "I read the book that she wrote."
  That's the teacher. I loved her class. = "That's the teacher whose class I loved."
  Eva remembers Marek. She visited Marek often. = "Eva remembers Marek, who/whom she visited often."
- Quick pairwork: Have your students identify the two sentences within some of the other sentences with adjective clauses in the reading.

Note 4   *(Exercises 2, 3)*
- Write *who/whom, that, which,* and *whose* in a vertical list on the board. Before each one, write *That's the one* or *That's the man*. After each one draw a long blank and then write a preposition at the end. Preposition suggestions: *for, to, about,* and *with*.
- On another part of the board, write *I donated blood for him. I gave my book to him. I wrote about him. I had lunch with his wife.*
- Quick pairwork: Ask students to fill in the blanks. They'll come up with sentences like these:
  That's the man who I donated blood for / for whom I donated blood.
  That's the man that I gave my book to.
  That's the one which I wrote about.
  That's the one whose wife I had lunch with.

  If they have trouble, you can prompt by putting two sentences on the board:
  I donated blood for a man. That's the man.
- Remind students that the relative pronoun refers to the object of the preposition, and that *which* is not used with people.

→ For additional practice, see the Supplementary Activities on page 95.

Note 5   *(Exercises 2, 3)*
- Point out the similarity of *then* and *when* (both time expressions) and *there* and *where*

(both place expressions). Some nouns refer to times and places; *when* and *where* are appropriate for use as relative pronouns with these expressions.
• Have students practice with the following examples:

You write		**They say**
Look at the big house. Ana lives there.	=	*"Look at the big house where Ana lives."*
It was a great day. I got a good job then.	=	*"It was a great day when I got a good job."*

Focused Practice (pages 211–214)

Exercise 1
steamy: full of hot water vapor or steam

adjoining: next to something

coil: to wind or twist into a round shape

anonymous: not known by name

overdress: coverall worn to protect clothing

oblique: not expressed in a direct way

eccentric: unusual or different

outwit: to outsmart, to trick by being clever

recitation: something spoken from memory

Exercise 2
first impression: first opinion or feeling you have about someone or something because of the way she, he, or it seems

feel pressure to do something: to feel that you have to do something because of someone else's wish

Exercise 3
sibling: brother or sister

get along: to have a friendly relationship with a person

Exercise 4
food stand: outdoor table or booth where food is sold

conduct business: to buy and sell something

Communication Practice (pages 215–218)

Exercise 5
• Work with your students to locate the desk, the chair, the mirror, the rug, and the guitar.
• Play the recording.
• Quick pairwork: Ask your students to make sentences about the rug, the guitar, the desk, and the mirror—using adjective clauses to show where they are in the room. *(The rug,*

which my sister put her bed on, is near the door. The guitar is on the bed where my sister kept it. The desk is near the window in the corner where there is good light. The mirror is on the wall between the two beds where both of us could use it.)

Exercise 7
• Some students might not have family photographs, so encourage them to use photos from magazines. Also encourage them to be creative in making up the stories.
• Quick pairwork: Have pairs of students practice together telling their stories.

Exercise 8
• Teach the concept of *paraphrasing.* Have small groups restate the ideas in each of the quotes in their own words.
• Have them share their paraphrases with the class.

Exercise 9
• Use the ideas in the paraphrases of the quotes to get students started.
• Brainstorm a list of places where people live, and write them on the board: *out in the country (rural areas), in small villages, in farming towns, in factory towns, in small cities with lots of business and industry, in big cities, on islands, in the forest, in barrios, in huge apartment buildings,* and so on.
• Quick pairwork: Ask students to choose two places and compare life in those environments.

Further Practice
1. Have some fun with this version of "The House That Jack Built." On cards or poster paper, draw the following: a house (square with a roof) with the words *Jack* and *built;* a mouse (two circles with pointed ears and a skinny tail) and *live;* a cat (fluffy tail and whiskers) and *caught;* and a triangle of cheese (add holes) and *was eaten.* Tape the pictures in order on the wall and have the students repeat after you, building the story: *This is the house that Jack built. This is the mouse that lived in the house that Jack built. This is the cat that caught the mouse that lived in the house that Jack built. This is the cheese that was eaten by the mouse that was caught by the cat that lived in the house that Jack built.* Then have students try it alone. Have students identify the nouns and object relative pronouns.

2. For this exercise you will need slips of paper—more than twice the number of slips as students—and two open shoe boxes or large plastic bowls. Create a game by having half of the students write sentence starters about people like these: *There's a person in my class . . . I know an old man . . . We all loved my grandmother . . . I met the most beautiful person in the world . . . I want to marry a person . . .* (You'll want more sentence starters than the number of students in the class.) Fold the slips and put them into an open box as students will be taking slips out of the box.

Have the other half follow the same procedure, but write adjective clauses that start with *who, whose,* or *that* like these: *. . . who always wears a red hat and something purple . . . whose car is 40 years old . . . that lives in a building that looks like a milk bottle . . . who sings opera while asleep.* To play the game, students choose one sentence starter and one adjective clause. Vote for the student whose sentence is the funniest.

GRAMMAR OUT OF THE BOX . . . . . .

Around the block. Have students go around their neighborhoods looking for unusual people, places, and things. Have them bring back reports of what they have found. Encourage them to use adjective clauses with object relative pronouns or *when* and *where.* Examples: *I saw a house which is painted purple with chartreuse and navy blue trim. I met a man whose three dogs were wearing ribbons.*

UNIT 15
Modals and Similar Expressions: Review

Unit Overview

Students will learn and practice modals for ability, advice, necessity, assumptions, and future possibility. Modals are auxiliary verbs that express a relationship between the subject of the sentence and its main verb as follows:

Modal verb	Ability	Advice	Necessity	Assumption	Future possibility
1. can	x				
2. be able to	x				
3. could/could not	x			x	x
4. can't	x		x		
5. must/must not			x	x	
6. have/has to			x	x	
7. have/has got to			x	x	
8. had better		x			
9. ought to		x			
10. should/shouldn't		x			
11. may/may not				x	x
12. might/might not				x	x

Grammar in Context (pages 226–228)

Background Notes

The appeal of reality TV might come from different aspects of human nature. We can imagine ourselves in the same situation as the people on TV (struggling against difficulties, feeling triumph). Another idea is that if someone else is dying, suffering, feeling hunger or thirst, those of us who are watching are not. A third reason may be the desire to have an audience, to be like the people on the shows.

Vocabulary

reality TV: TV programming in which real people show courage and fear

smash hit: very successful new play, movie, song, TV program

come in different flavors: to be available in many different forms

tune in: to watch or listen to a particular radio or TV program

Comprehension Questions

• Why do people watch reality TV? *(to see how people act and the emotions they show, to be able to discuss TV with friends)*
• When did reality TV shows first appear? *(in 1997)*

- What was the name of the first reality TV show? (Survivor)
- How do TV program producers determine the popularity of a show? *(number of viewers and number of hits on the website)*
- What's the difference between British and American reality TV? *(In American shows, the contestants must be glamorous.)*

Discussion Topics

- Are some of the things people have to do on reality shows cruel and embarrassing? Should people watch cruelty to others? Why or why not?
- How do you feel after you have finished doing something difficult? What are some of the most dangerous (or difficult) things you have ever done?

Grammar Presentation (pages 228–231)

Identify the Grammar

ABILITY
. . . *they simply can't change the channel.*

ADVICE
Why should producers pay for actors and writers . . . ?

NECESSITY
. . . *he thought there had to be a lot of people willing to try it.*

ASSUMPTION
That must be why they are tuning in by the millions!

FUTURE POSSIBILITY
. . . *they could use real people with real emotions.*

Grammar Charts

- Select one example sentence at a time from the reading and expand on the context to show students why each example shows ability, advice, etc. For example, read the sentence, "*. . . some might think a show is cruel and embarrassing . . .*" *(Assumption)*
- After a few examples, ask students to expand on the contexts. For example, from a chart in the book: *"You had better do this homework. If you don't, you won't be able to pass the test."*
- Quick pairwork: Write the five headers on the board: *Ability, Advice, Necessity, Assumption, Future Possibility.* Then have students, working in pairs, go through the reading

circling all of the modal and modal-like verbs. For each modal, students discuss with partners which column it should go in.

Grammar Notes

Note 1   *(Exercises 2, 3)*
- Point out that modals do not change: modal + main verb. Modal-like verbs do change because they have *be* or *have/has/had* as part of their form, and these words change according to time frame and person. Remind students of the importance of pronunciation and stress for modals: of the difference between *I can* (kən) *speak English* and *I can't* (kænt) *speak Greek.* They also should remember that the modal-like *be able to* and *have to* are almost always reduced.
- Quick pairwork: Say, "Name something you can do, something you can't do, and something you've always been able to do." The goal is accuracy with stress and reductions. *(I can cook, but I can't sew. I've always been able to sing.)*

Note 2   *(Exercises 2, 3)*
- Remind students that the positive and negative forms of *could* and *was/were able to* are used for long time periods in the past.
- Quick pairwork: Have student pairs make up three sentences about things that they *can* do now but *couldn't* (or *weren't able to*) do in the past: *Today I can skydive, but I couldn't in the past.* Then have student pairs make up three sentences about things that they *can't* do now but *could* (or *were able to*) do in the past: *When I was younger, I could do karate, but I can't anymore.*
- Point out that for specific times in the past, you can use the positive forms of *could* and both positive and negative forms of *was/were able to.*

Note 3   *(Exercises 2, 3)*
- Point out that *had better* is stronger than *should,* and *should* is stronger than *ought to. Ought not to* is not used often.
- Quick pairwork: Say, "Name something you ought to do, something you should do, and something you had better do." Point out that *had better* more often than not occurs as a contraction, and also includes the possibility of bad consequence: *I'd better move the car, or I'll get a ticket.*

Note 4 *(Exercises 2, 3)*
Point out the order from strongest to weakest: *must, have to, have got to, had better.*

Note 5 *(Exercises 2, 3)*
Point out that *must* and *couldn't* both mean certainty about assumptions. *Must not* and *could* are not nearly so certain.

→ For additional practice, see the Supplementary Activities on page 95.

Note 6 *(Exercises 2, 3)*
Quick pairwork: Students practice asking permission, switching the role of the person in authority. Class game for two or more teams: Play *Mother, May I . . . ?* Students take turns being "mother," the person who tells others to do small tasks. The others must, however, ask permission. For example, "Mother" says, "Carla, pick up your book." Carla must say, "Mother, may I pick up my book?" Mother then nods assent and says, "Yes, you may." If Carla does not ask permission, her team loses a point.

Focused Practice (pages 232–235)

Exercise 1
have a good shot at something: to have a better than average chance to do something
contestant: someone who competes in a competition

Exercise 2
turn up the volume: to make a TV or radio program louder
get kicked out: to be asked to leave a place like a restaurant or a place where one lives
the creeps: feeling of nervousness and fright

Exercise 3
shipwrecked: to have been in a ship that was destroyed by a storm or an accident

Communication Practice (pages 236–238)

Exercise 5
Ask the students to make observations about these two contestants even before they listen. Here are some ideas they might come up with: *Josh has made mistakes in the past. Others are upset with Josh. Pete didn't find the task easy.*

Exercise 6
• Begin a discussion about the different kinds of TV shows. Have students find examples of each type: reality TV, movies, sports, news, comedy, talk shows, music, quiz shows.

• Quick pairwork: Have students ask each other, "What kinds of shows do you like to watch?"

Exercise 7
Quick pairwork: Assign one of the eight questions to each pair of students. Ask them to survey their classmates to come up with answers.

Exercise 8
Try to reach consensus on the three most useless items to take *(book? computer? pen and paper? toothbrush?).* Try to reach consensus on the additional useful item to take *(fishing equipment? sunscreen? umbrella? blanket?).*

Exercise 9
Quick pairwork: Have students, working with partners, evaluate each of the items on the list, in Exercise 8.

Exercise 10
Look up the websites of two reality shows that you or others in the class watch.

Further Practice
People in some jobs give advice and guidance to others as part of their work. In a class discussion, have your students consider *judges* (who evaluate people's bad behavior and decide on punishment), *high school teachers and counselors* (who advise students about academic work, college, and careers), *coaches* (who evaluate athletes and encourage them to achieve high goals), *parents* (who make rules for behavior, encourage, discipline, and guide their children), and *police detectives* (who need to get information and make inferences and assumptions based on that information). Which modals are these groups of people likely to need?

Have pairs of students write scripts, practice, and perform a role play about one of the following situations: (a) a judge telling a person what to do to keep out of jail; (b) a school counselor advising a student about getting ready for college; (c) a coach encouraging an athlete to aim high; (d) a parent telling a teenager what the rules are for going to a party; (e) two police detectives discussing the meaning of a broken window, a shirt with blood on the sleeve, a missing television set, and a door that was left open.

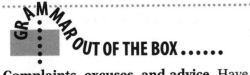

GRAMMAR OUT OF THE BOX ......

Complaints, excuses, and advice. Have students talk to coaches, counselors, dorm residents, and teachers to collect complaints and excuses. After the class has collected a series of complaints and excuses and the likely responses, have them role-play speaker and advice giver. For example:

A: My grades are terrible.

B: You might have to study more. / You must not be studying enough.

Advisability in the Past

Unit Overview

Students will learn and practice the use of *should have, ought to have, could have,* and *might have,* as well as the corresponding negative forms, to express advisability in the past.

Grammar in Context (pages 239–241)

Background Notes

When the magazine *Psychology Today* was first published about 35 years ago, most people thought that the writers would quickly run out of topics to write about. To their surprise, the magazine has grown in popularity and scope, covering subjects like dealing with regrets. Ask your students for reasons why a magazine that deals with how people think and what they think about is likely to be popular.

Vocabulary

destructive: causing severe or irreparable damage

regret: sadness that you feel about something because you wish it had not happened or that you had not done it

paralyzed: unable to move or function properly

disorder: disease or illness

cognitive psychologist: scientist who studies how our thoughts affect our emotions.

Comprehension Questions

• Where do feelings come from, according to psychologists? *(from the way we think about reality, not reality itself)*

• How can past mistakes help us? *(We can learn from them and improve.)*

• How can feeling deep regret be destructive? *(Some people think so much about missed opportunities that they become unable to do anything to improve their current situations.)*

• How can a person let go of regrets? *(by realizing that he or she really had no control over the situation anyway)*

Discussion Topics

• Have you ever regretted an educational or career decision you made? What was it? What could you have done better or differently?

• What should you have done differently when you were younger? What difference could that change have made?

Grammar Presentation (pages 241–242)

Identify the Grammar

... a student who fails a test learns that he or she *should have studied* more ...

"Write down an example of a way in which you *might have done* better."

"I *could have prevented* the injury. ...

"They *might* at least *have telephoned* me as soon as it happened."

Grammar Charts

• Use a new example statement—*She could have called them*—to show how the changes are made from statement to *yes/no* question to short answers to *wh-* question. Write the statement on the board; then erase *She* and *could,* rewriting them in question order: *Could she have . . . ?* Next erase *Could she* and *called them,* leaving *have* in place. Write in, *Yes, she could* in front of the *have.* Then erase the *Yes* and replace it with *No.* Ask the students what other change must be made (adding *'nt* to *could*). To end this change drill, write once more the *yes/no* question *Could she have called them?* and then add a *wh-* question word at the beginning: *Where could she have called them?*

• Write another statement—*I might have explained it*—on the board. Ask students, one at a time, to go to the board and make the changes that their classmates ask for. Remind the student at the board that he or she can ask another student to say what should be written on the board.

- Do a chain replacement drill in which pronouns, modal expressions, main verb phrase, and type of sentence (statement, *yes/no* question, *wh-* question, and affirmative and negative short answers) are changed, one element at a time.
- Review the contractions with the class. Remind students about the pronunciation of contractions: reduction of auxiliary verbs and stress on main verb rather than on the modal. Provide an example: *I might've explained it.*

Grammar Notes

Notes 1 and 2 *(Exercises 2, 3)*
- Point out that all of the modals that show advisability in the past in this chapter include a <u>modal + *have* + past participle</u>. With your students, expand similar sentences like these two: "I had a chance to travel around the world on a boat but I didn't go." *I should've gone because I might never get another opportunity like that one.*
  "I got into medical school, but I didn't go." *I should've gone to medical school. I could've become a doctor. I might've _____. Let* students supply verb, or prompt with examples such as *might've enjoyed it/might've helped people/might've become rich.*
- Also point out that *ought to have* is used rarely these days, and then mostly by people in authority (like parents to children) or a person's advice to himself or herself (*I ought to have studied more*). *Ought to have* is not used in questions. Also point out that the negative question is frequently used in giving advice politely: *Shouldn't you have reminded her about the appointment?* (polite) *You should have reminded her about the appointment.* (less polite)

Note 3 *(Exercises 2, 3)*
Demonstrate the pronunciation of reduced forms of modal phrases: *have* sounds like *of* or even *a.* You can mention that when native English speakers are learning to write as children, a very common error is to write *I should <u>of</u> done it.* Remind students that the contractions are not generally written: use *would have* instead of *would've* in writing. The negative contractions *(shouldn't've)* are never written, but usually pronounced in spoken English.

→ For additional practice, see the Supplementary Activities on page 95.

Focused Practice (pages 243–245)

Exercise 2
fire: to make someone leave his or her job

Exercise 3
inconsiderate: not caring about other people's needs or feelings

jog: to run slowly and in a steady way, especially as a way of exercising

Exercise 4
let someone go: to make someone leave his or her job (polite expression for *to fire*)

confront: try to make someone admit to a mistake

Communication Practice (pages 246–248)

Exercise 5
Point out to your students that each of the items in the list can be expanded into an advisability sentence. Before they listen to the recording, have them look at the list to predict what Jennifer will say: *Homework—I should have done my homework.*

Exercise 6
Ask your students what Jennifer did and didn't do. Then have them discuss what she *should have* and *should not have done.* Help them with vocabulary if they need it: *garbage, cockroaches, leave on, turn off (stove, water) put away (clothes). She should have taken out the garbage. She shouldn't have left food out to attract cockroaches.*

Exercise 7
Quick pairwork: Ask your students whether it is good to have a strong sense of obligation. Why or why not?

Exercise 8
Ask your students: "Was the reporter right to ask the questions?" *(Yes, he was / No, wasn't. He shouldn't have asked her.)* "Was Mustafa right to go back into the building?" *(Yes, he was / No, he wasn't. He shouldn't have gone back.)* "Was the insurance company right to refuse to pay for the medicine?" *(No, it should have paid . . .)*

Exercise 9
Help your students get started with this assignment by brainstorming possible dilemmas with your class: *Have you ever run out of money? Have you ever made a serious mistake at school, work, or home? Have you*

ever been unable to help a friend in need? In any of these situations, what could you/should you/might you have done? A possible title for this assignment is "That was a mistake!!" Encourage your students to be humorous, and remind them that not all mistakes are tragic or life-altering: *I shouldn't have bought those shoes that hurt my feet. I should never have asked for a pet monkey because a monkey is too much work!*

Exercise 10

Quick pairwork: Have students convert interview blunders into guidelines for interviewing. Assign one blunder to each pair of students.

Further Practice

Have three groups of students create lists of tasks (*household, school,* and *personal/general*) that they wanted to complete last week. Possible household tasks: *clean my room, take out the garbage, do laundry, pay my bills.* Possible school tasks: *study for the quiz, do my homework, get toner for my printer, buy the textbook I needed.* Suggestions for personal/general: *return books to the library, write home, clean up my e-mail, call my mother.* Then have them use past modals of advisability and obligation to talk about tasks they did and didn't do. Remind them that *should have* gives a message that the task was NOT completed. If they did complete the task, they need to change their statements to *I was supposed to . . .* or *I had to . . . and I did.* Ask them to give themselves advice about how they could have managed better and excuses why they didn't: *I should have cleaned my room, but I had to study for a big test.*

GRAMMAR OUT OF THE BOX ......

Twenty-twenty hindsight. Have students survey people they know outside of class about regrets, "roads they wish they had taken." Each student chooses one of the regrets and writes it on a card as a statement to put in a box. Then the cards are mixed up and each student chooses one and works with a partner. Card example: A car mechanic says, "I decided to become a mechanic instead of going to college to study mechanical engineering." The student changes the statement to something like this: "I should have gone to college to study mechanical engineering." Then the student and partner should expand with reasons and

excuses: "I needed money to buy a car of my own, but I might have made a lot more money, and I wouldn't have had to spend so much time now working with dirty, oily cars." Have students share the regrets and explanations that they have collected.

UNIT 17 Speculations and Conclusions About the Past

Unit Overview

Students will learn and practice *may have, might have, could have, must have,* and *had to have* as well as the corresponding negative forms to make speculations and draw conclusions about the past.

Grammar in Context (pages 249–250)

Background Notes

Prehistory (the time before written records are now available) is hidden from us. We have only physical evidence (the Nazca lines in Peru, the pyramids of Egypt and Mexico, the statues of Easter Island, and the great stones of Stonehenge in England) to help us guess why these things exist and how they came to be. Many theories (which can never be proved or disproved) have been published.

Vocabulary

speculate: to guess

landing strip: a level piece of ground that has been prepared for airplanes to use

spacecraft: vehicle that is able to travel in space

gigantic: extremely large

skeptical: having doubts about whether something is true, right, or good

Comprehension Questions

- How many Nazca forms are there? *(over 13,000)*
- What is Erich von Däniken's theory about the Nazca lines? *(They were made by visitors from another planet.)*
- What is the "proof" from Easter Island? *(The island could not have supported a population large enough to create the gigantic statues without help from outside.)*

Discussion Topics

• Why do people continue to read a book that was published in 1972?
• What other theories about strange phenomena have you heard?

Grammar Presentation (pages 251–253)

> ### Identify the Grammar
>
> *Xesspe may have been the first human . . . to recognize the designs.*
> *. . . how could an ancient culture have made these amazing pictures?*
> *. . . the people of those cultures must have believed that the visitors were gods.*
> *. . . the drawings might have marked a landing strip . . .*
> *Space visitors had to have built them.*

Grammar Charts

• Use a process similar to that of Unit 16. Begin with another statement (*I might have seen that movie*) and show how the changes are made from statement to *yes/no* question to short answers to *wh-* question. Write the statement on the board; then erase *I* and *might*, rewriting them in question order (*Might I have . . . ?*). Next erase *Might I* and *seen that movie?* leaving *have* in place. Write in *Yes, I might* in front of the *have*. Then erase the *Yes* and replace it with *No*. Ask the students what other change must be made (adding *not* after *might*.) To end this change drill, rewrite the *yes/no* question (*Might I have seen that movie?*) again and then add a *wh-* question word at the beginning: *When might I have seen that movie?*

• Start with another statement (*They must have built the hall*) on the board. Ask students, one at a time, to go to the board and make the changes that their classmates ask for. Remind the student at the board that he or she can ask another student to say what should be written on the board.

• Do a chain replacement drill in which pronouns, modal expressions, main verb phrase, and type of sentence (statement, *yes/no* question, *wh-* question, and affirmative and negative short answers) are changed, one element at a time.

• Remind students that the contractions of *might not* and *ought not* are not generally used.

Grammar Notes

Note 1   (*Exercises 2, 3, 4*)

• Point out to your students that speculations (some people call them inferences) are based on some evidence, but speculations can be wrong. Mention that there is very little difference between *might have, could have,* and *may have* in positive statements, and that these speculations are often preceded by "I don't know, but . . ."

• Quick practice: Ask students: "Who in this classroom got up earliest today? Was it [Gina]? Was it [Tomo]?" *I don't know, but it could have been [Gina]. She looks tired. I don't know, but it might have been [Tomo]. He was here first today.*

Note 2   (*Exercises 2, 3, 4*)

Point out that conclusions with *must have* are almost certainly true. Give an example: *His hair was all wet when he came in. It must have been raining.*

Notes 1–3

Draw a chart on the board to show the difference between positive and negative forms:

Positive		Negative
was	(100% sure)	wasn't
must have	(95%)	couldn't have
		can't have
	(less than 95% sure)	must not have
could have		
might have	(less than 50% sure)	might not have
may have		may not have

Use colored chalk, or underline, in order to point out how *might have* and *may have* don't change in degree of certainty between negative and positive, but *could have / couldn't have* are very different.

Notes 3–4   (*Exercises 2, 3, 4*)

Point out that although *must not have* and *couldn't have* are similar, *couldn't have* emphasizes that the action was impossible—or at least hard to believe. Because *might have* and *may have* are used to ask for permission (as in *May I have another piece of apple pie?* or *Might I have your attention please?*), *could have* is more commonly used for questions about possibility.

Note 5   (*Exercise 5*)

Point out that *be* is added to the short answer (*Yes, it could have been*) whereas other verbs are not. For a quick drill to practice this as well as reinforce the difference between *could have* and *must have* in the positive and negative, ask students questions with no clear answers:

Q: Was January 20, 2002 a Monday?

A: I don't know, but it could have been.

Q: Was it cold that day in Sweden?

A: It must have been.

Q: Did it snow that day in Sweden?

A: It must have.

Q: Was it cold that day in Rio?

A: It couldn't have been / can't have been.

Q: Did it snow that day in Rio?

A: It couldn't have. It hardly ever snows there.

→ For additional practice, see the Supplementary Activities on pages 95–96.

Note 6

Demonstrate how these modals are pronounced in their reduced forms. (*Could have* can sound like *could of* or *coulda*.) Have students answer quick questions or comment on situations with the reduced forms: *She bought a lottery ticket. She didn't win, but she might have / could have (mighta / coulda) won.*

Focused Practice (pages 254–258)

Exercise 1
archaeology: study of ancient societies by examining what remains of their buildings, graves, tools, etc.

Exercise 2
primitive: belonging to a society that has a very simple way of life, without modern industries and machines

hot-air balloon: very large cloth balloon filled with hot air, used for transporting people

Exercise 3
coral: a hard red, white, or pink substance formed from the skeletons of very small ocean creatures that live in warm water, often used to make jewelry

Exercise 4
become extinct: to cease to exist as a species or type of plant or animal

meteor: a piece of rock or metal in space and makes a bright line in the night sky when it falls through the Earth's atmosphere

kidnap: to take someone away illegally, usually by force, and demand money for returning him or her

Exercise 5
abruptly: in a sudden and unexpected manner

artifact: an object that was made and used a long time ago, especially one that is studied by scientists

Exercise 6
descendant: someone who is related to a person who lived a long time ago

paradise: a place or situation that is extremely pleasant, beautiful, or enjoyable

botanical: relating to plants or the scientific study of plants

Communication Practice (pages 259–261)

Exercise 7
Before students listen to the recording, have them speculate on the uses of the objects in the pictures and compare them to common objects today.

Exercise 8
Encourage students to be creative in their thinking and to come up with as many uses as they can. Once they have finished, you can tell them what the objects were really for:
1. Ceramic pillow from ancient China (ca. A.D. 900). Ceramic may have been used because it is cool in summer.
2. Bronze brooch from western or central Europe, probably from Italy. (ca. 600 B.C.). Both men and women have been found buried with similar brooches.
3. Razor and mirror, from Egypt (ca. 1400 B.C.) The mirror has a handle which is held in place by a small bronze peg, with an image of a woman's face with cow's ears.
4. Pair of snow goggles, from the Canadian Arctic, early 19th century. Goggles like these protected the eyes from the sun and the cold but also prevented the wearer from seeing the ground.
5. Navigation chart from Micronesia, made of sticks. Such charts are still made today, although they are not used for navigation.

Exercise 9
Point out that some of the information in the reading supports the von Däniken theory and some contradicts it. Have students write supporting and contradictory statements in two columns on the board.

Further Practice
Have students read and discuss the following mysteries.

1. Police have found an abandoned car in the mountains of British Columbia. It is almost new and in perfect condition. The tank is full of gas, and the keys are in the ignition. The car's owner lives about 500 miles away, but she is on a cruise around the world. She has been gone for two months.
2. Carol James has disappeared. She and her husband Chet have been planning a trip to Bermuda. They were supposed to leave in two days. However, the airplane tickets and a carefully packed suitcase of beach clothes were left, and Carol's car, her winter clothes, her mink coat, all of her jewelry, and all of the money in their bank account are missing. She left no note.
3. Archaeologists have found the frozen bodies of three children in a grave on top of a mountain. They were all wearing beautiful clothing and jewelry and were wrapped in nicely woven pieces of cloth. They all had serious head injuries. Tests show that these children died 3,000 years ago.

GRAMMAR OUT OF THE BOX . . . . . .

Who was this person? Ask students to bring in the oldest photographs they can find, either of family members or from books or magazines, but not of well-known people. Have students work in small groups. The groups exchange photographs and then make up stories about the people in the photos from the other group: *She's wearing a lot of beautiful jewelry. She <u>must have been</u> rich. He looks very tired. He <u>must have worked</u> very hard in his life. She's smiling. She <u>must have been</u> very happy.*

UNIT 18 The Passive: Overview

Unit Overview

Students will learn and practice the general principles of the passive.

Grammar in Context (pages 270–271)

Background Notes

Geography includes such varied aspects of the study of our planet as *physical geography* (the study of Earth's structure), *climatology* (study of weather patterns), and *cultural geography*.

Vocabulary

yawn: to open your mouth and breathe in deeply, usually because you are tired or bored

fulfill: to get, do, or achieve something you wanted, promised, or hoped for. If you fulfill a hope, promise, or wish, you achieve the thing that you had hoped for, promised, or wanted.

extend: to reach or spread

Comprehension Questions

- Where and when was the first issue of *National Geographic* published? *(nine months after the National Geographic Society was formed in Washington, D.C., in 1888)*
- How did the National Geographic Society change the meaning of geography? *(people used to think of geography as the names of countries and capitals, rivers, and mountain ranges, but the magazine shows how the world looks and feels, how people live, and how important the natural resources—animal, vegetable, and mineral—are)*
- What is the mission of *National Geographic*? *(to spread knowledge of and respect for the world, its resources, and its inhabitants)*

Discussion Topics

- Why do you think the National Geographic Society began publishing a magazine for young people?
- Consider people's interest in the *National Geographic* magazine, the television program about distant and different places, and people's desire to travel to distant places. What do these reveal about people all over the world?

Grammar Presentation (pages 271–273)

Identify the Grammar

National Geographic *TV programs <u>are watched</u> . . . in 145 countries.*
The National Geographic Society <u>was formed</u> in Washington, D.C., in 1888 . . .
They <u>were forced</u> to memorize the names of capital cities . . .
The Society's mission <u>has been fulfilled</u>.
. . . wonders of our world <u>have been brought</u> to life <u>by</u> fascinating reporting and beautiful photographs, . . .

Grammar Charts

- Call your students' attention to the title of the reading. Ask them to make up several other appropriate titles (possible examples: *The National Geographic Society; Our World; The True Meaning of Geography*). Have them write these alternative titles on the board and discuss what they all have in common (possible answer: *focus on the Earth and what is on it*). Ask the students who is doing the focusing. (It's not particularly important for the situation.)
- Point out the first example sentence on the board: *National Geographic TV programs <u>are watched</u> . . . in 145 countries.* Ask, "Who watches these programs?" Answer: *People in 145 countries.* Rewrite it as an active sentence: *People in 145 countries watch National Geographic TV programs.* Underline the object (*National Geographic TV programs*) and show with an arrow how it moves to the subject position in a passive sentence. Use a different color chalk to show the change to the verb. It remains in the present, but some form of *be* is added, plus past participle. Erase the *s* on *programs* and ask what happens to *are watched* (it changes to *is watched*).
- Ask what the difference is between the active and passive sentences. Point out that the subject of any sentence (the first part of the sentence) receives the most emphasis. *Who* or *what* did the action is sometimes less important than what was done.
- Ask your students to go through the sentences of the grammar charts, replacing *it* with noun phrases. Make sure that they understand that each noun phrase relates to the topic of the *National Geographic* magazine or the National Geographic Society.

Grammar Notes

Notes 1 and 2   *(Exercises 2, 3, 5)*
- Remind students of terminology: the *agent* is the person, persons, or thing that does or did the action. The *object* is the person, persons, or thing that receives (received, has received, will receive, will have received, etc.) the action.
- Point out that the passive requires the addition of some form of *be* (*is* or *are*) in the present, *was* or *were* in the past, and *has* or *have* + *been* in the present perfect. The verb also changes to the past participle in all tenses, including future.
- A sentence without a direct object cannot become a passive. (That is, only transitive verbs have active and passive forms.) Put a few examples of common student pitfalls on the board: *The earthquake happened. A fire broke out. He died.* And remind the class: no object = no passive form possible!

Note 3   *(Exercises 2, 4, 5, 6)*
Point out that there are three advantages to the passive. You *leave out unimportant or unrelated information,* you can *choose not to mention* who did something, and you can *keep a sharp focus on the main topic.*

→ For additional practice, see the Supplementary Activities on page 96.

Note 4   *(Exercise 5, 6)*
Point out that sometimes you want to keep a sharp focus on the main topic, but you also want to mention who or what did something. In such a case, use *by* + the agent: *The National Geographic Society was started by a group of scientists, mapmakers, and professors who were concerned about the Earth's future.* In this example, the focus is still on the National Geographic Society, but the *by* expression gives information that is also helpful. Remind students that if the agent is unimportant or obvious, it should be left out.

Focused Practice (pages 273–279)

Exercise 1
expedition: a long and carefully organized trip, especially to a dangerous place

newsstand: a place on a street where newspapers are sold

Exercise 3
cultural attaché: someone who works in an embassy and deals with the way of life of the society of that country

quinoa: edible grain-like seeds raised by the Andean Indians

llama: large South American animal with thick hair like wool and a long neck

naturalist: someone who studies plants, animals, and other living things

jaguar: large, wild South American cat with yellow fur and dark spots

Exercise 4
precaution: something that you do to prevent something bad or dangerous from happening

Exercise 5
charmed: pleased, delighted

boa constrictor: large snake that is not poisonous, but kills animals by crushing them

flourish: to grow or develop well

reed pipes: musical instrument made from tall woody grass plants

Exercise 6

trivia: detailed facts about history, famous people, sports, or anything else

goalie: the player on a sports team who tries to stop the ball from going into the goal, a goalkeeper

archer: person who shoots arrows from a bow

archery: the sport of shooting arrows from a bow

Exercise 7

humanitarian: concerned with improving bad living conditions and preventing unfair treatment of people

Communication Practice (pages 280–284)

Exercise 8

Before students listen to the recording, review the following words with them: *to hire/to be hired by; to train/to be trained by; to publish/ to be published by; to fire/to be fired by; to interview/to be interviewed by; to lay someone off/to be laid off.*

Exercise 9

hailstorm: rain and ice bits falling together

marble: a hard white rock that can be carved and polished

skillful: good at doing something you have learned and practiced

envy: to wish to have qualities that someone else has

• Point out that a great deal of wisdom is found within the proverbs of a group of people. Ask your students for some of their favorite proverbs and put them on the board. If they have trouble thinking of any, you can suggest one or two to help them get started: *No use crying over spilt milk.* (Remind students about the past regrets of Unit 16.) *We can cross that bridge when we come to it.* Write down two or three of the proverbs and discuss them with the students. Then have them try to do the exercise. Encourage the use of the form used in the example: "I think this means that . . ."

Exercise 10

Ask your students to explain the symbols on the maps: tobacco = one leaf, corn = a single ear, etc.

Exercise 11

Brainstorm a few inventions, some famous pieces of music, and some famous poems or novels. For the blank option, suggest and brainstorm athletes and sports, magazines and books, or cars/motorcycles/dirt bikes and people associated with them (include a topic that is likely to appeal to males).

Exercise 12

Do a dry run using local information, which the students are likely to know. Point out that many ideas can be expressed using either an active sentence or a passive one. Generate additional examples: *We are in southern Wisconsin, where dairy farming is an important industry. (Dairy cows are raised here.) The most important crops are animal foods like alfalfa, corn, and clover. (Alfalfa, corn, and clover are grown.) English is spoken widely, but in some communities you can still hear German, Polish, Italian, and some other European languages. (German, Polish and Italian are still heard.)* Then encourage students to expand on the information.

Further Practice

With the whole class, find a game that everyone knows how to play, perhaps a children's hide and seek game. List what happens on the board.

• The players gather.
• The rules are discussed: where "home" is, how far away the players can go, how long they can take to find a hiding place, whether they can move once to new hiding places once the seeker ("it") starts looking for the hidden players, etc.
• The game is begun. "It" hides his/her eyes and begins counting. Other players hide. "It" says, *Ready or not, here I come* and starts to look for other players. The first player who is found becomes the next "it."

After discussing the process with this example, have students, individually or in small groups, choose a board or outdoor game they know. They then write down what is needed to play the game, how the game is played, how the game is won, etc. Then have them teach the game to another student or group of students.

Optional: Students could describe their game without saying what the game is, other students could guess.

A: The game is played by two people. A board with red and black squares is used.

B: I think you mean checkers.

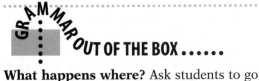

GRAMMAR OUT OF THE BOX . . . . . .

What happens where? Ask students to go to resort or apartment complex offices or websites or to find schematic drawings or maps. Have the students point out and then label the locations where certain activities take place. Examples: *This is the social center of the apartment complex. This part of the building is used for meetings and parties. This room is reserved for exercise because it holds all kinds of special equipment. Picnics are held in this part of the grounds because there are picnic tables. Renters' cars are parked here, and visitors' cars are parked in this special visitors' parking lot.*

Variation 1: Tell students that a wedding reception took place in this social center. Ask, "Where was the party held?" "Which area was reserved for dancing?" "Where were guests' cars parked?"

Variation 2: Ask students for other events that have been held there (such as a holiday crafts fair, a children's petting zoo, or a fashion show). Have students make up passive statements about how the facilities were used.

UNIT 19 The Passive with Modals and Similar Expressions

Unit Overview

Students will learn and practice modals and expressions like *has/have to* and *is/are going to* in passive constructions, with the corresponding negative forms.

Grammar in Context (pages 285–286)

Background Notes

In outer space, personal space for astronauts is limited. There is very little room inside space shuttles, but this is not really a problem, since astronauts do not spend much time there. Space stations, where people have to live for long periods of time, are different. Learning to live in these confined areas with people of other cultures, therefore, presents a great challenge for the astronauts who do it—as well as for the social scientists who study them.

Vocabulary

privacy: the state of being able to be alone and not seen or heard by other people

apprehension: worry that you will have to deal with something bad

master: to learn a skill or language so well that you understand it completely and have no difficulty with it

in the long run: over a long period of time

tolerance: the willingness to allow people to do, say, or believe what they want

harmony: a situation in which people are friendly and peaceful, and agree with each other

Comprehension Questions

- How long do astronauts usually stay on the space station? *(about six months at a time)*
- How is a space station a "trapped environment"? *(A person cannot simply decide to leave.)*
- What are some of the culture-related concerns of space station inhabitants? *(food, privacy, language barriers, religious matters like dietary restrictions)*
- Why do astronauts watch the TV show *Star Trek*? *(to observe people dealing with cultural differences)*

Discussion Topics

- How could sailors on a submarine be helped by cross-cultural training? Do they need such training? Why or why not?
- Think about body language. How does one person "show" rather than "say" messages like "I'm afraid of you" or "I don't believe you"? What are some other common body language messages? How are these body language messages different among different groups of people?

Grammar Presentation (pages 287–288)

Identify the Grammar

. . . decisions . . . <u>might not be made</u> quickly enough.
. . . privacy <u>may not be respected</u>.
. . . space tourists <u>can be transported</u> there for short stays.
. . . technical language <u>must be mastered</u> by everyone.
. . . How <u>should</u> preparation and cleanup <u>be handled</u>?
. . . they <u>have to be observed</u> and <u>experienced</u>.

Grammar Charts

- Point out that the passive + modal structure actually contains three elements:

1   2   3
The crew will be replaced next month.

- Put other example sentences from the reading on the board.
- Circle the *be* and the past participle in each example sentence from the reading using different colors of chalk as you explain that these are part of the passive construction.
- Point out that the modal is used in the short answers and that the *have to* and *going to* expressions use appropriate forms of *do* and *be* respectively. It might help some students to consider that *have to* is really *(do) have to* and *going to* is really *(be) going to.*
- Do a quick oral drill of short answers by asking various students in turn: "Should it be replaced?" "Can it be replaced?" "Will it be replaced?" "Does it have to be replaced?" "Is it going to be replaced?" "Do they have to be replaced?" Signal that you want a *yes* or a *no* answer by nodding or shaking your head as you ask. You can add humor by getting faster and faster as you move around the room. If the above sentences seem too easy for your students, you can make them longer and more complicated, just to make the point that even a very long sentence still gets a short simple answer: "Will the faulty computer that the astronauts brought on board the shuttle with them when they first arrived three months ago need to be replaced before it stops working completely?" *(Yes, it will.)*
- Remind students that although the *wh*-question is not included in a box, it follows the same formula as any other *wh-* question, that it is just formed from the *yes/no* question.
- Write these sentences on the board:
Will it need to be replaced?
What will need to be replaced?

Grammar Notes

Note 1   *(Exercises 2, 3)*
Use the same example sentences that are on the board from the grammar charts to remind students of the three necessary elements (modal, *be*, past participle).

Note 2   *(Exercises 2, 3)*
- Provide two sample sentences on the board for the students to use as they practice *will* and *be going to* to talk about the future:
Cross-cultural problems will be avoided.

The crew is going to be replaced.
You can then supply skeletons from which the students can make their own sentences: street/repair/next year (*The street will be repaired next year. / When will it be repaired?*) broken clock/replace/next week (*The broken clock is going to be replaced next week. / When is it going to be replaced?*)
- Ask your students what difference, if any, they see between the two ways of expressing future time (review from Unit 5).

Notes 3 and 4   *(Exercises 2, 3)*
Point out that the meanings of *can* and *could* for present and past ability and *could, may, might,* and *can't* for future possibility (or impossibility) are consistent with the meanings of these modals in active forms (Unit 15). The addition of the passive doesn't change the meaning of the modal.

Note 5   *(Exercises 2, 3)*
Point out that advisability, obligation, and necessity as expressed by *have (got) to, had better, should, ought to,* and *must* are also consistent with the meanings of these expressions in active sentences (Unit 15).

→ For additional practice, see the Supplementary Activities on page 96.

Focused Practice (pages 289–292)

Exercise 1
module: a part of a spacecraft or any other structure that can be separated from the main part and used for a particular purpose

Exercise 2
dehydrated: waterless, dried (food)

utensil: a tool or object that you use to prepare, cook, or eat food

Exercise 3
simulation: something you do or make in order to practice what you would do in a real situation

whisker: facial hair on men

Exercise 4
restraint: something that prevents someone from moving freely

Communication Practice (pages 293–295)

Exercise 5
- Before students listen to the recording, review these words with them:

meteorite: a small meteor

manual: a book that gives instructions about how to do something such as use a machine

- Review the stress patterns with positive and negative forms of *can:*
  It can be **helped**. (one stress) / *It* **can't** *be* **helped**. (two stresses)

Exercise 6
Quick pairwork: Have students, working with partners, choose the three most important issues to consider. Then have two pairs of students (four students) compare their selections and discuss why they made their selections. Ask them to come to consensus.

Exercise 7
Prepare students for this exercise by asking what could or should be done to improve their classroom. Ask them for reasons why these improvements are advisable. Remind them again about intonation and stress: that modals and auxiliary verbs are stressed less than the past participle. Remind them, also, to use contractions and reductions whenever possible: *It has got to be replaced. = It's gotta be re***placed**.

Exercise 8
- Have students brainstorm social problems in addition to public housing that require lots of money: *job development, hunger, natural disaster recovery work, fighting health issues such as the spread of AIDS, care for the elderly,* etc.
- Quick pairwork: Have pairs of students prioritize these social needs and come up with reasons why they think the most important one should be addressed first.

Exercise 9
- Have your students use some of the ideas from the discussion for Exercise 8 in their paragraphs.
- Quick pairwork: Write *could be done, should be done, must be done* on the board. Ask pairs of students to come up with two things for each category.

Further Practice
Have students form "committees" to evaluate several different aspects of the school: the physical plant (condition of the classrooms, restrooms, the grounds); the teaching equipment (video machines, computers, TV monitors, tape and CD players, screens, overhead projectors); students' supplies and immediate environment (textbooks,

dictionaries, desks, work areas, boards); and activities schedule (time in class, time in labs, school trips, extracurricular activities). They can ask questions and then make recommendations.

GRAMMAR OUT OF THE BOX ......

What about twins? How should twins be treated? Should twins have names that are similar? Should parents dress twins alike? Should twins be in the same class with the same teacher? Should twins be treated the same? Ask your students these questions and encourage them to make up more questions about how twins should be treated. Write these questions on the board, and when there are six questions, have the students copy them. They should ask three people outside of class for their opinions. Then they can compare the answers they got. Remind students that besides practicing the passive, this is a chance to review the grammar that they learned in Unit 8. For example: *I asked four people the questions, and so did Kadir. All of my friends thought twins should be dressed alike, but none of Enrique's friends did. Yuko's respondents thought that twins should be placed in the same class, and mine did too.*

UNIT 20 The Passive Causative

Unit Overview

Students will learn and practice the causative as it is expressed through a passive-like form using *get* or *have*.

Grammar in Context (pages 296–297)

Background Notes
People all over the world are concerned with making themselves look good. After body shape and clothing choices, hair and skin treatments are the most obvious adornments.

Vocabulary
aftercare: the care or treatment of someone recovering from a medical procedure or operation

Comprehension Questions

- What are some ways to change your appearance? *(changing hairstyle and hair color, using makeup or paint, getting a tattoo, adding jewelry to pierced body parts, cosmetic surgery)*
- Why is getting a tattoo an important decision? *(It's not easy to reverse a tattoo.)*
- What is the most expensive form of changing your appearance? *(cosmetic surgery)*

Discussion Topics

- What is your opinion of uniforms for medical, military, or school populations? How does wearing a uniform affect a person?
- Consider cosmetic surgery. What parts of your body can you have changed easily? Why do people choose cosmetic surgery?

Grammar Presentation (pages 298–299)

Identify the Grammar

The Passive Causative

. . . men and women *have their hair permed.*
But you can also *have it bleached white* or *get it dyed blue, green, or orange!*
. . . *having one [a tattoo] applied* is still a big decision.
Getting your hair done is the easiest way to change your appearance.

Grammar Charts

- Point out that there are two main forms for the passive causative: *get (something) done* and *have (something) done.* Ask students to find the verb phrases that are used with each form in the reading and show them that either *get* or *have* will work in all cases. Point out that for this form of passive causative, there is no difference between *get* and *have.*
- Remind students that *have/get* + object + past participle means that another person performed the action.
- Point out that *be going to* can be used for future meaning with the two causative forms: *She is going to have her hair permed, and then she is going to get her nails done,* and that, as in Unit 5, there is little or no difference between *be going to* and the present progressive.
- Be sure that your students see that normal rules for *yes/no* questions and *wh-* questions are followed in making passive causative questions, and that they are using *do/does/did*

for the questions (rather than "Has she her hair cut once a month?").

Grammar Notes

Note 1 *(Exercises 2, 3)*
- With your students, make a list on the board of all the things that can be done to hair *(wash it, shave it, cut it, bleach it, curl it, perm it, straighten it, dye it, lengthen it).*
- Quick pairwork: Have students make up sentences about their own hair or someone else's, with the two passive causative forms and the various hair-related vocabulary. Encourage the use of more complicated tenses: "My mother has never had her hair permed, but she's been having it colored for years."

→ For additional practice, see the Supplementary Activities on page 96.

Note 2 *(Exercises 2, 3)*
- Point out the difference between these two similar sentences:
Ted always washes his car on Saturday. (Ted does it himself.)
Ted always has his car washed on Saturday. (Another person washes Ted's car.)
- With your students, make a list on the board of all the things that you can *have done* to your car *(wash it, paint it, change the oil, tune up the motor, clean it, rotate the tires on it, fix it).*
- Quick pairwork: Have students work in pairs to make up sentences with the two passive causative forms: *I'm going to have my car painted. Bill Gates doesn't wash his car(s) himself; he gets it (them) washed.*

Note 3 *(Exercise 3)*
Point out the difference between these two similar sentences:
Ted always has his car washed on Saturday. (It doesn't matter who washes it.)
Ted always has his car washed by the Boy Scouts. (The Scouts having a car-washing service is important because Ted likes to support the Scouts.)

Focused Practice (pages 300–303)

Exercise 1
waxed: (floors) having a thin layer of wax to make the correct degree of smoothness or beauty

Exercise 2
barber: a man whose job it is to cut men's hair and sometimes shave them

Exercise 3

it's up to you: (idiom) it depends on you and what you decide to do

Exercise 4

caterer: a person or organization who provides and serves food and drinks at a party, meeting, etc., usually as a business

Communication Practice (pages 303–305)

Exercise 5

Prepare students for the listening by asking whether they could do the things on Amber's list themselves or whether they would have them done by others. You also could have them personalize the vocabulary, by asking each other, in pairs, "Do you cut your hair yourself, or do you have it cut?" If you choose this option, circulate to check pronunciation: "your**self**" and "do you have it **cut**?"

Exercise 6

Quick pairwork: You're going on a trip and you have no time, but you do have money to hire people to help you. *Your best shirt is missing a button. Your coat is dirty and needs to be dry cleaned. Your best shoes are covered with mud. Your blue jeans have a tear in the pocket.* Use the causative passive forms!

Exercise 7

Quick pairwork: With a partner, have students list three cosmetic changes people make if they can afford them *(teeth straightened, ears pierced, nails manicured, tattoos removed, hair cut).*

Exercise 8

Ask your students to make an opinion questionnaire on the various kinds of body art in this chapter. Which kinds do they like? Which kinds are out of favor? Encourage recycling of the material from Unit 8: *So do I./Neither do I.*

Exercise 9

• Discuss the concept of "special occasions" with your students.
• Quick pairwork: Have student pairs choose one special occasion and decide what they would do to dress up for it.

Exercise 10

Ask the whole class to brainstorm a list on the board of things that will change the appearance of a room: *new curtains or window shades, new light fixtures, new carpet or other floor covering, different furniture, new pictures on the wall, new wall colors.* Then have students, working in

pairs, use the *have/get* + object + past participle form to list things they would have or get done.

Further Practice

Usually a hairstylist cuts hair, but what if your hairstylist did something unusual, like pulled out a loose tooth? *I had my loose tooth pulled out by my hairstylist.* Have the class make a list of specialists (doctor, dentist, auto mechanic, dressmaker, plumber, fortune teller, tattoo artist, electrician, aerobic instructor, choir director, professor) and a list of actions (hair cut, bathtub fixed, wedding music planned, exercise routine planned, car fixed, tooth fixed, appendix removed, new suit made, fortune told, tattoo applied, course of study outlined). Then see how many funny sentences using the causative passive they can make, working in pairs.

GRAMMAR OUT OF THE BOX ......

Back to the future. Have students go to the Internet or to a historical society for historical photographs and modern photographs of the same scene or building. Examples: the White House in 1850 and today, photos of a family home picture taken 50 years ago and today, the old farm and the farm now. Make up eight sentences describing what people had done to make the changes: *Dad got the old fence taken down. The new owner had a lot of trees planted and some flower gardens planted.*

UNIT 21 Present Real Conditionals

Unit Overview

Students will learn and practice present real conditionals in statements and questions.

Grammar in Context (pages 314–315)

Background Notes

Shopping online is becoming more and more popular as companies without doors offer goods and services through the Internet. However, shopping online (or selling online) can be risky because of confidentiality and security with money transactions.

Vocabulary

surf (the Internet/Net/Web): to look quickly at different places on the Internet for information that interests you

dispute: to say that something such as a fact, idea, or charge is not correct or true

enter: to press "enter" on a computer keyboard

print out: to print from a computer

precaution: something that you do to prevent something bad or dangerous from happening

Comprehension Questions

- Why should you be sure that you buy only on a secure site? *(If you enter your credit card number and the site is not secure, someone else could use your credit card.)*
- Why are prices generally lower from Internet companies? *(They don't have to pay for a store, lots of employees, or a large stock.)*
- Why is a receipt important? *(If you don't like what you bought, you can return it. A receipt proves that you bought it.)*

Discussion Topics

- When supermarkets became popular, shoppers began to buy from people they didn't know. They began to shop once a week, or even less often. The result is more isolation. Will more online shopping mean more isolation, just as supermarkets did? Is online shopping a positive change?
- What precautions must a person take with credit cards, besides the ones mentioned in the reading? (You could also remind students here of the information about credit cards that they discussed in Unit 6.)

Grammar Presentation (pages 316–317)

Identify the Grammar

If the site isn't secure, don't enter your credit card information.
Always pay by credit card if you can.
If you don't know the company, ask them to send you information.
What happens if you don't like the product?

Grammar Charts

- Use the first two sentences of the target grammar points *(If the site isn't secure, . . .* and *Always pay by credit card . . .)* to point out that an *if* clause at the beginning of a sentence is always followed by a comma and that no

comma is necessary for an *if* clause at the end of a sentence. You can do this by asking, "What's the difference between the first and the second sentence?" Be sure that students understand the grammar terminology "*if* clause" and "result clause" (colored chalk is helpful).
- Point out that in both *yes/no* and *wh-*questions, the *if* clause usually comes at the end.

Grammar Notes

Note 1   *(Exercises 1–2)*
Be sure that students understand that general truths (and scientific facts) are phenomena that do not change. Examples: *Credit cards are always faster, but also more expensive to use. If I drop a glass on the floor, it breaks.*

Note 2   *(Exercises 2–4)*
- Point out that *when* can often be used instead of *if* in present real conditionals. *When I sleep, I think too. = If I sleep, I think too. When* is used for habits or things that are likely to happen many times. *I take my dog out very early every morning. When we leave the house, it is still dark.*
- Quick pairwork: Have students list five things that they do every day. Have them expand their statements into *if* clause (or *when* clause) statements: *I get up at seven. If I don't get up at seven, I'm late for everything else all day.* Encourage students to include some negative sentences, and sentences with *he/she/it: If I forget to set my alarm clock, it doesn't ring, and I don't get to school on time.*

Note 3   *(Exercise 2)*
Point out that modals change the meaning of the verb in the result clause. Remind students that modals are not generally used in *if* clauses.

→ For additional practice, see the Supplementary Activities on pages 96–97.

Note 4   *(Exercise 2)*
Quick pairwork: Have students practice giving advice. Put some *result* clauses on the board:
. . . *wear a hat.*
. . . *phone home.*
. . . *don't tell your mother.*
Have students work with a partner to create conditions (with *if* or *when* clauses) under which the partner would carry out the imperative in the result clause. Examples: *If it's cold, wear a hat. If you run out of money, phone home. If you feel homesick, phone home. If you*

have a car accident, phone home. If you get a tattoo, don't tell your mother. Encourage students to restate some of their sentences to include *then.*

Note 5 *(Exercise 3)*
Quick pairwork: Tell students to use their sentence ideas from Note 4, but have them reverse the order, with the *if* or *when* clauses at the end. Check pronunciation to be sure that there is no pause when the comma is removed.

Focused Practice (pages 317–321)

Exercise 1
bargain: to discuss a price with a seller in order to get a fair or better price

trick: a secret strategy

vendor: someone who sells things, especially in the street

negotiation: a discussion between two people or groups who are trying to agree on something

Exercise 2
crafts: skilled activity in which you make something using your hands

Exercise 3
field: a subject that people study or are involved in as part of their work

such as: for example

Communication Practice (pages 322–325)

Exercise 6
- Quick pairwork: Have students work with a partner to make a sequence of what to expect as announcements before boarding an airplane, as they board the plane, and after they are on the plane.
- Quick pairwork: Have students discuss safety on board an airplane. Items to consider include baggage, tray tables, oxygen masks, seat belts.

Exercise 7
Quick pairwork: Have students discuss with a partner the importance of these aspects of travel—the right kind of shoes, layers of clothing, what to pack for easy access. The model can be:

A: What's important to you when you travel?

B: When I travel, I always bring comfortable shoes.

Exercise 8
Quick pairwork: Have students work with a partner to discuss the categories and where the cities are *(far north, near the equator, . . .).* This is also an opportunity for review of Unit 3: "Have you ever been to . . . ?"

Exercise 9
Before students work in pairs, have the whole class brainstorm a list of important purchases besides a camera or a car *(laptop computer, special software, a new printer, . . .).*

Exercise 10
- Check that your students are familiar with general shopping vocabulary: *to try on, to fit, too small, too tight, too loose, my size.*
- Quick pairwork: Have student pairs decide how long they are willing to wait between the time they buy something (an item of clothing, a piece of jewelry, a best-selling book, a piece of sports equipment) and having it in their hands. Example: *Are you willing to wait three days for the book you need?* Answers: *Yes, I am, for a better price. / No, I'm not. I want the book when I first see it.* Ask them to decide how much it is worth to them to have the item instantly. Have student pairs compare answers.

Exercise 11
After students have done their writing, ask them to revise the *if* clause sentences so that they are using *when* clauses. Note the changes that are necessary.

Further Practice
Your students are interested in renting apartments. You either have students go to apartment rental offices, bring in apartment renting information yourself, or use this information from one apartment complex:
- Apartments can be rented by the month, but they cost 25 percent more than apartments leased for a year.
- A six-month lease is available, but the cost is more than for a year-long lease.
- Renters must pay a deposit equal to the first- and last-month's rent when they sign a lease.
- Apartments have washers and dryers, but there is a charge for using them.
- There is a $300 pet deposit for each cat or dog.

- Each apartment has one covered parking space. Additional parking places cost $30 a month each.
- Apartments on the second floor are $20 a month more than apartments on the first floor.
- The complex has sports facilities (weight room, swimming pool, exercise equipment), but residents must join the Health Club to use them. Membership is $100 a year for the first resident of an apartment and $50 for each additional resident of the apartment.
- The second year of a lease entitles a resident to one month's free rent.
- Packages can be delivered at the main office for a $2 pickup fee.

Have students use the information to make statements using present real conditionals. Example: *If you have a package delivered to the main office, you have to pay $2 to pick it up.*

GRAMMAR OUT OF THE BOX ......

But what if I . . . This activity, based on real life, will be different for every student. Each student should think of a daily activity that involves another person and that doesn't vary much from day to day (buying a train ticket, getting a cup of coffee on the corner, speaking with a family member or roommate about preparing a meal). The student then thinks of a possible change to this activity and asks the other person (family member, ticket agent, roommate) about the possible consequences: *What if I only buy a three-zone ticket and then I stay on the train for four zones? What if I spill the coffee on the counter, will you give me a paper towel? What if you forget to buy rice today?* Students write down their possible questions and bring them to class for a role-play exercise in pairs:

A: You're my sister. You always cook dinner. I ask you, "What if you forget to buy rice?"

B: If I forget to buy rice, I send *you* out to buy it!

UNIT 22 Future Real Conditionals

Unit Overview

Students will learn and practice the meaning and use of future real conditional expressions.

Grammar in Context (pages 326–327)

Background Notes

Many cultural beliefs are based on ideas that are superstitious, rather than logical or rational. However, many superstitions have a basis in fact. A black cat may not be bad luck, but a person might trip over a black cat in the dark because the cat is not easy to see. A ladder in itself is not dangerous, but walking under a ladder puts a person in a position where something heavy might fall and cause injury.

Vocabulary

confident: sure that you have the ability to do things well or deal with situations successfully

Comprehension Questions

- Superstitions are cause-and-effect sentences. What are real consequences of the following circumstances?
  —You break a mirror. (*You have to sweep up the broken pieces and buy a new mirror.*)
  —A black cat runs in front of you. (*You have to be careful not to trip over it.*)
  —You walk under a ladder. (*Nothing, unless something falls on you! Then you have to take care of your injury.*)
- What are the superstitions that people might have about the same circumstances?
  —*A broken mirror means seven years of bad luck.*
  —*You will have bad luck.*
  —*You risk injury.*

Discussion Topics

- Sports stars tend to be superstitious. They wear lucky hats, take their showers at specific times, refuse to dust themselves off if they fall. What reasons can you think of for this kind if behavior?
- What is a lucky number? Do you have one? Why is it your lucky number?
- What happens if you lose a lucky piece?
- Quick pairwork: What are some other superstitions? Why did they develop?

Grammar Presentation (pages 328–329)

Identify the Grammar

If X happens, then Y will also happen.
If the pen makes you feel more confident, you might improve your score.
. . . your lucky pen will be powerless unless you study.
. . . he'll be more successful if he owns pet fish.
If the palm of your hand itches, you're going to get some money.

Grammar Charts

- Point out that the *if* (or *unless*) clause can come at the beginning of the sentence or at the end of the sentence. It requires a comma if it comes first.
- Show students that the *if* or *unless* clause can precede a *wh-* question: *If she doesn't pass the exam, what will she do? Unless she passes the exam, what will she do?*
- Point out that *might* can be used in some result sentences in place of *will* or *be going to*: *If you feel confident, you might improve your test score. If you feel confident, you will improve your test score.*

Grammar Notes

Notes 1, 2   *(Exercises 3, 4, 5)*
- Point out that the purpose of future real conditionals is to state a condition and the result that will occur as a result. *If you spend the money, you won't have it anymore.* (Don't spend the money, and you will still have it.)
- Point out that there is *no* future marker (modal or modal-like expression) in the *if* clause. The meaning is future anyway. *If you <u>are</u> confident, you'<u>ll do</u> well on the test.*

Note 3   *(Exercise 4)*
Quick pairwork: Have student partners change around the order of the conditional sentences in the reading.

Note 4   *(Exercise 2)*
Because *unless* is so tricky for nonnative speakers of English, it is useful to do a quick teacher-directed oral drill here: Give students a (simple) *if* situation and have them transform it into a sentence with *unless*:

TEACHER: If I'm not hungry, I don't eat.

STUDENTS: You don't eat unless you're hungry.

TEACHER: If you don't ask, I won't tell you.

STUDENTS: You won't tell us unless we ask.

TEACHER: If you don't study, you won't pass the test.

STUDENTS: We won't pass the test unless we study.

→ For additional practice, see the Supplementary Activities on page 97.

Focused Practice (pages 329–333)

Exercise 1
backwards: with the back part in front

Exercise 2
miracle: something very good or lucky that you hope will happen, but that does not seem likely

Exercise 3
itchy: if part of your body is itchy, it feels unpleasant and you want to rub it

Exercise 4
pessimist: someone who always expects that bad things will happen

career move: a change in job or profession

Exercise 6
campaign: to work to try to get elected to office

get into: to be accepted, particularly into a school

Communication Practice (pages 333–335)

Exercise 7
Before students listen to the recording, have them work in small groups to explore the concept of communication. Ask, "What are the ways people communicate?" *(speech; writing memos, letters, e-mails; body language)* "What makes one person a good communicator and another person not?" *(Some people are better than others at stating the main idea. Some people ramble. Some people cannot give examples.)*

Exercise 8
- Prepare for this exercise by asking *If . . . , then what . . . ?* questions like these:
"If you keep careful records of your money, then what?" *(You'll know where it went.)*
"If you have house rules where you live, then what?" *(There won't be arguments about small things.)*

- Point out that in order to do this exercise, students will need to come up with vocabulary which is not in the book, so some critical thinking is necessary here. In the example in the book, they would have needed to think of *police, landlord,* or *move.* If students are having trouble with number 2, you can prompt them with *aspirin, doctor, rest,* or *vacation.*

Exercise 9
Have students invent some superstitions by completing these *if* clauses:
- If your ears itch, then . . .
- If your feet itch, then . . .
- If your nose itches, then . . .

Exercise 10
Have students prepare for this writing assignment by answering questions like these in small groups, which should prompt the kind of campaign promises required in the assignment.
- What do students need to make studying easier? *(study areas in student unions and classroom buildings, soft music, desks and chairs, . . .)*
- What do students need so that education is not so expensive? *(computer labs, public transportation, . . .)*
- What can make going to school more enjoyable? *(more on-campus activities, clubs, free concerts, . . .)*

Further Practice
Have student groups or teams compete with others in the class. One student starts with an *if* clause and a result clause. The next student continues the story by changing the result clause to an *if* clause and making a new sentence. Here is an example:

A: If I get a part-time job, I'll have more money for entertainment.

B: If I have more money for entertainment, I won't study as much.

C: If I don't study as much, my grades will go down.

D: If my grades go down, I'll lose my scholarship.

E: If I lose my scholarship, I'll have to drop out of school.

F: If I drop out of school, I'll have to pay back my student loans.

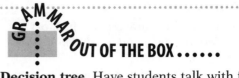

GRAMMAR OUT OF THE BOX . . . . . .

Decision tree. Have students talk with friends outside of class about making a decision such as whether to buy a secondhand car, whether to get a part-time job, whether to change majors. Have them use the decision-making model in Exercise 5 *(What if . . .)* and create future real conditional sentences about the decision.

UNIT 23 Present and Future Unreal Conditionals

Unit Overview

Students will learn and practice the meaning and use of present and future unreal conditionals.

Grammar in Context (pages 336–338)

Background Notes
Cultural values are often taught to children through stories like fairy tales, stories in which magical things happen. This story is both a fairy tale and a *fable*—a story that presents a moral lesson: Ask for what you need, be willing to work for it, and be satisfied when you have what you need.

Vocabulary
pigpen: a place on a farm where pigs are kept, a dirty place

enchanted: something that is enchanted has been changed by magic so that it has special powers

cottage: a small house in the country, especially an old one

utensils: tools or objects that you use to cook, prepare, or eat food

chandelier: a frame that holds lights or candles, hangs from the ceiling, and is decorated with small pieces of glass

marble: a hard rock that can be polished and used for buildings, statues, etc.

throne: the chair on which a king or queen sits

satisfied: pleased because something has happened in the way that you want

pitch black: completely black or dark

Comprehension Questions

- Who are the main characters of the story? *(a fisherman, his wife, and a fish who is an enchanted prince)*
- Where did the fisherman and his wife live at the beginning of the story? *(in a pigpen)*
- Where do the fisherman and his wife live at the end of the story? *(in a pigpen)*
- What kind of human being is the fisherman? *(kind-hearted, satisfied, rather shy)*
- What kind of human being is the fisherman's wife? *(dissatisfied, unhappy)*
- What is the personality of the enchanted prince-fish? *(reasonable, willing to help)*
- Why do the fisherman and his wife end up with nothing? *(because the woman is so greedy)*
- What is the lesson, or moral, of the story? *(A person who asks for too much gets nothing.)*

Discussion Topics

- The fisherman and his wife both have serious weaknesses in their personalities. What are they and how do they bring about their downfall?
- The writer of the fable tells us about the thinking and mood of the enchanted prince-fish in an interesting way. What is it? *(the color of the seawater and the height and strength of the waves)*

Grammar Presentation (pages 338–340)

Identify the Grammar

If you knew my real identity, you wouldn't kill me.
If we had a cottage, I would be a lot happier.
If I asked for a cottage, the fish might get angry.
I wish we had a nice little cottage.

Grammar Charts

- Write an *If . . . , would/could . . .* sentence and an *I wish* sentence on the board. Point out also that the *if* clause looks like the past tense. Show that each sentence represents a situation in which an unreal condition is stated as a proposition or a wish. If the proposed or wished for proposition were true (but it's not) then another result would follow.
- Point out the similarity between sentences with *if* and the sentences with *wish: If I were king, I would own all this land. I wish I were king of all this land.* In these two sentences, the essential meaning is the same: *I am not*

king, and I do not own the land. I want to be king because then I would own all the land.
- Point out that in both *yes/no* questions and *wh-* questions, the modal *would* is used in the main clause and *had* or *were* in the *if* clause. Normal word order is used. Short answers follow normal modal-use rules.

Grammar Notes

Notes 1 and 2   *(Exercises 2, 3, 5)*
- Point out that if the clause in a sentence about a real situation is positive, the clause in the related present unreal conditional sentence is negative. Examples: *I am rich, so I live in a palace. = If I weren't rich, I wouldn't live in a palace.*
- Also point out that, in a similar way, if the clause in a sentence about a real situation is negative, then the clause in the related present unreal conditional sentence is positive. For example, *I don't live in a palace, so I don't give big parties. = If I lived in a palace, I would give big parties.*
- Quick pairwork: Have students write true simple present tense sentences about situations in their lives that they don't like and the results. Then ask them to imagine that the situation is now different and write related present unreal conditional sentences. Examples: *I'm a student, so I don't have much money. If I weren't a student, I would have more money.*
- Remind students that *would* is not used in the *if* clause.
- Point out that the correct form of *be* in present and future unreal conditionals is always *were*. (Though some speakers use *was*, many people consider it incorrect. To be correct as far as everyone is concerned, use *were*.)

Note 3   *(Exercises 2, 3, 5)*
- Point out that the most common modal in the result clause is *would* because it shows certainty: *If X were true, the result would be Y.*
- Remind students that sometimes ability to do something is part of the condition, so *would* is replaced with *could* in the result clause: *If X were true, then Y could do Z.*
- If the result is not certain, then *might* or *could* can appear in the result clause: *If X were true, then (maybe) the result might be Y. If X were true, then (maybe) the result could be Y.*

Note 4   *(Exercises 3, 5)*

- Point out that the order of the main clause and the *if* clause can be reversed. Examples:
If you knew my real identity, you wouldn't kill me. = You wouldn't kill me if you knew my real identity.
If we lived in a big stone castle, I would be much happier. = I would be much happier if we lived in a big stone castle.
- Point out that the comma is needed only for an initial *if* clause.

Note 5

Quick pairwork: Have student pairs practice giving advice to the fisherman, his wife, and the fish. Examples:
- (to fisherman) *If I were you, I wouldn't do everything your wife asked you to do.*
- (to fisherman's wife) *If I were you, I would be happy with a nice cottage.*
- (to fish) *If I were you, I'd grant fewer wishes.*

Note 6   *(Exercise 4)*

- Point out that in sentences with *wish*, the result is not stated, but implied: *I wish I had a nice cottage to live in. = If I had a nice cottage to live in, I would be happier.*
- Have students transform their *if* sentences from the Note 2 pairwork activity into wishes.

→ For additional practice, see the Supplementary Activities on page 97.

Focused Practice (pages 341–345)

Exercise 2
moan: to make a long low sound expressing pain or sadness

therapist: someone who has been trained to give a particular form of treatment for mental or physical illness

beggar: someone who lives by asking people for food or money

genie: a magical creature in old stories who can make wishes come true (point out that *abracadabra* is a word spoken to help magic succeed when performing magic tricks)

Exercise 3
balance (a checkbook): to check the amounts of money deposited to and withdrawn from a bank account

Quick pairwork: These excuses could be expanded into role plays. One student plays the role of the psychologist, and the other role-plays the client.

Exercise 6
intriguing: interesting because it is strange or mysterious

catastrophic: relating to a lot of destruction or suffering

pump gas: to put gas into your car

warlike: threatening war or attack, or seeming to like war

Communication Practice (pages 346–347)

Exercise 7
Talk with your students about things they would wish for if they had a magical wish. (A practical person would ask for an unlimited number of wishes.)

Exercise 8
Alternative questions: What would you do/ Where would you go if you could travel into the past/future?

Exercise 9
Quick pairwork: Have partners ask each other, "What would you change about this school?" Encourage students to exchange creative ideas such as: *add more classes, get air conditioning, have a restaurant.*

Exercise 10
Quick group work: Have students in pairs or small groups start with the sentence *If I were famous, I wouldn't have any free time,* then change the result clause to the *if* clause and continue. *(If I didn't have any free time, I wouldn't have time to spend with friends. If I didn't have time to spend with friends, I would lose all of the people I love.)* Have groups compete to see who can keep the chain going longest.

Exercise 11
Go back to Exercise 6. Point out that *The Disappearance* was published in 1951. Prompt a class discussion with the following questions: Have ideas about men's and women's abilities changed since the novel was published? If so, how? Do you agree with Wiley's ideas? Do you agree with the student's ideas in the last paragraph? Why or why not? Does the fable at the beginning of the unit show any stereotypes about men and women that you agree or disagree with?

Further Practice
With your students, make a list of professions in which people can become famous and

maybe also rich like computer billionaire Bill Gates *(scientist, inventor, actor, political leader, clothing designer, musician, athlete, movie star).* Then have them name a real person for each profession and create interview questions for that person using present and future unreal conditionals. For example, for Bill Gates: *Bill, what would you do if you lost all your money? Bill, what would you do if someone invented something better than computers and software?*

GRAMMAR OUT OF THE BOX . . . . . .

Fantasy. Give students newspaper reporter assignments to find out what people would do if they had a year off work and enough money so they could go anywhere and do anything. Encourage students to ask other teachers, parents, people they work with, hairstylists, and people they meet at places like coffee shops. Have them report others' fantasies to the class.

UNIT 24 — Past Unreal Conditionals

Unit Overview

Students will learn and practice the meaning and formation of past unreal conditionals.

Grammar in Context (pages 348–349)

Background Notes

The movie *It's a Wonderful Life* was made in 1946, but its timeless message makes it appropriate for audiences today. It is shown regularly during the winter holiday season in North America. Originally it was a black-and-white film, but color has been added. Also, the sound has been improved with modern technology, and the film is available in DVD format.

Vocabulary

episode: an event, or a short time that is different from the time around it

boarding house: a private house where you pay to sleep and eat

heartwarming: making you feel happy, calm, and hopeful

Comprehension Questions

- Who is the main character of the movie? *(George Bailey)*
- What kind of person is he? *(the kind of person who sacrifices his own dreams to help other people)*
- Who is Clarence? *(an angel sent to help George)*
- What does Clarence do to help George understand that his life has been meaningful? *(He shows George what life would have been like for the people in his community if George had not been born.)*

Discussion Topics

- Explain the movie title: *It's a Wonderful Life.*
- What other titles might be appropriate for this movie?
- Think about how the things we say and do make a difference in other people's lives. Think about someone you've helped in your life. If you had acted in a different way, what would have happened?

Grammar Presentation (pages 350–351)

Identify the Grammar

What would have happened if you had never been born?
He could have gone to college if the family business hadn't needed him.
If George hadn't been alive, he couldn't have saved Harry's life.
Harry would have never grown up to be a war hero.
We see . . . how the lives of those around him would have been different if he hadn't known them.

Grammar Charts

- Point out that for past unreal conditionals, the past perfect is used in the *if* clause: *If George <u>had not been born</u>, . . .* The result clause uses *would have* + past participle form of the verb:
  . . . , many people's lives <u>would have been changed</u> for the worse.
- Review the contractions: *Would have* and *would not have* are contracted as *would've* and *wouldn't have* (or *wouldn't've*, in speech).

Grammar Notes

Note 1 *(Exercises 2, 4)*

• Remind students that ideas expressed in unreal past conditionals and the results are untrue (perhaps impossible) or imagined. Example: *If I had not gone to college, I wouldn't have become a teacher.* (I went to college [the *if* clause is untrue] and I <u>did</u> become a teacher, so the result is also untrue.)

• Point out that explanatory sentences starting with *but* can be added to boldfaced sentences in the reading. For example: *What would have happened if you had never been born?* (*But I was born, so this sentence is unreal.*) Quick pairwork: Have student pairs choose several boldfaced sentences from the reading and add *but* clauses to them.

Note 2 *(Exercise 2)*

• Quick oral practice: Ask students, "What would you have done if you hadn't come to class today / yesterday / last week?" (*I would've gone to the beach / stayed home / gone to work / slept late . . .*) Point out an easy, quick trick for remembering all the parts of this structure: Use the thumb and fingers of your hand to count off all the parts. Demonstrate as you say, "I <u>would</u> (thumb) <u>have</u> (index) <u>stayed</u> (middle) home if I <u>hadn't</u> (ring) <u>come</u> (pinky) to class." Put the first part of the model question on the board (*What would you have done if . . .*) and have students get up and circulate to ask each other the question, while you check for grammar (especially *have*; use the counting-off-on-fingers trick) and pronunciation/reduction: *What wouldja've **done** if you hadn't **come** to class?*

• Have students circle the verbs in the *if* clauses and the result clauses in the boldfaced sentences in the reading. Point out that the common elements in the *if* clauses are *had* + past participle and the common elements in the result clauses are *would / could have* + past participle.

Note 3 *(Exercises 2, 4)*

Point out that past condition can influence present result as well as past result, depending on the verb and the situation: *If I hadn't taken this class, I never would have met you* (past result) / *I wouldn't know you* (present result).

→ For additional practice, see the Supplementary Activities on page 97.

Note 4 *(Exercise 4)*

Quick pairwork: Have the students reverse the order of the *if* clauses and the result clauses in the examples in the reading. Remind them about the need for a comma with an initial *if* clause.

Notes 5 and 6 *(Exercises 2, 3)*

Quick pairwork: Have students think of some situation in which they felt regret, and express it with both an "I wish" statement and a past unreal conditional. *(I wish I had saved my money instead of putting it into a machine at the airport in Las Vegas. If I had known that I would lose every nickel, I wouldn't have put any money into that machine at the airport in Las Vegas.)*

Focused Practice (pages 352–356)

Exercise 2

deaf: physically unable to hear, or unable to hear well

honeymoon: a vacation taken by two people who have just gotten married

desperate: willing to do anything to change a very bad situation, and not caring about danger

Exercise 3

yell at: to scold someone

Exercise 4

(the) lead: the main acting part in a play

Parkinson's disease: a serious illness in which your muscles become very weak, and your arms and legs shake

Exercise 5

come out: (idiom) to become publicly known or available

Communication Practice (pages 357–358)

Exercise 6

• Point out that listening to contractions is very important in understanding conditionals.

• Review the contractions in the grammar chart in the Grammar Presentation (*would've, wouldn't have*). Mention that spoken English also uses a double contraction (*wouldn't've*) which is not written.

Exercise 7

Quick pairwork: Have students use these situations to think of creative solutions and to compare and discuss ethics.

Exercise 8

Brainstorm past regrets to prepare students for the exercise (*a lost friendship, a problem at school, trouble with a family relationship, saying or doing the wrong thing, a missed opportunity for study or travel*).

Exercise 9

Ask students to imagine a change in their past and how it would have affected their lives. "What if I hadn't decided to study English/left my hometown/met my husband (wife)?" "What if I had been born somewhere else/at a different time/into a different family?" "What would have happened instead?" A few minutes of discussion will help students prepare for the writing assignment.

Further Practice

Go back to Unit 16, Exercise 8: Ask your students to consider what *would have happened* if Sheila had been willing to tell the reporter about her mistake and decision never to cheat again (Case 1), if Mustafa had not gone into the building to get the records (Case 2), and if Pierre had not gotten an extra job (Case 3).

 OUT OF THE BOX ......

Facing problems. Tell students to take note of some common personal problems in the outside world and be prepared to describe them in class. Suggest that they might find such problems by reading newspaper advice columns, by watching a soap opera or reality television show, by observing, or by asking friends. Each problem should be defined in one or two sentences. For small group work, then, each group will have a number of problems to discuss. Encourage the groups to come up with solutions using present unreal conditionals. Example: *I saw a woman standing by her truck on the side of the freeway. An armchair had fallen out of the back of her truck and was in the middle of a five-lane freeway where it could cause a terrible accident. If that had happened to me, I would have called 911 and gotten police help.*

Direct and Indirect Speech

Unit Overview

Students will learn and practice the uses and forms of direct and indirect speech.

Grammar in Context (pages 368–369)

Background Notes

To some people, there is a difference between a lie and a *white lie*, a simple untruth told to avoid hurting the feelings of another person. Some people simply avoid saying what they really think; if another person asks, "Do you like my new hairstyle?" the first person will answer, "It's really modern" or "It's an interesting new trend," rather than giving a completely honest answer. Other people lie to avoid an unpleasant truth or situation: They might tell a bill collector that the check is in the mail even though it has not yet been sent at all.

Vocabulary

fiancée: the woman whom a man is going to marry

born yesterday: (idiom) new and unfamiliar, naïve and simple-minded

Comprehension Questions

• What is unusual about the title of this reading? (*The words* truth *and* lying *have opposite meanings.*)
• What reasons are given for telling white lies? (*to get something fast or avoid an unpleasant situation, to appear better or feel better, to make a polite excuse, to protect someone's feelings*)
• What is the trend in regard to lying? (*People lie more today than they did in the past.*)

Discussion Topics

• Reread the quote at the end of the reading: "All men are born truthful and die liars." What is your opinion?
• What white lies have you told recently?
• Under some circumstances, people decide not to tell the truth at all and feel good about the decision. Is it, for example, good to tell a person who is very ill that she or he is dying? What other circumstances might make people consider not telling the whole story?

Grammar Presentation (pages 369–371)

Identify the Grammar

DIRECT SPEECH

"The check is in the mail," Rick replied quickly.
. . . Vauvenargues . . . wrote, "All men are
born truthful and die liars."

INDIRECT SPEECH

Arriving late, Rick told his client that traffic
had been bad.
Each time, he told himself that sometimes the
truth causes too many problems.

Grammar Charts

- Point out that a person's words can be reported as direct speech or indirect speech. Direct speech (the exact words of the person) requires quotation marks.
- Point out these three things about indirect speech:
  1. It sometimes requires a change in verb form.
  2. It does not need quotation marks.
  3. It often includes *that* as a clause introducer for the indirect statement, the reworded quotation.

Grammar Notes

Note 1

Point out that direct speech is a quotation; therefore, you need to tell who *said* the words. Another person's exact words always require quotation marks. Remind students to follow the punctuation rules for direct speech in Appendix 26, page A-13.

→ For additional practice, see the Supplementary Activities on page 98.

Note 2

- Point out the similarities between *say* and *tell*. They mean essentially the same thing. However, *tell [someone]* is followed by the name of the listener or a personal pronoun *(me/you/him/her/us/them)*. *Say [to someone]* (that is, to the listener) is less common. *Say* is usually used alone. Thus, if the listener is mentioned, it is more common to use *tell*.
  Sam told Sally that he got a new job.
  (Sam said to Sally that he got a new job.)
  Sam said, "Sally, I got a new job."
  Sam said that he got a new job.

Notes 3 and 4   *(Exercises 2, 3)*

- Point out that in indirect speech the verb form changes if the statement was made some time ago:
  He said, "Jim is a great guy."
  He said that Jim was a great guy.
- Quick teacher-directed drill:

  TEACHER: I talked to my mother three weeks ago. I said, "I'm coming to see you!" (ask students) What did I say?

  STUDENTS: You said you <u>were</u> coming to see her.

  TEACHER: I told her, "You sound happy!" What did I tell her?

  STUDENTS: You told her she <u>sounded</u> happy.

Note 5   *(Exercise 4)*

Remind students that for a newly made statement or an unchanging fact, we use the present:
He said he's aware of the problem.
He said that the world really is flat.
The astronauts said that the earth is round.

Note 6   *(Exercises 2, 3, 4)*

- Point out that simple present stays simple present, especially in newspapers:
  Psychologists <u>say</u> that lying <u>shows</u> a lack of control.
- Bring in some newspaper polls or surveys, and have students report on them in groups: "Our survey says that 50 percent of Americans prefer blue cars."

Focused Practice (pages 372–375)

Exercise 1
risky business: not a good idea, something that could get you in trouble in the future

credits: successfully completed parts of a course at a university or college

short: (idiom) to not have enough

discrepancy: the difference between two details or facts that should be the same

Exercise 2
smashed: broken

funny look: a questioning facial expression

Exercise 4
starting salary: the rate of pay you receive when you begin to work for a company

Exercise 5

hoax: a trick that makes someone believe something that is not true

sunscreen: a cream that you put on your skin to stop the sun from burning you

Communication Practice (pages 376–378)

Exercise 6
Before students listen to the recording, review the weekly planner and what is already scheduled.

Exercise 7
Quick pairwork: Have each student disclose a white lie she or he recently told. Ask them to justify it, using one of the four reasons for telling a white lie given in the reading, or ask them to use the pictures on page 373 for the pairwork.

Exercise 8
Ask students how often they believe others when they blame traffic for their being late. Ask what other statements or excuses seem like white lies.

Exercise 9
Help students generate ideas for this contest *(has participated in a marathon, has a twin, has lived in three other countries, has had cosmetic surgery, has won a contest . . .).*

Exercise 10
Quick pairwork: For writing practice, have students paraphrase one or two of the quotes and then share their paraphrases with the rest of the class.

Exercise 11
Discuss with the students how they know when someone is upset (besides the things they say). Ask them to describe some body language clues.

Further Practice
Write the following three proverbs about honesty on the board:
Honesty is always the best policy.
The truth will out. (You may have to explain that this is a short way of saying that the truth will *come* out.)
A person who always tells the truth doesn't have to remember as much as a person who lies.

Have students work in small groups to discuss these proverbs. Then have them discuss which ones they agree or disagree with. Encourage them to support their reasons with examples. Finally have the groups report their findings to the class using indirect speech *(Marcus said that he agrees with . . . , but Alma said that she . . .).*

Politics. In class, have students identify three political issues. They can decide to use campus issues, like the need for emergency phone stations; local issues, like changes in parking regulations; or global concerns, like global warming, or the spread of AIDS. Have groups of students make survey statements about each of the issues chosen. *(Parking should be free on Sundays.)* Then send students out with survey forms to interview three people each with answers such as: *agree strongly, have no opinion, disagree somewhat,* and *disagree strongly.* Have them write up the responses they gather and report them to the class in indirect speech. Tally the responses. Summarize the responses with indirect speech *(Most of the people in our survey said that they . . .).*

UNIT 26 Indirect Speech: Tense Changes

Unit Overview

Students will learn and practice the tense changes in indirect speech.

Grammar in Context (pages 379–381)

Background Notes
Floods are usually caused by long rainstorms and the rapid melting of snow. For this reason, people hope for gentle rain over a period of months and a long cool spring. The flood in this reading was caused by one heavy late summer storm.

Vocabulary

evacuation: the process of moving people from a dangerous place to a safe place

stream: to move quickly and continuously in one direction (water or people)

slosh: to walk through water or mud in a noisy way

stand: to tolerate something, deal well with a difficult situation

jumble: a messy mixture of things

gape: to look at something for a long time, usually with your mouth open, because you are very shocked or surprised

global warming: an increase in the world temperatures, caused by an increase of carbon dioxide around the earth

Comprehension Questions

- What caused the flood in central Europe in 2002? *(heavy rain)*
- What things are most endangered by floods? *(buildings and bridges along rivers and the materials in the buildings)*
- How do sandbags work? *(Sandbags are stacked along river banks to create natural walls that can hold a river inside its normal channel. The bags hold the sand so the water cannot wash it downstream.)*
- What could have caused the great amount of rain? *(global warming, a change in weather patterns)*
- What do experts believe could stop the weather-related disasters? *(government policies and laws that will control the causes of weather changes)*

Discussion Topics

- Land along rivers, lakes, and oceans is beautiful. What are some possible problems with building houses in such places?
- What seems to be the reason for global warming and changes in weather patterns? What could be done to stop global warming?

Grammar Presentation (pages 381–383)

Identify the Grammar

. . . Hooper reported <u>that it had been raining</u> for more than 24 hours straight.
Hooper noted <u>that evacuations had already started</u> in Prague . . .
. . . Nemec told reporters <u>that the historic Old Town should remain safe.</u>
. . . he said <u>he was back</u> in his hometown that summer to help.
He said <u>it would have been</u> too cruel to bear.

Grammar Charts

- Have students change the example sentences (and other sentences in indirect speech in the

reading) to direct speech, with appropriate capitalization and punctuation:
—*Hooper reported, "It has been raining for more than 24 hours straight."*
—*Hooper noted, "Evacuations have already started in Prague."*
—*Nemec told reporters, "The historic Old Town should remain safe."*
—*He said, "I am back in my hometown this summer to help."*
—*He said, "It would be too cruel to bear."*

- Point out to students that direct quotes are easier because the exact words of the speaker are used. Also point out, however, that indirect quoting (indirect speech) is much more common and natural.
- Next point out that moving from direct to indirect speech is moving one step into the past. Put on the board:

Write	Students supply
is	was
are	were
move	moved
moved	had moved
am looking	was looking
have looked	had looked
can go	could go
have to go	had to go
will stay	would stay
may stay	might stay
must visit	had to visit

Point out that the only verbs that do not change are those that don't really have another form, like past modals:

should go	remains	*should go*
ought to go	remains	*ought to go*
could go	remains	*could go*

Past perfect verbs (including present and past unreal conditionals) have no further past form to move to, so they stay the same:

had seen	remains	*had seen*

Grammar Notes

Notes 1–5 *(Exercises 2, 3, 4)*
Use what you have written on the board during the presentation of the Grammar Charts for oral practice of all of these forms. Give your students a sentence, and then ask them, "What did I say?" For example, "It's a nice day. What did I say?" *(You said it was a nice day.)* "He must leave this place. What did I say?" *(You said he had to leave this place.)*

→ For additional practice, see the Supplementary Activities on page 98.

Focused Practice (pages 383–388)

Exercise 1

forecaster: someone who says what is likely to happen in the future, especially the person on television who predicts the weather

emergency relief workers: a group of people who replace other people who have been working in a dangerous situation

Exercise 2

run out of something: to use all of something so that there is none left

Exercise 3

widespread: happening in many places

Exercise 4

stubborn: determined not to change your opinions, beliefs, etc., because you believe you are right

Communication Practice (pages 389–390)

Exercise 6

Before students listen to the recording, go over the questions because the information will come very fast and they will need to be familiar with the content and the choices. Be sure that they know the meaning of the word *advisory:* having the purpose of giving advice.

Exercise 7

Point out that students should <u>not</u> repeat what they have said.

Exercise 8

Point out that hurricanes and typhoons are wind and rainstorms that can cause a lot of damage over a broad area.

Exercise 9

Suggest that students make up the name of a weather reporter or several reporters to quote in doing this assignment.

Further Practice

On individual index cards, write statements using some modals. Make as many cards as you have students. Here are some examples:
- My grandmother is sending me a check for a thousand dollars.
- You can have my two free tickets to Hawaii for spring break.
- You should pay the electricity bill as soon as possible.
- You ought to get the windshield on your car fixed.
- I'm going to start a new job tomorrow.
- My family has to find a new place to live because of the fire in their building.
- I have to write an essay for class tomorrow.

Then pass out the cards to groups of three students. Student A picks up a card and reads it out loud. Student B asks, "Would you say that again?" Student C repeats the message using indirect speech. Example:

A: My grandmother is sending me a check for a thousand dollars.

B: (to C) What did she say?

C: She said that her grandmother is/was sending her a check for a thousand dollars.

When each group has finished with its cards, it can pass them along to another group of students.

 GRAMMAR OUT OF THE BOX . . . . . .

Extraordinary reporter. Have students look up news articles about weather events of the past. Possible topics are unusual weather conditions, a natural disaster like a forest fire or an earthquake, a crime that made headlines, a sports event of some importance. They then report back to the class about what happened.

Storytellers Many communities have storytellers' clubs. Have your students find out if there is one in your area, and if so invite them to class to tell stories which the students can then write up using indirect speech.

UNIT 27 Indirect Instructions, Commands, Requests, and Invitations

Unit Overview

Students will learn and practice how to give indirect instructions, commands, requests, and invitations.

Grammar in Context (pages 391–392)

Background Notes

Sleep disruption, according to psychologists, is a major reason for emotional and other mental disturbances. People who are deprived of sleep tend to be more nervous, hold more water in their bodies, and have more headaches. They are also more easily angered, frustrated, and moved to tears.

Vocabulary

snooze: a short period of sleep

insomnia: the condition of not being able to sleep

What's the big deal?: (idiom) Why is this important?

drowsy: tired and almost asleep

fatigue: extreme tiredness

astounding: very surprising

caffeine: a chemical substance found in coffee, tea, and some other drinks that makes people feel more active

remedies: cures or solutions

scrub: to clean something by rubbing it very hard with a stiff brush or rough cloth

monitor: to watch carefully, listen to, or examine something over a period of time, to check for any changes or developments

Comprehension Questions

• Who is the director of the Sleep Disorders Clinic? *(Dr. Thornton Ray)*
• What is the topic of the interview? *(sleep disorders, particularly insomnia)*
• In Dr. Ray's opinion, why is insomnia a problem? *(It causes costly accidents.)*
• What recommendations does Dr. Ray make for people with sleep deprivation problems? *(Stop drinking coffee and cola later in the day, eat a high carbohydrate snack before going to bed, exercise regularly but not just before going to bed, and do something boring when you can't sleep.)*

Discussion Topics

• Are you a morning person or a night owl? When do you do your best studying? Your best creative work?
• What happens to you when you are tired? Are you able to express yourself as well as usual? Are you as fast in the work you do?
• Have students, working in groups of three or four, find out how many hours of sleep the group averages per night. Have them discuss whether they think it is enough.

Grammar Presentation (page 393)

Identify the Grammar

We've invited Dr. Thorton Ray <u>to talk to us</u> about insomnia.
I always tell people <u>to think of the biggest disaster</u> that they've ever heard of.
Then I ask them <u>to think about</u> what can happen if they drive when they're tired.
My doctor told me <u>to get more exercise.</u>
I would tell you <u>to stop.</u>
I advised one patient <u>to balance his checkbook.</u>

Grammar Charts

• Point out that commands (direct speech) use the base form of the verb, with the subject not mentioned, but understood to be "you": *Stop smoking. Don't drink alcohol. Lie down.*
• In indirect speech, the infinitive (*to* + base verb form) is used: *He said to stop smoking. He told her not to drink alcohol. He advised them to lie down.*
• Have students change the example sentences to direct speech, noting that there may be more than one way to effect the change:
  —We've invited Dr. Thorton Ray <u>to talk to us</u> about insomnia. → We said, "Dr. Ray, please talk to us about insomnia."
  —I always tell people <u>to think of the biggest disaster</u> that they've ever heard of. → I said, "Think of the biggest disaster that you've ever heard of."
  —Then I ask them <u>to think about</u> what can happen if they drive when they're tired. → Then I ask them, "Can you think of what could happen if you were driving when you were tired?"
  —My doctor told me <u>to get more exercise.</u> → My doctor said, "Get more exercise."
  —I would tell you <u>to stop.</u> → I would say, "You should stop."
  —I advised one patient <u>to balance his checkbook.</u> → I advised him, "Balance your checkbook."

Grammar Notes

Note 1 *(Exercises 2, 3)*
• Point out that Appendix 13, on page A-5, has a list of verbs for giving instructions, making commands and requests, and making invitations. Discuss which verbs are used for each purpose.

- Quick pairwork: Have pairs of students look at Appendix 13 and use the listed verbs to create at least two sentences each for instructions, commands, requests, and invitations. Have them share their sentences with their classmates. Possible examples:

A: Could you open the window?

B: She said, "Could you open the window?" She asked me if I could open the window.

A: Give me the pen.

B: He said, "Give me the pen." He asked me to give him the pen.

→ For additional practice, see the Supplementary Activities on page 98.

Note 2   *(Exercises 2, 3)*
- Point out that *not* precedes the *to* of the infinitive.
- Quick pairwork: Have the students make negative instructions, commands, requests, and invitations out of their sentences from the previous quick pairwork.

Focused Practice (pages 394–397)

Exercise 1
travel light: to travel with very little luggage

cozy: small, comfortable, and warm

impulse: a short electrical signal sent in one direction along a wire or nerve, or through the air

Note that not every reporting verb in this exercise is used to give an indirect instruction, command, request, or invitation. Point out to students that some phrases are not followed by infinitives. Have them identify them. They are:
Only the video camera and cable told me I was in a sleep clinic.
. . . he told me that the disks, called electrodes, would be connected to a machine . . .
He told me that I had healthy sleep patterns, . . .

Exercise 2
soothe: to make a pain stop hurting as much

cramp: a severe pain that you get when a muscle gets very tight

ease: to make something less severe or difficult, or to become less severe or difficult

rash: a lot of red spots on someone's skin, caused by an illness or reaction to food, plants, medicine, etc.

Quick pairwork: After students complete this exercise, ask them what Helen *says* to do for a sore throat, stains on one's teeth, insomnia, an itchy poison ivy rash, leg cramps, and bugs:
For _____, Helen says to _____.

Exercise 3
panic: to suddenly feel so frightened that you do things without thinking clearly, or to make someone feel this way

Exercise 4
journal: a written record that you make of the things that happen to you each day

Communication Practice (pages 398–400)

Exercise 5
Before students listen to the recording, have them read and discuss the eight suggestions. Ask if they think there is likely to be any truth about these suggestions. Tell them that you will play the recording three times. The first time they listen have them make a small X next to the items they hear. Have them check "Not Mentioned" for the remaining items. For the second listening, suggest that they listen for what the experts told Juan NOT to do. The third time they listen, they should check what Juan was told to do.

Exercise 6
- Review possible new vocabulary—*hiccup:* (usually plural) a sudden repeated stopping of the breath, usually caused by eating or drinking too fast; *blister:* a swelling on your skin containing clear liquid, caused for example by a burn or continuous rubbing.
- Possible answers: put cold water and then aloe vera on minor kitchen burns; drink warm milk for insomnia; make a paste of baking soda and water and put it on insect bites; take aspirin for headaches; turn the snoring sleeper on his or her side; swallow a spoonful of dry sugar fast to stop hiccups; take vitamin C for colds; wash the skin with strong soap and avoid scratching for poison ivy; drink hot water with lemon juice and honey for sore throats.

Exercise 7
Be sure that students know the meaning of the word *nightmare:* a very frightening dream.

Exercise 8
Quick pairwork: Have student partners tell each other about good dreams or nightmares in preparation for this assignment. Have the partners take notes for each other.

Further Practice
Form small groups. Have each group choose a different person to give advice to (a person

looking for an apartment, someone buying a used car, a college student). Then have the group create a list of instructions and advice for that person using imperative statements like *Find a good advisor.* Next have the groups exchange lists and change the imperative statements to indirect instructions and commands: *They told me to find a good advisor.*

GRAMMAR OUT OF THE BOX . . . . . .

In the community. Begin this activity by brainstorming places where a person can get help in the community. The Chamber of Commerce helps new business owners; the tourism office helps businesses that are related to tourism and tourists too; the newspapers help people buy and sell things; various government entities (like social security offices, the post office, employment) give instructions and advice on many different topics. With your students, create a list of places to go and what to ask. Send students (in pairs or groups of three) to get information, instructions, and advice. Have them report their findings to the class or make a poster that can be displayed in the classroom.

UNIT 28 Indirect Questions

Unit Overview

Students will learn and practice how to make and use indirect questions.

Grammar in Context (pages 401–402)

Background Notes

There are laws that prevent employers from asking specific kinds of questions of prospective employees so that all people have equal chances to get good jobs, regardless of age, religion, marital status, gender, and race. For example, without these laws, a woman of 40 who has five children to support might not get a job even if she is well-qualified because an employer might think she would miss a lot of work time because of her children's needs and might decide not to hire her for that imagined reason.

Vocabulary

hostile: very unfriendly and ready to fight or argue with someone

legitimate: fair or reasonable

lose one's cool: to become upset, ruffled, excited

Comprehension Questions

• What is the purpose of a stress interview? *(to determine whether a job candidate can handle pressure of the kind that a job might include)*
• How did Melissa react to the stress interview? *(She was shocked.)*
• What reason might an interviewer have for telling a job candidate that he or she is probably not the best person for the position? *(to see what kind of reaction the person has to that idea)*
• Why aren't all job interviews stress interviews? *(Not all jobs require that a person be able to handle stress.)*
• What disadvantage might a stress interview have for a company? *(A good candidate for a job might decide he or she does not want to work for a company that would stress a candidate so much during an interview and refuse the job offer.)*

Discussion Topics

• How can a person prepare for a stress interview? Do you think it helps to be prepared for a stress interview? How so?
• What kind of investigation into a company should any job applicant do? Why is it important to know about the company?
• Is it a good idea to send thank-you cards to people who have interviewed you when you are looking for a job? What is the effect of such a personal communication as thanking an interviewer for having taken the time to talk with you?

Grammar Presentation (pages 403–405)

Identify the Grammar

First, the interviewer asked her why she couldn't work under pressure.
. . . he asked if she had cleaned out her car recently.
Then he wanted to know who had written her application letter for her.
She asked the interviewer whether he was going to ask her serious questions.

Grammar Charts

- Be sure that students know the word *spreadsheet:* a computer program that can show and calculate financial information.
- Point out that *yes/no* questions that become indirect questions use *if* or *whether (or not).*
- Point out that *who* and *what* can take the place of the subject, so no change in word order is required with these two *wh-* words: *Who told her about the job?* → *He asked who told her about the job.*
- Point out that when the *wh-* word takes the place of part of the predicate, the helping verb *(do/did)* is dropped and any modal (such as *can* or *might*) moves to the regular sentence word order position after the subject: *Where did I work?* → *He asked where I worked. What can a cook make with tomatoes?* → *The chef asks what the cook can make with tomatoes.*

Grammar Notes

Note 1   *(Exercises 2, 3)*
Quick pairwork: Have students ask each other two questions that start with *Do you* and two that start with *Are you.* Then go around the room having students report what they asked their partners *(I asked my partner if he likes pizza. I asked my partner whether she is comfortable with spreadsheets.)*

Note 2   *(Exercises 2, 3)*
- Write *when, where, how, why,* and *how much* on the board.
- Quick pairwork: Have your students ask each other questions with each of the *wh-* words on the board and then role-play one question for the rest of the class using this sequence:

  STUDENT A: Where do you want to live?

  CLASS, TO STUDENT B: What did your partner ask?

  STUDENT B: He asked me where I want to live.

Note 3   *(Exercises 2, 3)*
Point out that the *be* verb after *who* or *what* requires a change in word order and sometimes a change to the past: *Who is that man?* → *I want to know who that man is. / I asked who that man was.*

→ For additional practice, see the Supplementary Activities on page 98.

Note 4   *(Exercises 2, 3)*
- Point out that an indirect question is not a true question, so it does not need a question mark.
- Repeat the rule that *do, does,* and *did* are not needed because statement word order is used.

Focused Practice (pages 406–409)

Exercise 1
tricky: something that is difficult to deal with because it is complicated and full of problems

snap decision: a decision or judgment made quickly, especially one made without enough thought or preparation

Exercise 2
Quick pairwork: Ask student pairs to come up with four questions they would want to ask about a job (where, how much pay, how many hours a week, benefits, any flexibility of schedule). Then have them report to the class using indirect question form. *(We want to ask how much the pay is. We want to know whether this job has benefits.)*

Exercise 3
job performance: how well you do your work

layoffs: workers lose their jobs because the company doesn't have enough work

Exercise 4
keep one's poise: to maintain a calm, confident way of behaving, to be able to control how you feel

Communication Practice (pages 410–412)

Exercise 5
Have students prepare for the recorded interview by changing the elements in both lists into questions and then indirect questions. Remind them of the stress and vowel change in the pronunciation of statements with *can* and *can't:* You /kən/ ASK vs. You /kænt/ ASK.
What is your name? → *You can ask what a person's name is.*
How old are you? → *You can't ask how old a person is.*

Exercise 6
Point out the term *associate's degree,* and explain that it is a two-year degree from a community college.

Exercise 7

Point out that the acceptability of some personal questions (about, for example, one's origins, family, financial matters, marital status, education, life goals, weight, age) varies from one culture to another. Discuss with your class what things are inappropriate to ask before they interview one another.

Exercise 8

Collect some of the questions that students were asked and determine which questions were difficult to answer. Help the students come up with ways of avoiding such questions. Sometimes the best way is with another question: *Is the number of languages I can speak an important part of this job?*

Exercise 9

Quick pairwork: Have your students practice changing their questions into indirect questions before they begin to write.

Further Practice

For this activity, students work in groups of three. Prepare two information cards for each group, one for Student A and one for Student C.

Student A's card says:
- I'm arriving at the airport at three o'clock on Thursday afternoon.
- Can you pick me up then?
- Do you have a bed for me so that I can stay overnight?

Student C's card says:
- Which airline are you coming in on?
- Will you have a lot of baggage?
- How long are you going to stay with us?

If possible, set up the chairs so that Students A and C have their backs to each other, and Student B is between them. Student A and C are talking on the phone, but they have a very bad connection, and it is difficult for them to hear each other. Student B is the operator, helping them to understand each other's questions.

A: I'm arriving at the airport at 3:00 on Thursday afternoon.

C: (to B) What did he say?

B: He said he's (or, he was) arriving at the airport at 3:00 on Thursday.

C: (to B) Ask him which airline he's coming in on.

B: (to A) Which airline are you coming in on? OR He wants to know which airline you're coming in on.

Continue until all the questions have been asked and answered. If you make the question cards slightly different for each group (for example, I'm arriving at the train station. Can you send a taxi for me? Can you reserve a hotel room for me?) the groups can exchange cards and roles and do the activity again, so that everyone has a chance to be Student B.

GRAMMAR OUT OF THE BOX . . . . . .

Want ads. Have students bring in Want Ads from the local newspaper. Have them work with a partner to choose jobs that appeal to them (whether they are presently qualified for those jobs or not). Have them create a list of five questions for each job. Have them role-play the interviews in pairs. Then join two pair groups and have each pair explain to the second pair (using indirect questions) what they asked.

UNIT 29 Embedded Questions

Unit Overview

Students will learn and practice the use of embedded questions with *if* or *whether*, *wh-*words, and infinitives.

Grammar in Context (pages 413–414)

Background Notes

Tipping for good service is a custom that is common in many places. However, both who is tipped and how much he or she is tipped vary significantly from place to place. Most commonly, food servers, bartenders, and taxi drivers expect tips. Hotel housekeepers, doormen, hairstylists, manicurists, and delivery people may also expect tips. In the United States, tips for good service range from 10 to 20 percent. The title *Tips on Tipping* contains a double meaning: A tip is both the money you leave for a service performed and also a piece of advice or a hint.

Vocabulary

tip: (1) a small amount of additional money; (2) a hint or piece of advice

illogical: not sensible or reasonable

contradiction: a difference between two facts, stories, or the like, that means they cannot both be true

Comprehension Questions

- What is the main idea of the reading? *(Customs about tipping vary from place to place.)*
- Where did it used to be illegal to tip? *(China)*
- Where is a tip added to the bill so that there can be no mistake as to how much is expected? *(Germany)*
- What is the meaning of a small tip? *(The customer thinks the service was bad.)*

Discussion Topics

- What is your opinion of the custom of tipping?
- Tipping makes many people feel uncomfortable. They want to follow the social customs, but they don't know what they are. When you travel, what do you do about tipping?

Grammar Presentation (pages 415–417)

Identify the Grammar

Tell me why you decided to write a book about tipping.
Does your book explain who to tip?
Suppose I don't know whether to tip someone, . . .
People . . . will tell you what most customers do.
Usually travel agents know what the rules are for tipping in each country.

Grammar Charts

Point out that questions are embedded in two ways: The whole question is embedded (*People will tell you what most customers do.*) or a wh- word + infinitive structure is used (*Does your book explain who to tip?*).

Grammar Notes

Note 1 *(Exercises 2, 3)*
Quick pairwork: Have students convert the embedded questions in the reading into direct questions. Examples: *Tell me why you decided*

to write a book about tipping. → *Why did you decide to write a book about tipping?*

Note 2 *(Exercises 2, 3)*
- Be sure that students know the meaning of the term *service charge:* an amount of money that is added to the price of something in order to pay for extra services that you use when buying it.
- Point out that direct questions sometimes seem abrupt and impolite, but embedded questions are softer: *Can/could you tell me? Would you mind telling me?*
- Quick pairwork: Have students ask each other personal questions such as, "How old are you?" using the polite embedded question form. Their partners can then answer, "I'd rather not say."

Note 3 *(Exercises 2, 3)*
Point out that embedded *yes/no* questions are like the indirect questions of Unit 28. The difference is that the verbs are more likely to be ones such as *know, wonder,* or *can't decide* rather than *say* or *tell.*

Note 4 *(Exercises 2, 3)*
- Note that the rules for use of *do/does/did* are the same as for indirect questions.
- Point out that the word order changes for *wh-* questions are the same as for indirect questions.

Note 5 *(Exercise 4)*
- Have students identify the embedded questions that use the infinitive in the reading.
- Quick pairwork: Have the students expand the embedded questions with infinitives into full questions. *Does your book explain who to tip?* → *Does the book explain who I should tip?*

Note 6 *(Exercises 2, 3)*
Have students write some direct questions about tipping and then use the question openers in Note 6 to practice making embedded questions.

→ For additional practice, see the Supplementary Activities on page 99.

Focused Practice (pages 418–422)

Exercise 1

fiancée: the woman whom a man is going to marry

hostel: a cheap place for young people to stay when they are traveling

Exercise 2

insult: to do or say something that offends someone, by showing that you do not respect him or her

fixed fee: an amount of money for a service, tax, tip, etc., which is limited to a certain value

Exercise 5

dilemma: a situation in which you have to make a difficult choice between two or more actions

Communication Practice (pages 422–426)

Exercise 6

Prepare students for the exercise by anticipating (inferring from the information there) what the first two questions might be. (If the correct answer to the first question is *Between 15 and 20 percent of the total bill,* and the wrong answer is *The waiter,* then the question must be about how much to tip a waiter in a restaurant. Clues for Caller Two show that the question must be about a taxi ride, and whether a driver should be tipped. (Note that this anticipation gives the students more practice with making embedded questions.)

Exercise 7

Point out that there is one advantage that tipping provides. In a place where there is no tipping, servers are less likely to smile and be pleasant, to be quick about serving you, or to check to be sure you are happy with the food or other service. During the discussion, encourage the use of *I wonder/I'm not sure/I don't know* to elicit the embedded question forms.

Exercise 8

Prepare students for this exercise by reviewing terms they might not know: *catch of the day, soup of the day, side dishes, "da Luigi."*

Exercise 9

Model a first-time experience for your students: "I remember the first time I went skiing. I didn't know whether everyone there would know how to ski really well. I didn't know what I should bring. I didn't know if I would need my own skis. I didn't understand what the customs were about getting skiing lessons. And I didn't know if I should have money for tips for the instructor or where to keep that money."

Exercise 10

Have students practice in pairs, and then ask for volunteers to perform for the whole class.

Exercise 11

Students might find a brainstorm of vocabulary helpful for this assignment. Make a list of the kinds of problems they are likely to have had and then add related words. Examples: *MONEY—cash, travelers' checks, coins, ATM, receipt; TRANSPORTATION—ticket, ticket sellers, kiosk, conductor, bus driver, transfers.*

Further Practice

People who have jobs at information booths have to give information, advice, and guidance to others as part of their everyday work. In a class discussion, have your students consider what a new interpreter at a tourist information office will have to ask the expert to give good answers to the questions he or she is asked to provide. Have pairs of students write scripts, practice, and perform a role play with questions from foreign visitors about the distance to a tourist site, how long it takes to visit the site, what to take along, whether there is any danger in visiting the site, etc. Tell students that these particular foreign visitors are very polite, and don't want to risk offending anyone by asking questions too directly!

GRAMMAR OUT OF THE BOX ......

Let's be tourists. Have students visit tourist attractions, agencies, or offices to collect tourist brochures and other information. They might contact embassies or consulates to find information on tourist attractions they know well (a historical site, museum, palace, park, shrine, or gallery). Then ask them to imagine that they have been asked to work at a tourist information booth. Have them write down questions with embedded questions inside that they might be asked. Then have them share their questions with the class. Posting the brochures with the questions would make a nice display.

Supplementary Activities

Unit 1   Note 1

Write on the board: *At home I _____, but (right) now I'm _____ing _____.*

Then say the following sentences as examples: *At home I wear slippers, but now I'm wearing shoes. At home I wear old clothes, but right now I'm wearing a nice shirt.*

Ask various students to complete the sentence on the board. You may want to choose the first student and then have that student pick the next person to complete the sentence. Go around the whole room. If necessary, you may want to write some verbs on the board before you begin the activity, for example, *speak, eat, wear, talk, smile, listen.*

Unit 2   Note 4

Write on the board: *What were you doing _____? I was _____.*
                    While you were _____, I was _____.

Ask a student: *What were you doing yesterday morning at 6:30?* Possible student answer: *I was having breakfast.* Then say: *While you were having breakfast, I was working out.*

Repeat the procedure with various students. You may want to have students pick the next student and ask the questions while the class listens. Or you may want to form pairs or small groups.

Unit 3   Note 3

Gesture to a student and ask: *When did you get your watch?* Tell the student to use *ago* in the answer. Possible student answer: *Three years ago.* You say: *So, you've had it for three years.*

Continue asking various students *When did you get . . . ?* and then using the present perfect to say how long they have had the object. You may want to go around the room and have students pick other students and ask the question. You can also have students walk around the room and do this activity with five classmates.

Unit 4   Note 7

Write a model time line with events on the board:

finished university	*got my first job*	*bought a new car*	*started a new job*
1999	2000	2002	[last year]

Have each student work alone to create a personal time line on a separate piece of paper. Encourage students to include at least four events. You may want to brainstorm types of events they can include: *bought a car, learned to drive, left my hometown, got married.*

Choose two students to role-play a conversation comparing your lives. For example,

TEACHER: By 1999 I had already graduated from the university. How about you?

STUDENT A: By 1999 I hadn't finished my studies, but I had traveled around Europe.

TEACHER: How about you?

STUDENT B: By 1999 I had [already] gotten married.

Unit 5   Note 3

Write on the board: *When I'm old, I'll _____ .*

Then say the following sentences as examples: *When I'm old, I'll be rich. When I'm old, I'll have a little house with a big garden. When I'm old, I'll live near my children.*

Have each student write their own sentence on a separate piece of paper. Encourage them to complete the sentence with information that shows something about their personalities and / or dreams.

Ask students to fold their papers and put them in a mixed pile on your desk. Have one student at a time come up to choose and read one of the papers. The class should guess who wrote it!

Unit 6   Note 3

Write on the board: *When did you _____ ?*
                            By next year you will have _____ .

Ask a student: *When did you start studying at this school?* Possible student answer: *I started studying here one year ago.* Then say: *By next year you will have been studying here for two years.*

Ask students to brainstorm more *When* questions: *When did you move to this city? When did you get married? When did you get to school today?* You may want to write them on the board. Then have students work in small groups or pairs to follow the model on the board: 1. ask a *When* question 2. say the amount of time 3. make a new statement with *By next year . . .*

Unit 7   Note 3

First prepare a list of statements that students can add tag questions to. Use a variety of tenses, as well as singular and plural forms.

Examples:	Possible tag questions
1. *It's hot,*	*isn't it?*
2. *Those aren't your books,*	*are they?*
3. *He speaks French,*	*doesn't he?*
4. *We don't have any homework,*	*do we?*
5. *She didn't come to class today,*	*did she?*
6. *We've done this already,*	*haven't we?*
7. *He's going to call you,*	*isn't he?*
8. *We'll see you tonight,*	*won't we?*

Tell students that you will say a statement and they need to provide the correct tag question. Students can say the answers (the tag questions) out loud or write them on a piece of paper. Reviewing the answer after each item helps students identify and understand their mistakes before moving on to the next items.

Option: If you feel your students only need a brief review of tag questions, write a list of statements on the board. Set a (short) time limit and have students individually or in pairs write as many tag questions for the items as they can. Review the answers and make necessary corrections.

Unit 8   Notes 2–4

Form small groups. Tell students they are going to talk about the different foods and drinks they like and don't like. Ask one student in each group to be the "secretary" and write *too, either,* and *but* four times each on a piece of paper.

Have students take turns saying sentences about their food and drink preferences. They should use *too, either,* and *but* as often as they can. Possible group conversation:

A: *I like grapes.*

B: *I like grapes too. I don't like apples.*

C: *I don't like apples either.*

The "secretary" should cross out a word on the list each time it is used correctly. When a group uses all 12 words they should say "finished!" Walk around and make necessary corrections.

Unit 9   Notes 2 and 3

Write on the board 15–20 verbs that can be followed by an infinitive or a gerund. Use Appendices 3 and 4 of the Student Book.

Form pairs or small groups. Tell students they are going to write a short story using at least 10 of the verbs on the board. You may want to brainstorm story ideas, for example, *Write a story about a magic fish, about something that surprised you, about a funny/unbelievable thing that happened to you.* Set a time limit. Walk around and provide help as needed. Collect the groups' papers.

Options: 1. Read various stories out loud to the class. Ask the class to identify and correct any mistakes with the verbs. You can correct stories you don't read and return them during the next class. 2. Give the stories to different groups and have them underline and correct any mistakes with verbs. Return the papers to the original groups so they can review their work. 3. Make a list of common mistakes found in the stories and use them to do a review with the whole class.

Unit 10   Notes 1–3

Write the following on the board and ask students to study the causative verbs and common phrases with causative verbs.

make	*have*	<u>*try to get*</u> *someone* <u>*to do*</u> *something . . .*
help	*let*	<u>*used to make*</u> *me . . .*
get (someone/something) to		<u>*didn't want to let*</u> *me . . .*

Tell students they are going to talk about their childhood and various things they remember. They should use as many causatives as possible. To provide a model, tell students some things you remember about your childhood (real or imagined). Ask students to listen for the common verbs/phrases used with causatives (column 2).

> *My parents always <u>tried to get</u> me <u>to eat</u> vegetables, but I never liked them. They <u>used to make</u> me <u>practice</u> the piano every day after school, and they always <u>helped</u> me <u>do</u> my homework. They <u>didn't want to let</u> me <u>stay out</u> late as a teenager, but I always <u>tried to get</u> them <u>to let</u> me.*

Form pairs or small groups. Set a time limit. Remind students to use as many causatives and common phrases from column 2 as possible. Walk around and provide help as needed. If you have time, you may want to ask various students to tell the class about their childhood memories.

Unit 11   Notes 3–5

Preparation: Count the number of students in your class. Make a list of phrasal verbs using the verbs from the unit notes on pages 160–161 and from Appendices 17 and 18 of the Student Book. Cut out a small piece of paper for each student in the class. On each paper write the "meaning" of a phrasal verb from your list. (Do not write the actual phrasal verb). For example, if *come back* is on your list, then write *return* on a piece of paper. If *figure out* is on your list, write *understand* on a piece of paper.

Form pairs. Give each student a piece of paper. Tell students that they will make a sentence with the verb on their paper. Their partner must then use the corresponding phrasal verb to say what the sentence means / restate the sentence. Possible student conversations:

A: (paper = remove) *I removed my coat.*

B: *You took off your coat.*

B: (paper = return something) *I returned a book that I borrowed from a friend.*

A: *You gave back your friend's book.*

Tell students that when you clap your hands, each pair should pass their papers to the next group. (Decide if students will pass to their right or left.) Continue this activity until all students have worked with all of the pieces of paper. You may want to review any phrasal verbs that students had problems with.

Unit 12   Notes 2, 4, 5

Write 10–15 inseparable phrasal verbs on the board. (See Appendices 17 and 18.) Form pairs. Have students choose eight verbs from the board and write eight sentences together. Encourage students to write sentences that are true about their lives. Then have each pair change partners with another group and share their sentences. Walk around the room and provide help as needed.

Unit 13   Note 3

Write on the board: *who—man, woman, a group of children, police*
                      that—book, chicken, guitar,

Form groups of four. Tell students they are going to play a memory game using adjective clauses. Have students study the words on the board. One student makes a sentence, using a relative pronoun and a noun from the list on the board. Another student says what the first student did, then adds a new sentence, and so on. Possible student conversation:

A: *I read a book that was very boring.*

B: *You read a book that was very boring, and I saw a man who was carrying a chicken.*

C: *He read a book that was very boring, you saw a man who was carrying a chicken, and I have a dog that barks at the TV.*

D: *He read a book that was very boring, she saw a man who was carrying a chicken, you have a dog who barks at the TV, and I saw a group of children who were playing guitars.*

Set a time limit. After this time ends, write new words in the lists on the board and ask students to find a new group of four. Walk around the room and provide help as needed.

Unit 14   Notes 3 and 5

Follow the teaching notes for the activity in Unit 13. Add to the list on the board:
whose—teacher, classmate, model
where—the store, the beach, the building
when—the day, the morning, the evening

You may want to review each relative pronoun and the purpose of its relative clause. (Review the Grammar Notes in Units 13 and 14.)

Unit 15   Note 5

Write the following in one column on the board: 1. He must be rich. 2. He might be rich. 3. He might not be rich. 4. He must not be rich. 5. He couldn't be rich.

Tell students they are going to write sentences about why the "comments" on the board may be true. Possible student sentences: 1. *He drives a big car and he doesn't go to work every day.* 2. *She goes on vacation for two months every year.* 3. *I think he buys a new car every year.* 4. *He said he had to work overtime to earn money if he wanted to go on vacation.* 5. *He has 10 children and his shoes have holes in them.*

Form pairs. Set a time limit. Point out that each student may have his/her own interpretation of why "he" may or may not be rich!

Unit 16   Notes 2 and 3

Write on the board: *You _____.*
            I'm sorry I _____. I shouldn't have _____.

Tell each student you are going to "accuse" them of doing something. Students should apologize using the simple past and then say what they shouldn't have done.

Possible conversation:
TEACHER: *You took the last piece of cake!*
STUDENT A: *I'm sorry I took it. I shouldn't have taken it.*
TEACHER: *You forgot my birthday!*
STUDENT B: *I'm sorry I forgot. I shouldn't have forgotten.*

Include irregular verbs in order to provide practice with the past participles of irregular verbs, for example: *stolen, forgotten, taken, driven, left.* Also point out this common reduction in spoken English: *I shouldn't've. . . .*

Unit 17   Notes 1–5

Tell students they are going to listen to a description of a situation. They need to speculate about what they think happened. (Note: There is no correct answer; students should just speculate.) If necessary write on the board:

        may (not)
        might (not)
[person] could (not) + have + [past participle] + [information]
        must (not)
        had to

Tell the story: *Last night my car was parked in front of my house. Around midnight, I heard a loud noise, and when I went out this morning there was a big dent and some blue paint on the side of my car. Here are some things I do know. Who do you think could have done it?*

Write on the board:
1. Jim has a blue car, but he was out of town.
2. Bob has a red car, but sometimes he drives his wife's blue car.
3. Julie has a blue car, but she always goes to bed early.
4. Mary has a blue car, and she is a very bad driver.

Unit 18   Notes 2 and 4

Write on the board: *pull someone over, steal something, tow something (away), arrest someone, stop someone, break into something*

Tell students these are common verbs that describe things that happen to cars or to people when they are driving. Form groups of three. Ask students to write at least five questions using the vocabulary + the passive + *ever*. Examples: *Have you ever been towed? Has your car ever been stolen? Have you ever been pulled over for speeding by the police?*

Ask various groups for their questions, make necessary corrections, and write them on the board. Then have the class play "Find Someone Who _____." Set a time limit. Students should walk around room asking the questions from the board and writing down names. To finish, do a survey to see who had the experiences on the board happen to them!

Unit 19   Notes 2, 4, and 5

Write on the board some common combinations of modals + passive:

could have been stopped	*will be changed*
must be seen	*shouldn't be completed*
might be invited	*has got to be provided*
shouldn't be told	*can't be taught*

Form pairs or small groups. Tell students they are going to write a short story using as many as possible of the modal + passive combinations on the board. Their stories can be funny, serious, true, or imagined. Walk around the room and provide help as needed. To finish the activity have groups combine to share their stories or ask groups to read their stories to the class.

Unit 20   Notes 1 and 2

If you feel your students will not be comfortable sharing information about the following personal issues, you can have students talk about movie stars and famous people instead. Have students ask each other questions about various changes to their appearances using *ever* and *When?* Remind students to use the passive causative forms in this unit. Examples:
How old were you when you had your ears pierced?
Have you ever had your hair colored?
Would you like to have a tattoo done?
Can you have a tattoo removed?

Unit 21   Note 3

Write on the board: *If I go to _____, what should / must I see or do?*

Ask a student: *If I go to your hometown, what should I see?* Possible student answer: *If you go to my hometown, you should see the new sports stadium.* Then have the student fill in the blanks and ask you a question. Possible conversation: S: *If I go to Paris, what should I do?* T: *If you go to Paris, you must go up the Eiffel Tower!*

Set a time limit. Have students walk around the room and talk to at least five classmates. Students should ask and answer a question each time.

Unit 22   Note 4

Write on the board: *If _____ , [not] _____ .*

Say various sentences as models. Examples: *If I don't have any money, I won't go shopping. If it doesn't rain, I won't take an umbrella. If Bob and Mike don't go to the party, I won't go either.* Then ask students to write two negative *if-* conditional sentences on a separate piece of paper.

Tell students they are going to use *unless* to transform their sentences. Transform the examples you provided: *Unless I have money, I don't go shopping. Unless it rains, I won't take an umbrella. Unless Bob and Mike go the party, I won't go either.*

Form pairs. Have students exchange papers. Tell them to write the new sentences with *unless* on the same paper. Remind students not to change the meaning of the original sentences. Then have students check each other's work. Walk around and provide help as necessary.

Unit 23   Notes 2 and 6

Write on the board:
I wish I were _____ . If you were _____ . . .
I wish I [simple past] _____ . If you [simple past] _____ , you would [simple past] . . .

Tell the class you are going to do a chain substitution drill (for the material in Grammar Notes 2 and 6). Say the following sentences to show a model of the substitutions. Tell students that to make a chain means each person will say something.

I wish I were king of the world.
If you were king of the world, you'd be very busy! I wish I had a million dollars.
If you had a million dollars, you'd have a lot of friends! I wish I lived on the beach.
If you lived on the beach, you'd have to learn how to swim. I wish people in this city were nicer.

Option: You may want to do this activity in (small) groups.

Unit 24   Note 3

Write on the board: *1. I didn't have breakfast today.*
                        2. I was hungry all morning.
                        3. If I'd had breakfast, I wouldn't have been hungry.

Form pairs or small groups. Tell students they are going to write three sentences: 1. say what happened (real or imagined) 2. say a result of what happened 3. use the past conditional to say something about what would have happened if #1 had not happened.

If necessary, share these examples with the class:
Example: *1. I didn't study hard last week. 2. I got a bad grade on the test. 3. If I'd studied harder, I would have gotten a better grade on the test.*
Example: *1. I went to bed late last night. 2. I couldn't wake up on time this morning. 3. If I'd gone to bed earlier, I would have been able to wake up on time this morning.*

Unit 25   Notes 2, 4, and 7

Have students turn to page 2 in their Student Books. Form pairs or groups of three. Tell students they are going to practice converting direct speech—the words of the speaker—into indirect speech. Have students take turns reading sentences in the texts about Yevdokiya and Jorge and converting the sentences to indirect speech. Examples:

Hi. My name is Yevdokiya Ivanova. = You said your name was Yevdokiya Ivanova.
I'm from Russia. = You said you were from Russia.
This year I'm living and working in Canada. = You said that this year you were living and working in Canada.

Unit 26   Note 2

Form groups of three. Students take turns playing the roles of speaker, listener, and "translator." The speaker says something using *will, can, may,* or *must.* The listener thinks he / she didn't hear correctly. And the "translator" uses indirect speech to repeat what the speaker said. Example:

A. *It may rain this morning.*

B. *What did you say?*

C. *She said it might rain this morning.*

Walk around the room and provide help as needed. Encourage students to make the necessary tense changes. Remind students to change roles with each conversation.

Unit 27   Note 2

Form groups of six. Students go around the circle and take turns. One person says a problem he/she has, the second person gives some advice, the third person tells the rest of the group what the advice was. Examples:

A: I need to lose five pounds.

B: Don't eat so many sweets.

C: She told her not to eat so many sweets.

Make sure the person giving advice uses the command form and the person reporting the advice uses indirect speech. Walk around and provide help as needed.

Unit 28   Note 3

Write on the board: *"Where do you live?"*
                    I asked him *where he lived.*

Form small groups. Set a time limit. Have students write five questions they would like to ask a celebrity or political figure. Then have them imagine they asked the question and to report the question to the class. Examples:

I asked the president if he was going to improve the education system.
I asked the prime minister whether she had decreased unemployment.
I asked [actress] why she hadn't responded to my fan letter!
I asked [actor] why he had accepted a role in such a bad movie.

Write on the board:

I'd like to know. . .	*Could you explain. . .*
I'd like to find out. . .	*Can you tell me. . .*
I'm not sure. . .	

Form small groups. Tell the students that they are going to live in a different country. Have them write questions they have about their move. Students should create embedded questions. Examples:

I'd like to know how long I can stay on a tourist visa.
I'd like to find out where to find an affordable apartment.
Could you explain how to get a work permit?
Can you tell me where the post office is?
I'm not sure whether people leave tips in restaurants there.

Then have groups combine to work together. Each group takes turns asking their questions. The other group should answer the questions based on what they know about this country. Example:

A: *I'd like to know how long I can stay with a tourist visa.*

B: *A tourist visa? I think that's for 60 days.*

Scoring Rubric for Speaking

Tips for using the speaking rubric

- Give a copy of the rubric to the class before you use it.
- Tell students that you will evaluate their speaking using the rubric.
- The speaking rubric can also be found in a printable format on the Power Point® presentations CD-ROM found in the back of this Teacher's Manual.
- Give feedback for the different areas identified in the rubric: vocabulary, grammar, pronunciation, fluidity, topic organization, and communication. Use language that a student can understand and give examples of what the student did or didn't say when possible. Example comments: *You used a lot of vocabulary and expressions from the unit.* OR *You need to work on verb forms. Review the verb forms needed for the future conditional.* OR *Your sentences were usually complete and clear, but sometimes you hesitated a lot.*
- It's recommended that you discuss the assigned rating and your feedback with each student in a timely manner in order to be most effective and helpful.

SPEAKING RUBRIC

Rating	Vocabulary	Grammar	Pronunciation	Fluidity	Topic	Communication
4	Uses variety, with few errors	Uses a variety of structures, with few errors	Almost always clear and accurate	Speaks smoothly, little hesitation	Successfully organizes and develops topic	Communicates information and opinions effectively
3	Uses variety, makes some errors in word choice	Uses a variety of structures, makes some errors	Usually clear and accurate, some problem areas	Speaks with some hesitation, does not usually interfere with communication	Topic is organized, needs more development	Most information and opinions are communicated clearly
2	Uses limited vocabulary and expressions, some errors	Uses basic structures, makes frequent errors	Errors sometimes make it difficult to understand student	Speaks with hesitation, frequently interferes with communication	Topic not organized, needs development	Information and opinions are not clear
1	Uses basic vocabulary and expressions, makes many errors	Uses basic structures, makes many errors	Very weak; student cannot be understood	Hesitates frequently when speaking, interferes with communication	Does not stay on the topic	Is not able to communicate information and opinions

Scoring Rubric for Writing

Tips for using the writing rubric

- Give a copy of the rubric to the class before you use it.
- Tell students that you will evaluate their writing using the rubric.
- The writing rubric can also be found in a printable format on the Power Point® presentations CD-ROM found in the back of this Teacher's Manual.
- Give feedback by writing comments for the different areas identified in the rubric: topic, sentence structure, vocabulary, grammar.
- Use language that a student can understand and, when possible, give examples of what the student did or didn't do. Example comments: *You addressed the topic and gave very clear examples to support your ideas.* OR *You tried to use a lot of vocabulary and expressions from the unit, but review the meanings of the items I marked in red.* OR *You need to work on verb forms. Review regular and irregular verb forms in the simple past.*
- It's recommended that you discuss the assigned rating and your feedback with each student in order to be most effective and helpful.

Rating	WRITING RUBRIC
5	• Topic is addressed and well organized; includes clear explanations or details • Includes mostly complex sentence types, with few errors • Uses a variety of vocabulary and idiomatic expressions; makes few errors in word choice • Uses complex grammar structures, with few errors
4	• Topic is addressed and generally well organized; includes some explanations or details • Includes some variety of sentence types, but with occasional errors • Varies vocabulary and expressions, but makes occasional errors in word choice • Uses some complex grammar structures, but with errors
3	• Topic is not addressed completely, but writing is organized; explanations or details need more development • Uses little variety in sentence type, but does not have many errors • Attempts to vary vocabulary and expressions, but makes some errors in word choice • Does not use complex grammar structures, but does not make many grammar errors
2	• Topic is somewhat addressed, but writing is not organized and lacks explanations or details • Uses only basic sentence types and makes frequent errors • Uses limited vocabulary and with frequent errors • Uses simple grammar structures, but with some errors
1	• Topic is not addressed; there are no explanations or details • Most sentences have errors • Has many errors in vocabulary usage, even at the basic level • Uses only simple grammar structures, and makes many errors

Audioscript

Unit 1

Exercise 4 (page 7)

A: Hi, Janine. What are you doing?

B: Looking at photos. Wanna see?

A: Sure. I love photos. Oh, who's that?

B: My niece Alex. Isn't she cute?

A: Alex? Isn't that a boy's name?

B: Not anymore. Well, maybe some people still consider it a boy's name, but more and more parents are giving *girls* names like Alex, too.

A: Now, *he's* kinda cute.

B: Who?

A: The guy who's wearing glasses.

B: Oh. That's my friend, Red.

A: Red?

B: Yeah. You can't tell from this photo, but he's got *really* red hair.

A: Who's that?

B: My nephew, Michael. But everyone calls him "Bozo."

A: "Bozo," as in "Bozo the clown"? Gee, that's kind of insulting, isn't it? I bet he hates it.

B: Not really. He knows we mean it affectionately. Anyhow, he just makes a joke out of it—like with everything else.

A: Oh. Does he always act like this?

B: Yep. He's always fooling around. Just like in this picture.

A: And who's that?

B: That's my cousin. We call her "Sunshine."

A: Sunshine? How come?

B: Because she smiles so much.

A: But she's not smiling in *this* picture! In fact, she looks pretty serious.

B: You're right. She doesn't look happy at all. Well, so much for nicknames!

A: That guy looks familiar. Who is he?

B: Oh, you know who that is! That's my brother, Karl.

A: Karl! I didn't recognize him. Doesn't he wear glasses?

B: Yeah. Usually. But he doesn't like how he looks in them, so he's wearing contact lenses for the picture.

A: Guess which one is Bertha.

A: Bertha? That's easy. Bertha's the woman who's wearing the hat.

B: Wrong! That's my Aunt Vicki.

A: You're kidding! She looks more like a Bertha to me!

B: Why?

A: Oh, I don't know. The name Vicki sounds like it belongs to someone young and sexy—like the other woman.

B: Nope. Bertha's her daughter!

A: Strange.

Unit 2

Exercise 6 (page 17)

INTERVIEWER: So, how did you and your husband meet?

WOMAN: Well, actually it's a pretty romantic story. John and I were both working for a newspaper. We didn't know each other well at the time, but one day we got an assignment together. (I was a photographer, and he was a writer.) Well, we were doing this story outside when it started to storm. I mean, it was *really* coming down hard. When it started lightening and thundering too, we ran into the nearest coffee shop we could find. As soon as we sat down, lightning struck nearby and the place lost its electricity. Luckily, the coffee shop had candles on the table, so it was no problem.

INTERVIEWER: Oh. So while it was thundering and lightening outside, the two of you were sitting there talking by candlelight. How long did the storm last?

WOMAN: Oh, I guess about an hour.

INTERVIEWER: So you both got to know each other pretty well.

WOMAN: Yes. You know, at work there was never enough time to talk—we were always working against some deadline. So anyway, John was just beginning to tell me a little about his childhood when the lights came back on. We were going to leave and get back to work, but then we just sat there another two hours talking. When we finally left, the sky was clear and the sun was shining. It all seemed so symbolic. A month later, we were married.

Unit 3

Exercise 5 (page 26)

JASON: Hi, honey. I'm calling from the passport office. You wouldn't believe the lines down here. I've been waiting for 40 minutes.

JOY: Well, that's what happens when you leave things till the last minute. What about the plane tickets?

JASON: I picked them up on the way over here.

JOY: Is there anything you can do while you're waiting? What about that skydiving guide I gave you to read?

JASON: I've read it. I found some great locations. I'll tell you about it later. That reminds me—have you made the hotel reservations?

JOY: I've been calling all morning, but I haven't gotten through. Oh—I went to the post office to arrange for our mail to be held. The lines were long there too. I had to wait more than half an hour.

JASON: Well, at least it's taken care of. Have you found a bathing suit?

JOY: I've been looking, but . . .

JASON: Oops, gotta go. It's almost my turn. See you later.

JOY: Love you.

JASON: Love you, too.

Unit 4

Exercise 9 (page 40)

HOTLINE: Good evening and welcome to the Monday edition of *Hotline*. Today I'm talking to Richard Valdez. Richard and his wife Molly are the producers of the prize-winning movie *People Like Us*. Richard, you didn't start out in the movie business. What had you been doing before you came to New York?

VALDEZ: Before we moved here, Molly had been teaching filmmaking at a college in Utica, and I'd been working for a newspaper, selling advertising. We lived in Utica for three years before we moved here. Through Molly, I had also started to get interested in small, independent filmmakers.

HOTLINE: How did you find your first film?

VALDEZ: A former student of Molly's from film school had been writing screenplays for a couple of years, but he hadn't sold any. One evening he

showed us a short film that he'd made in film school. I thought, "This is terrific. Why isn't this guy famous?" By the end of the evening, Molly and I had decided to form a company and produce one of his screenplays. I knew how to use the telephone to ask people for money, and Molly knew how to make films. After we'd sold a couple of small films, we knew we needed to move to a larger city.

HOTLINE: What was it like to move from a small city to a city like New York?

VALDEZ: It wasn't easy at first. We didn't know anyone in New York, so we lived in an awful hotel for about a month. Molly got a job as a teacher right away, and I tried to raise money for our next movie. But I didn't have any success at first.

HOTLINE: Did you ever consider just going home?

VALDEZ: Yes, we sure did. We had been discussing going back home to Utica when our luck suddenly changed. We found an apartment, and we could actually afford it!

HOTLINE: When did you meet Lynn Costello, who wrote *People Like Us?*

VALDEZ: We'd only been living in the new apartment for about a week when we got a phone call. This woman said, "You probably don't know me. My name is Lynn Costello." Actually, we'd been interested in Lynn's work for a long time—but we never thought we'd have the chance to produce one of her screenplays.

HOTLINE: I guess Molly was pretty happy about that.

VALDEZ: Oh, yeah. She'd been supporting us both since we moved to New York. This gave her a chance to do what she really loved.

HOTLINE: So do you and Molly consider yourselves New Yorkers now?

VALDEZ: Definitely. We'd been discouraged about moving here—I admit that. But after we moved into our apartment and Lynn called us, that changed. Now we love New York.

Unit 5

Exercise 7 (page 62)

LORNA: You know, interest is really growing in housing development on Venus. We should try to organize a conference there this summer.

JENNIFER: Good idea. But I don't think it's going to be possible for us to find a time we're all available. We're all so busy.

BRIAN: Well, we won't know unless we try. Jennifer, what are your summer plans?

JENNIFER: I don't know exactly, Brian. I do know that I'm taking a vacation with my family the last two weeks of August. What about you, Brian?

BRIAN: Well, I don't have any vacation plans yet. But I'll be going on a business trip to Mars in the second and third weeks of July. Lorna, what are your plans?

LORNA: Well, it's already the end of June, and I'll need at least two weeks' advance notice for work.

BRIAN: Hmmm. So, let's see. That means the earliest you could go would be the third week of July. Tranh, what about you? Any plans?

TRANH: I hate this planet in the summer. Too many intergalactic tourists. I'm going to be getting away from Earth as much as I can.

LORNA: Really? Where will you be going?

TRANH: Well, I'll be flying to Mars to visit my sister every other weekend, starting the second week in July.

BRIAN: Hmmm. Every other weekend starting the second week of July . . . the conference has to run through the weekend, so the second and fourth weeks of July are no good.

LORNA: And the second and fourth weeks of August aren't good either. What about the rest of the time, Tranh?

TRANH: Well. I'll be doing research the third week in July, and with a little luck, I'll be traveling to Jupiter with my new girlfriend the third week in August.

BRIAN: Well, according to my calculations, that leaves only one week that we all have free . . .

Unit 6

Exercise 6 (page 77)

THEA: The kids' summer vacation will be over in a month, and we won't have even left Seattle. Next year I want to *go* somewhere during the summer.

DON: Well, we'd better start planning right now if we want to save enough for next year.

THEA: OK. Let's get out the budget and calculator . . . Hmmm . . . You know, our food budget seems awfully high. Why don't you try packing your lunch?

DON: Do you really think it's worth it?

THEA: Well . . . let's figure it out. How much do you spend on lunch every day?

DON: Uh . . . about $7 . . . five days a week . . . uhmm . . . That's $35 a week.

THEA: Well, it only costs me $4 a day at the most to pack my lunch, so I only spend about $20 a week . . . Hmmm . . .That means you can save $15 a week on lunch.

DON: OK—so figure 50 weeks of work. That means by the end of the year I'll have saved . . . uhmm . . . $750. Good grief. That's a lot of money!

THEA: Uh-huh. It adds up, doesn't it?

DON: Now, you're going to need some new clothes this year. How much do you want to budget for that?

THEA: Actually, I think I'll only need about $400. That's only half of what I spent last year. I can just buy some new scarves and earrings to make my suits look new.

DON: OK, if you're sure you don't mind. And if Ned and Valerie'll wear some things from the thrift shop, we can save another $400 on *their* clothes.

THEA: I think they will. They know they'll be saving for a special vacation.

DON: Great. So, by next August, we'll have saved $800 on clothes.

THEA: That's terrific. Now, let's look at transportation. You know, I've been thinking that we could save some money taking the commuter shuttle instead of driving into the city. Two monthly shuttle tickets cost $150.

DON: Well, right now we're spending about $250 a month on gas, tolls, and parking downtown.

THEA: OK. Let's try the commuter shuttle, then. We'll save $100 a month. So, how much will we have saved by next summer?

DON: Let's see . . . If we go on vacation in August, that's 12 months from now. We'll have saved $1,200. Wow! Why didn't we think of this sooner?

THEA: Can we cut back on entertainment?

DON: I think so. We could rent DVDs online instead of going to the movies and order a pizza instead of eating dinner in a restaurant. By next summer, we'll have saved $540 just by watching movies and having pizza at home.

THEA: How did you figure that?

DON: Look—we go out for dinner and a movie about once a month, and we spend $65 every time for our meal, movie tickets, and snacks at the movie. DVDs cost $4 each to rent, and a large pizza costs, $15, delivered. We save approximately $45 a month, times 12 months.

THEA: This is going to be a nice vacation. What's our total so far?

DON: Well, so far I figure we'll have saved . . . let's see . . . uh . . .

Unit 7

Exercise 7 (page 98)

Conversation 1

A: Karen, hi! I haven't seen you for a while. I'm glad it's finally stopped raining.

B: Hi, Ken. I was in New York for a week. It's a nice day, isn't it?

Conversation 2

A: Hi, Lou. It's Pam. Do you have time for coffee this morning?

B: Hi. Uhmm, I think so. But don't you usually work on Fridays?

Conversation 3

A: I helped Kay pack all morning. What a job! She has at least two of everything.

B: Really? She isn't moving again, is she?

Conversation 4

A: I just found a great apartment in New York. I'm glad my sister was with me. She knew just where to look.

B: Oh, that's right. Your sister's from New York, isn't she?

Conversation 5

A: What's wrong? You seem a little depressed.

B: I'm just tired. I've been working a lot.

A: That's right. You're working on a new screenplay, aren't you?

Conversation 6

A: You're home early! What happened?

B: They canceled Tina's soccer game because of bad air quality. They told us to go home and stay inside with the air conditioner on.

A: Isn't this smog terrible!

Conversation 7

A: There must be ten black umbrellas here. Oh . . . here's mine.

B: That's not your umbrella, is it? It's ripped.

Conversation 8

A: Look! The sun just came out. It's going to be a nice day after all.

B: Great. So we really don't need our umbrellas do we?

Conversation 9

A: I just read Tom's new screenplay. He made all the changes we asked for.

B: I know. Isn't it great?

Conversation 10

A: Let's go and see that new Eddie Murphy comedy.

B: I'd rather see *Heartbreak in Las Vegas*.

A: Don't you like comedies?

Unit 8

Exercise 7 (page 112)

MAN: This is a great restaurant. I really love Italian food.

WOMAN: So do I. Do you cook?

MAN: Not really.

WOMAN: I do. I love trying out new recipes.

MAN: I eat out a lot.

WOMAN: Oh, so do I.

MAN: Or I buy some take-out food after work and rent a DVD. I love old movies.

WOMAN: I do too . . . Uh . . . do you like to read?

MAN: Uh-hmm. Especially biographies.

WOMAN: So do I! What about novels?

MAN: I don't read much fiction.

WOMAN: I don't either . . . what about sports?

MAN: I don't really play any sports. What about you?

WOMAN: I do. I play tennis and volleyball every week. But I never watch sports on TV.

MAN: Me neither. I watch a lot of news programs, though.

WOMAN: So do I. In fact, there's an interesting documentary on tonight at eight. It's about identical twins.

MAN: Hmmm. It's seven o'clock. If we leave now, we can watch it.

WOMAN: I think that sounds good.

MAN: So do I.

Unit 9

Exercise 6 (page 134)

LILY: Yuk!

VICTOR: I warned you not to get the meat loaf, didn't I?

LILY: I don't remember your saying anything. Yuk! I can't wait to fill out that survey.

VICTOR: Let's do it now. How about lending me a pencil?

LILY: Here you are.

VICTOR: OK. First question. Do we support introducing Burger Queen? Yes! We do! There's my check.

LILY: Wait a minute. I refuse to check that one. It's wrong to sell fast food in a school dining hall. It has too much fat and salt. They shouldn't encourage students to eat it.

VICTOR: Come on—you're not the food police. You can't keep students from eating fast food.

LILY: I guess not. But you can avoid selling it to them. I think showing fat and calorie content of foods is a good idea, though. That way, you can choose between having a burger with 18 grams of fat and a piece of chicken with 8.

VICTOR: I don't feel like seeing that information before I eat. It ruins my appetite. No, I definitely don't want to know about fat and calories. But I'm not opposed to offering more healthy choices.

LILY: I think that's a good idea, too. Look at the next one. Do you care about lowering prices? The food is already pretty cheap.

VICTOR: You're right. It is.

LILY: Then I would like them *not* to lower prices, but to improve the quality of the food—starting with this meat loaf!

VICTOR: That's a good point. I agree with you on both items. Now, you can't object to their offering Chinese food.

LILY: That would be great. But they'd better hire a chef to prepare it. Remember, they can't cook meat loaf here.

VICTOR: They'll probably hire someone to do it. Having some international foods make sense since we have so many international students here now.

LILY: Right. So we both approve of offering Chinese food.

VICTOR: Uh-oh. I'm not happy about their starting breakfast earlier.

LILY: Why not? I run early in the morning. I'd be happy to be able to buy breakfast at 6:30.

VICTOR: I work here for breakfast, remember? I can't imagine getting up any earlier.

Unit 10

Exercise 5 (page 146)

SIMON: Hi, Ms. Jacobson. I wanted to talk about my essay. I'd like to change my topic.

MS. JACOBSON: Let's see. You're writing about playing the guitar. It's a good topic, and you've done a lot of work on it. Why don't you keep this topic and add more details to the second paragraph?

SIMON: OK, but that's my problem. I can't think of anything more to say.

MS. JACOBSON: Didn't your uncle help you learn to play? I remember your writing about him in your journal.

SIMON: Oh, yeah. He was great. He taught me a lot of funny old songs. He even wrote one for me.

MS. JACOBSON: Why don't you include that in your essay?

SIMON: OK. I'll try. Is that what you meant about adding details?

MS. JACOBSON: That's part of it. You could also try answering some *wh-* questions. For example, why did you decide to learn guitar? Where were you living at the time?

SIMON: Oh, we were living in El Salvador. Everyone in my family plays a musical instrument. OK. I see what you mean. I'll use *wh-* questions to add details.

MS. JACOBSON: Great. Anything else?

SIMON: I'm confused about this sentence. Like, why can't I say, "Play guitar professionally is my dream"?

MS. JACOBSON: When you use a verb form for a subject, what should you do?

SIMON: Uh . . . use a gerund? So should I say, "Playing guitar professionally is my dream"?

MS. JACOBSON: Right. Good!

SIMON: Would you mark all the gerund mistakes on this paper? I'd like to work on them.

MS. JACOBSON: Why don't *you* go through the paper and underline the gerunds? Then we'll talk about any problems you're having.

SIMON: OK. Can I make an appointment for another conference on Wednesday?

MS. JACOBSON: Sure. I can see you again at 3:00. And don't worry, Simon. It's going to be a great essay!

Unit 11

Exercise 6 (page 166)

Conversation 1

AMY: How's the temperature in here?

BEN: It's a little too cold for me. Do you mind if I turn the air conditioner down?

Conversation 2

AMY: What did you think about that information on feng shui?

BEN: I haven't had the chance to look it up yet.

Conversation 3

AMY: Have you finished redecorating your office?

BEN: Almost. I'm going to IKEA today to pick out a new couch.

Conversation 4

AMY: The living room is a mess. Your books are all over the place.

BEN: Don't worry. I'll put them back as soon as I'm done with my homework.

Conversation 5

AMY: I really don't like those new curtains.

BEN: Neither do I. I'm going to take them down tomorrow.

Conversation 6

AMY: This mattress isn't as comfortable as it used to be.

BEN: I know. I think we need to turn it around.

Conversation 7

AMY: What color should we paint the kitchen?

BEN: I don't know. Let's discuss it when we get back.

Unit 12

Exercise 6 (page 178)

MR. CHEN: Hello?

BRENDA: Hi! This is Brenda Williams from Cheatim Telecommunications? Is this Mr. Chin?

MR. CHEN: No, this is Mr. *Chen*.

BRENDA: Well, Mr. Chen, it looks like you've been paying too much for your phone service. We think we can help you out with our new low rates.

MR. CHEN: Oh, really?

BRENDA: That's right . . . When you sign up for our Get Together Program, you'll be paying just 5 cents a minute on all your long distance calls.

MR. CHEN: Actually, I'm only paying 5 cents a minute now . . .

BRENDA: But wait till you hear the rest! The Get Together Program offers cell phone service! When you add on our cell phone service, you'll get unlimited cell phone minutes for just one low monthly fee! You will never run out of minutes again!

MR. CHEN: How much is the program?

BRENDA: Just $49.95 a month. And what a lot of people like is, we put all your phone charges together on one convenient bill. So, can I sign you up today?

MR. CHEN: Are there any other charges?

BRENDA: Just a small fee for setting up the new plan.

MR. CHEN: How much?

BRENDA: That will be just $20. It'll show up on your first bill.

MR. CHEN: How about activation fees?

BRENDA: Well, sure, there's a small charge to program your cell phone and turn the service on. That's just $30.

MR. CHEN: And how about the phone? Is that free?

BRENDA: We have a great offer for you! Normally, we charge $50 for the cell phone. But if you sign up right now, we'll send you a rebate card with the phone. Send in the card, and we'll give you $20 back!

MR. CHEN: So the cost of the phone comes out to . . . $30. You know, I have to talk this over with my wife. It sounds like we might end up paying more after all these fees. Can I call you back?

BRENDA: I'm really sorry, Mr. Chin . . .

MR. CHEN: Chen.

BRENDA: . . . Mr. Chen, but I can only make this offer for one day. If you put it off until tomorrow, you won't have another chance. Think about it! Low long distance rates and unlimited cell phone minutes. This is too good to pass up.

MR. CHEN: I guess I'll just stick with the service I have. But thanks.

Unit 13

Exercise 6 (page 201)

WOMAN: Wow, people have really changed!

MAN: You're not kidding! Can you recognize anyone at that table over there?

WOMAN: Uhmm. Let's see. Isn't that Bob Gramer?

MAN: Which one?

WOMAN: The man who's standing up.

MAN: You know, I think you're right! He actually looks even taller!

WOMAN: And isn't that Ann Richardson over there?

MAN: Where? The woman sitting next to Bob?

WOMAN: No. The one who's wearing a scarf.

MAN: You're right! That is Ann! And that's Kado!

WOMAN: Where?

MAN: The man who's talking to Ann.

WOMAN: So, who's the woman sitting next to Bob?

MAN: You know, that must be Pat. Remember Pat Wayne? She and Bob used to work on the school newspaper.

WOMAN: Do you think they both became writers?

MAN: I don't know. Maybe. Who's the woman who's wearing all the jewelry?

WOMAN: You mean the one sitting across the table from Bob?

MAN: Uh-huh. Do you think that could be . . . uhmm . . . what's-her-name . . . Kasha?

WOMAN: You mean Asha!

MAN: Yeah, that's the one. Didn't she always use to wear a lot of beautiful jewelry, even to school?

WOMAN: Yep! You're right! That's Asha all right.

MAN: She got married to Raza Gupta, right?

WOMAN: Yeah, but that's not Raza who's sitting next to her, is it?

MAN: No. It looks more like Pete Rizzo.

WOMAN: Pete Rizzo? Who's he? The name sounds familiar.

MAN: Oh, you remember Pete. He was the guy who ran for class president in our senior year.

WOMAN: Uh-huh. He's changed a lot, but I'm sure it's Pete.

MAN: Why don't we go over and find out?

WOMAN: Good idea. Then we can find out who the couple is that's sitting between Asha and Pat.

MAN: Yeah. I don't have a clue who they are!

Unit 14

Exercise 5 (page 215)

I remember my childhood bedroom very well. It was a small room, which I shared with my older sister, Katie. There were two beds. The one which I slept in was in a corner. My sister's bed, under which was a large beautiful old rug, was in the middle of the room against the wall. To the left of my bed was a window through which we could see a tree. There was also a big wall mirror in which we both enjoyed looking at our own reflections. That was in the corner that was nearest my sister's bed. Across from my bed was a desk at which we both did our homework after dinner, which we always ate in the kitchen with the rest of the family. My sister, whose greatest passion in life those days was music, kept her guitar on her bed, where she would practice for hours after our homework was done. I remember those as happy times, when we were both young and full of hope and excitement.

Unit 15

Exercise 5 (page 236)

JOSH: We've got to climb the hill today. I should go first.

TARA: OK, Josh, but you'd better not mess up this time.

JOSH: Why is everybody so mad at me? They must know I'm really a nice guy.

TARA: Very funny. Well, we have to work together today, and they know it.

JOSH: Are you worried? That hill couldn't be very hard to climb.

TARA: We have to go down the other side. It's almost straight down to the water. Pete might not be able to do it.

JOSH: You ought to help him climb down.

TARA: Oh, really? You must not know what's he's been saying about me.

JOSH: I know . . . but let's face it, Pete'll be able to help us in the next challenge.

TARA: Hmmm. We've got to find our team's flag in the water near the rocks.

JOSH: It's got to be very deep out there.

TARA: So I shouldn't let Pete know that *I* know that he's been plotting against me?

JOSH: You know you can do it. And tonight I'll get him voted off the island.

TARA: I don't know about that. He's got to be the most popular guy here.

JOSH: And everybody hates me. Never mind. I can make it happen.

Unit 16

Exercise 5 (page 246)

What a day! I really messed up in a big way. For starters—I should've done my homework. Now I've got to get up early tomorrow morning, and it's already midnight. What a bummer! And I shouldn't have walked to work today. I was late again, and I could see that Doug was really annoyed. Then, I got a notice from my bank that one of my checks bounced! Now, I'm afraid I'm going to bounce another one. I really should've made that $100 deposit today. I'll never learn. Speaking of money, I shouldn't have bought a new coat. My old one's good enough, and I could use the extra money. I just don't have any self-control. Oh, and now Aunt Rose is furious with me. I didn't send her a card for her birthday. I might've at least called to wish her a happy birthday. I only think of myself. On the other hand, I shouldn't have called Ron. All he does is complain. He regrets this, he regrets that . . . It's so depressing, but I guess I asked for it! Let's see . . . what else? Uh, oh yeah. I ought to have gone to the supermarket before it closed. I never plan ahead. And now there's nothing in the house to eat. Oh. And I should've finished that David Burns book. Maybe then I'd know how to feel better. Oh well, there's always tomorrow.

Unit 17

Exercise 7 (page 259)

Conversation A

A: Wow! Look at that! It's got a blade. And this looks like a handle.

B: Yeah. It might've been used as some sort of cutting tool, like a sickle.

A: A sickle? What's that?

B: It's a kind of farming tool. Something used to cut down high grass.

A: You mean like wheat?

B: Yeah. They could've harvested wheat with this.

Conversation B

A: That's a strange-looking design.

B: Yeah. They must've seen one of those astronauts that von Däniken writes about.

A: Right. What do you think they used it for?

B: Well, look at the hole. They may have worn it on a string around their necks for good luck or something.

A: That's right. They could've.

Conversation C

A: Look at this ring. What do you suppose they used it for?

B: Hmmm. It could've been part of a shoe.

A: Part of a shoe? What do you mean?

B: Like an eyelet. They could've pulled some kind of shoelace through the hole, and then tied the laces.

A: Oh. I see.

Conversation D

A: That's beautiful. What do you think it came from?

B: Well, from the round shape and from the design, I'd say it must've been part of a vase.

A: Or it could've been a cooking or serving utensil.

B: Yeah, the design looks like some kind of border.

A: It could've been part of the base.

B: No, it's too narrow. It must've been part of the neck. They could've poured things out of it.

A: You're right.

Conversation E

A: That looks like a pretty sophisticated instrument!

B: Is it a pump?

A: I don't think so. I remember reading about something like this in one of our books. I think they could've used this to make fire!

B: Really? How?

A: Well, they could've had a tinder inside the cylinder . . .

B: A tinder?

A: Uh-huh. Something that burns easily. Look—when you push this piece down into the cylinder, it quickly compresses the air. That makes the air hot, and the tinder could start to burn.

B: Incredible! They must've been really intelligent to have figured that out!

A: Yeah, really!

Conversation F

A: What's that you've got there? It looks just like a rock.

B: I don't think it's a rock. Look at the shape. It's too clear. Someone must've made it.

A: You know, you're right. It couldn't have just formed like that naturally. Someone must've chipped away at it to produce all those different angles. What do you think it was used for?

B: I think it must've been used as some kind of tool.

A: Hmmm. They could've used it to cut hard material—like wood.

B: You mean like a hand axe?

A: Exactly. Like a hand axe.

Unit 18

Exercise 8 (page 280)

Conversation 1

A: How long has Jill worked here?

B: Jill? Let's see. I think it's been about 15 years.

A: Fifteen years? Was that before or after Bob started working here?

B: After. Jill was hired by Bob.

Conversation 2

A: How did you learn to use all those new computer programs? Did you take classes?

B: Yeah. I took some classes at the college. The company sent me.

A: Minna really knows a lot too. Did she take classes there too?

B: No. *I* trained Minna.

Conversation 3

A: Have things changed a lot since you've been here?

B: They sure have. When I started, we were just a small company. There were just 10 employees.

A: What about the magazine itself?

B: First of all, it was just about half the size it is now, and it was published just six times a year.

A: Wow.

Conversation 4

A: I haven't seen Jill lately. Is she on vacation?

B: No. Haven't you heard what happened?

A: No. What happened?

B: Tony fired Jill.

A: You're kidding! How come?

B: Well, you know, she really made a lot of mistakes on that Bolivia article.

A: That's terrible.

Conversation 5

A: Are they going to replace Jill?

B: They have to. They need another writer.

A: Are they interviewing for the position?

B: Uh-huh. They started interviewing last week. They're trying to fill the position with someone from within the company.

A: Really?

B: Yes. In fact, Diana is applying for the position.

A: That's interesting. Did her own boss interview her?

B: No. She was interviewed by Jay.

Conversation 6

A: Do you know Ed Bly?

B: The name sounds familiar. Who is he?

A: A sportswriter.

B: Oh, right. I think I know who you mean. He was laid off.

Unit 19

Exercise 5 (page 293)

PICARRO: Spaceship *Endeavor* calling Earth . . . This is Captain Picarro speaking. We've been hit by a meteorite.

EARTH: Is anyone hurt?

PICARRO: No, everyone is safe.

EARTH: You'd better start repairing the damage immediately.

PICARRO: It can't be repaired out here.

PICARRO: We'll be approaching Planet CX5 of the Delta solar system in a few hours. Is their language on our computer, Dr. Sock?

SOCK: I'm checking now . . . We don't have a language for CX5 on the computer, but we have one for CX4. Shall we try it?

PICARRO: We'd better be very careful. Our messages could be misunderstood.

LON: OK. I'm ready. Let's go.

RAY: What about oxygen?

LON: Isn't the atmosphere on CX5 just like Earth's?

RAY: I think you've been in space too long. Read your manual. Oxygen must be used on other planets.

PICARRO: I've lost contact with Lon and Ray. I hope their equipment works on CX5.

SOCK: Don't worry. They'll be picked up by the radar.

LON: Look at those plants. I want to take some back to the ship.

RAY: They can't be grown in space. We've already tried.

LON: That's right. I forgot.

CX5: What do you want to ask us, Earthlings?

RAY: Our vehicle was hit by a meteorite. We request permission to land on your planet.

CX5: Permission granted. Our engineers will be ready for you.

RAY: Thank you. As you know, we have to be helped with the repairs.

Unit 20

Exercise 5 (page 303)

JAKE: Hi, Amber. It's Dad. How are things going with your new apartment?

AMBER: Great. I really like my roommate, and I can drive to school in 15 minutes.

JAKE: Good. Hey—speaking of driving, remember that you have to change the oil in your car every 3,000 miles. It must be almost time.

AMBER: I remembered. I had it changed today.

JAKE: Did you change the locks on your apartment door?

AMBER: Of course, Dad. I got them changed right after we moved in. Don't worry. This is a really safe neighborhood.

JAKE: OK, but you know we can't help worrying a little. Your mother said the apartment needs painting. Maybe I could come up next weekend and paint it for you. You probably need some bookshelves, too. I could put those up, too.

AMBER: That's OK, Dad. We had a painting party last weekend. Li and I invited some friends over, and we painted the apartment ourselves. It looks great. And I got the bookshelves put up as soon as the paint was dry.

JAKE: Wow. It sounds like you've really settled in.

AMBER: Just about. I had to buy a computer desk and some lamps. They fit right into the car, so I didn't even have to have them delivered.

JAKE: Well, your mom and I would really love to see you soon—even if you don't have any chores for us to do.

AMBER: I'd love to see you too, Dad. Why don't you come up next weekend? Oh, I should warn you. I had my hands painted. Don't be shocked when you see me.

JAKE: OK. I'll warn your mother. Anything else we should know about?

AMBER: I cut my hair, too. It's pretty short now. And I had it colored.

JAKE: Hey—will we be able to recognize you?

AMBER: Well . . . Maybe we'd better meet at the apartment!

Unit 21

Exercise 6 (page 322)

Announcement Number 1

Flight 398 nonstop to Taipei will be ready to board at Gate 8C in just a few minutes. Please have your boarding passes ready. If you have more than two pieces of carry-on luggage, you must check them at the gate. We will begin boarding in about five minutes.

Announcement Number 2

Flight 398 nonstop to Taipei is now ready for boarding. If you are traveling with a small child, or if you need extra time, please go to the gate now. If you are flying standby, please wait until all other passengers have boarded. If you are sitting in rows 17 to 24, please proceed to the gate for boarding. All other passengers, please wait until your row is called.

Announcement Number 3

Flight 398 is now continuing to board. If you are sitting in rows 7 to 16, please proceed to the gate for boarding. Please have your boarding pass ready. If you are traveling standby, please continue to wait until all other passengers have boarded.

Announcement Number 4

Welcome to Flight 398 nonstop to Taipei. Please pay careful attention while the flight attendants review some important safety procedures. In the unlikely event that the cabin loses pressure, oxygen masks will automatically descend from the overhead panels. If you are traveling with a child, put your own mask on first. Then assist the child. This cabin is equipped with six emergency exits. Please take the time to locate the one nearest you.

Announcement Number 5

Good morning. This is Captain Huang Wen-Chu speaking. We hope you're enjoying the flight. We are flying at an altitude of 35,000 feet, with light winds and clear skies. For passengers sitting on the left—if you look out your window, you can see the lights of Tokyo. We're expecting to arrive on schedule, and the weather in Taipei should be good.

Announcement Number 6

We are beginning our initial descent into the Taipei area. The temperature is a comfortable 26 degrees Celsius—that's around 78 degrees Fahrenheit—and the skies are pretty clear. If you need information about a connecting flight, be sure to check the overhead monitors in the airport terminal. Please put your seats and tray tables in an upright and locked position and make sure all carry-on luggage is safely stowed under the seat in front of you or in the overhead compartments. We should be landing in Taipei in approximately 10 minutes. We thank you for flying UPAir and hope you have had a pleasant trip.

Unit 22

Exercise 7 (page 333)

INTERVIEWER: Welcome to "Meet the Candidates." Tonight we are talking to Yuki Tamari, who, as most of you know, is running for student council president. Welcome, Yuki.

YUKI: Thanks, Daniel. It's a pleasure to be here.

INTERVIEWER: What will you do first if you become our student council president?

YUKI: If I'm elected, I'm going to improve communications with students. I want to be available to students and hear what they have to say.

INTERVIEWER: How do you plan to do that?

YUKI: First, by a lot of personal contact. If I'm elected, I'll have informal lunch meetings with students. In the evenings, I'll be at the Student Union and other places where students meet. Unless I talk to a lot of students personally, I won't be able to hear their concerns. That has been the problem of our student council for a while.

INTERVIEWER: What else do you have in mind?

YUKI: Again, I want to talk about communication. If I become president, I am going to appoint a committee to improve the student council's website. A lot more information should be available to students. Teacher evaluations, for example. If we publish evaluations on the Web, it will be much easier for students to choose their courses. The e-mail addresses of student council representatives should also be on our website. Students can't participate in student government unless they know how to contact their representatives.

INTERVIEWER: Do you have any plans for other student services?

YUKI: Many, but I'll just mention one right now. If I become president, I'll try to get the college to provide a bus service from the airport to the college at the beginning and end of every semester. It won't be free, but if students use the bus, they won't have to pay for those very expensive taxi fares. This will also be a much friendlier welcome for international students when they arrive here for their first semester.

INTERVIEWER: What about educational issues?

YUKI: The college should offer more majors. A lot of students are interested in mass communications, for example, but there's no mass communications major. International studies is another important major that the college does not offer. If I'm elected, I'm going to encourage the administration to develop more major areas of study. Many students will take these courses if we offer them.

INTERVIEWER: College tuition has been increasing very quickly. Is there anything the student council can do about that?

YUKI: This is a state college, but our tuition has been rising too. Unless we can keep tuition costs down, a lot of good students aren't going to be able to afford a college education. If I'm elected, I will ask our student council to create a committee to meet with state lawmakers. Many state colleges have committees that do this. If I get support for this idea here, we will be able to discuss tuition costs with the state government.

INTERVIEWER: Thanks, Yuki. You have a very ambitious platform. Good luck at the polls tomorrow.

YUKI: Thank you.

Unit 23

Exercise 7 (page 346)

Once there was a young girl named Cindy who was very good at math, sports, and languages. She wanted to be a scientist when she grew up so she could help many people. One day, while Cindy was playing soccer in the park with her friends, the ball flew into the woods. She looked and looked for the ball, but she couldn't see it anywhere.

"I wish I could find that soccer ball," Cindy muttered angrily. At that she heard a strange sound. "Ree-beep. Ree-beep. Over here! Your ball is over here." She looked in the direction of the sound, and she saw the soccer ball in the middle of some bushes. Next to the ball was a large toad.

"Thanks for finding the ball," she told the toad. "You're welcome," said the toad. "But before I give it to you, you have to grant me one wish." Cindy started to run toward the ball, but she couldn't get through the bushes. There was some sort of magic spell around them. "What's your wish?" she asked the toad. "Please hurry up. We want to finish our game."

"I wish that you would marry me." "Yuk!" screamed Cindy. "You're a toad. I'm a girl. I can't marry you." "I'm not really a toad," he replied. "I'm under a spell. If you married me, you would break the spell. I would become a handsome prince. And if I were a prince, you would be my princess."

Cindy thought about the princesses she had read about in magazines. "I don't think so, Toad," Cindy told him. "You see, I plan to become a scientist and help a lot of people when I grow up. If I were your princess, I'd have to spend a lot of time having my photograph taken and going to ceremonies. If I did that, I'd be too busy to study science. But thanks anyway." Cindy turned to leave the woods.

"Wait!" shouted the toad. "If you really wanted to help people, you wouldn't leave me here in these bushes." Cindy stopped. "If you give me back the soccer ball, I'll try to help you. But no wedding." The toad agreed, and Cindy picked up the ball.

"So, who put you under the spell?" she asked.

"A magician turned me into a toad. He also gave me some magic powers. He keeps telling me that if I used my powers properly, I'd find a way to become a prince again. But so far, nothing has worked."

"Can you grant wishes?" asked Cindy. "Just one," replied the toad.

"Then I wish you would turn me into a scientist right now. If I were a scientist, I would find a way to turn you back into a prince."

In a flash, Cindy and the toad found themselves in a large, modern laboratory. Cindy thought hard and worked long hours. At last she succeeded in turning the toad back into a prince. The prince became a good king, and Cindy worked hard in her laboratory. Her discoveries helped many people.

Unit 24

Exercise 6 (page 357)

Conversation 1

A: I haven't seen Stephanie lately. Have you?

B: No. Why wasn't she at David's party last weekend?

A: Uh, I don't know.

B: Hmmm. If I'd had her number, I would've called her.

A: Oh. Isn't it in the phone book?

B: I looked, but I couldn't find it.

Conversation 2

A: You know, I didn't see Jean-Claude at the party. I thought the two of you were good friends. What happened?

B: I would've invited him if he'd been in town.

A: He was out of town? Where was he?

B: Chicago.

Conversation 3

A: Brian seemed kind of depressed.

B: He was. He's unhappy with his job. Remember that job offer he had? He turned it down.

A: Oh, how come?

B: If he'd changed jobs, he wouldn't have gotten the same benefits.

A: Oh, I see why he didn't do it, then.

Conversation 4

A: After the party, we all watched *It's a Wonderful Life* on TV. Have you ever seen it?

B: Many times. It's on TV every year around the holidays. What did you think of it?

A: I would've liked it better on a big screen.

B: Yeah. Sometimes screen size really makes a big difference.

Conversation 5

A: How do you know Tania?

B: She was in my class last year. How do *you* know her?

A: She's a friend of my sister's.

B: I wish David had invited her.

A: Me too.

Conversation 6

A: That woman Rosario seemed really nice.

B: Oh. Did you ask for her phone number?

A: No. Do you think I should have?

B: *I* would have.

A: Well, maybe I can get it from John.

B: Good idea.

Conversation 7

A: Was Holly at the party?

B: Yeah. Holly was there.

A: What about Greg?

B: He was there, too. Holly was avoiding him all night.

A: Oh. That must've really been hard for both of them.

B: I know. If I'd invited Holly, I wouldn't have invited Greg.

A: Me neither.

Conversation 8

A: Where were Tony and Rosa? I don't remember seeing them at the party,

B: They weren't able to come.

A: Oh, that's too bad.

B: If the party hadn't been on a Saturday, they could've come.

A: Oh. Is Tony still working on weekends?

B: Yeah. That's why he couldn't make it. And Rosa didn't want to go without him.

Unit 25

Exercise 6 (page 376)

Conversation 1

ALEX: Hi, Lisa. This is Alex. Let's have dinner together Saturday night. I know you don't like to eat meat, but I found this great new vegetarian restaurant on the West Side.

LISA: I'd really love to, Alex, but my parents are in town for the weekend. I want to spend some time with them on Saturday night. Let's do it another weekend, OK?

Conversation 2

LISA: So, what do you do in your spare time, Ben?

BEN: I like to go to the gym when I get a chance. I usually work out about three times a week.

LISA: Oh really? So do I. I'm even taking aerobics on Sunday, and I love it. I never miss a class.

Conversation 3

LISA: Hi, Mark. This is Lisa. How's the report coming?

MARK: Pretty well. Let's see . . . Today's Monday. I'll have it ready for you tomorrow morning.

LISA: Gee, Mark. I really need to have it today.

MARK: Oh? What's the rush?

LISA: Our weekly staff meeting is Monday afternoon. I need to have the report before the meeting.

MARK: OK. I'll do my best.

Conversation 4

LISA: Dinner looks absolutely wonderful, Chris.

CHRIS: Try the meat sauce. I want to know what you think.

LISA: Mmmm. I love it. It's just delicious. How did you make it?

CHRIS: Oh, it's an old family recipe. But I can give it to you if you like.

LISA: Yes, please do. I'd love to make this sauce.

Unit 26

Exercise 6 (page 389)

The weather service has issued a winter storm warning. About a foot of snow has fallen in our area since early this morning, and more snow is expected during the day. All schools closed by ten o'clock. We advise students, teachers, and other employees to return home immediately. Schools may remain closed tomorrow, so keep listening for further reports.

Snow and high winds are causing dangerous conditions on the roads. Drivers must drive slowly and with a great deal of caution to avoid accidents. If possible, everyone should avoid driving until conditions improve. If you *must* drive, you should take along extra clothing and blankets. You should also make certain you have plenty of gas.

Many government offices will close today. Libraries are closing at 1 P.M. However, post offices will stay open until five o'clock. All government offices will be closed tomorrow.

Many businesses in the area are also closing early because of the storm. Banks are closing at noon to allow employees time to get home safely. Most supermarkets and gas stations will remain open until this evening. You are advised to stock up on food and other necessities since driving could be difficult for several days.

Unit 27

Exercise 5 (page 398)

ANN: Hi, Juan. How are you doing?

JUAN: Oh, well, actually not that great. I've been having a lot of headaches lately. In fact, I just got back from a headache clinic.

ANN: Really? What did they tell you?

JUAN: Let's see . . . They said to get regular exercise. Oh, and they also told me to get eight hours' sleep. They said that fatigue causes headaches.

ANN: That's interesting. You work at a sleep clinic and you haven't been getting enough sleep. Did they give you some painkillers?

JUAN: No. They told me not to take painkillers right now. They said to try to treat the headaches without medication first.

ANN: That sounds good. What did they suggest?

JUAN: Uhmm . . . they said to use an ice pack.

ANN: That's a good idea. How about massaging around your eyes?

JUAN: They didn't tell me to do that. Does it help?

ANN: I think so. What else did they say about preventing headaches?

JUAN: Oh, they said not to eat three big meals a day. They told me to eat several small meals instead.

ANN: Do you have to avoid certain foods?

JUAN: Yeah. Chocolate. They said not to eat chocolate.

ANN: How about cheese? I've heard that cheese can cause headaches.

JUAN: They didn't tell me to avoid cheese. Hey, you seem to know a lot about this.

ANN: Oh, I've been going to a headache clinic for a long time. Let me show you how to massage around your eyes. That really helps me.

Unit 28

Exercise 5 (page 410)

INTERVIEWER: Your resume is very impressive, Ms. . . . uhmm . . .Tsourikov.

TSOURIKOV: That's Tsourikov.

INTERVIEWER: Tsourikov. So, tell me, Ms. Tsourikov, why did you leave your job at Q & L Enterprises?

TSOURIKOV: Well, I had worked there for more than 15 years. Two years ago, I went back to school and got my degree in accounting. I want a position that uses my new skills, and there's nothing available at Q & L.

INTERVIEWER: Fifteen years. Hmmm. That's a pretty long time. How old are you?

TSOURIKOV: Let's just say that I'm old enough to have a lot of valuable experience and still young enough to bring a lot of energy to the job.

INTERVIEWER: I'm sure you are. Are you married?

TSOURIKOV: Er, yes. I'm married and I have two grown children.

INTERVIEWER: I see. What do you know about this company? I mean, why do you want to work for us?

TSOURIKOV: I know you're one of the three leading producers of household appliances and that your products have a reputation for excellence. I would like to be part of your company, and I know I could make a significant contribution.

INTERVIEWER: Tsourikov. That's an unusual name. What nationality are you?

TSOURIKOV: Well, I took my husband's last name . . .

INTERVIEWER: Oh, yes. What does your husband do, Mrs. Tsourikov?

TSOURIKOV: Tsourikov. He's a data processor.

INTERVIEWER: Do you owe anyone any money?

TSOURIKOV: Uh . . .We owe some money on our credit cards . . . and uhmm, we do still have a mortgage on our home . . .

INTERVIEWER: OK . . . Tell me, what computer programs are you familiar with?

TSOURIKOV: I've used Word, Filemaker Pro, and Excel.

INTERVIEWER: Have you ever been arrested?

TSOURIKOV: Excuse me?

INTERVIEWER: Have you ever been arrested?

TSOURIKOV: Er, no. Why do you ask?

INTERVIEWER: Just checking. We have to be very careful who we hire these days . . .Why don't you tell me a little more about yourself. Do you consider yourself successful?

TSOURIKOV: Yes. I was very successful at my last job, as I'm sure my employer would tell you.

INTERVIEWER: Good. How tall are you, Mrs. Tsourikov?

TSOURIKOV: How tall am I? I'm sorry, but before I answer that question, can you tell me how it specifically relates to this job?

INTERVIEWER: Yes? . . . Uhmm, would you excuse me a moment? I have to take this call.

Unit 29

Exercise 6 (page 422)

HOST: Good morning. You're listening to WYAK talk radio. I'm your host, Ed Collins, and our topic this morning is tipping—when, who, where, and how much. For those of you who've just tuned in, we've been talking to Alicia Marksen, who owns and operates a travel agency. Ms. Marksen is now ready to answer any and all of your questions about tipping. Caller number 1, you're on the air.

CALLER 1: In Norway, where I come from, restaurants add a service charge to the bill, so we usually don't leave a tip. Can you tell me how much to tip in a U.S. restaurant?

HOST: Caller number 2, go ahead.

CALLER 2: I don't take taxis very much, and I never know exactly how much to tip the driver. Sometimes I think I overtip.

HOST: Caller number 3, you're on the air.

CALLER 3: I just got to this country, and I've been eating out a lot in restaurants where, you know, you pay at the cashier. My problem is this—I'm never sure where to leave the tip.

HOST: Caller number 4, you're on the air.

CALLER 4: I'm going to France on business, and I'll probably go to the theater. Someone told me something about tipping in a French theater. Can you tell me who I'm supposed to tip?

HOST: Caller number 5, please ask your question.

CALLER 5: I just had an awful experience in a restaurant. Our server was slow, forgot things, and on top of it all, wasn't even polite. Please tell me what to do if I don't like the service in a restaurant.

HOST: Caller number 6, please go ahead.

CALLER 6: I recently started going to a hairdresser. I know I'm supposed to tip the person who washes my hair, but when I'm ready to leave, she's often busy with another customer and I don't want to interrupt. Besides, her hands are all wet! Can you tell me where I should leave the tip?

HOST: Caller number 7, what's your question?

CALLER 7: I travel a lot, and my travel agent doesn't have cultural information for all the places I visit. I wonder how to find information on tipping practices before I travel.

HOST: We have time for just one more question. Caller number 8, please go ahead.

CALLER 8: My roommate and I are exchange students from Pakistan. We need to find out how much to tip when we order takeout. It's kind of urgent! We just ordered a pizza.

Student Book Answer Key

NOTE: In this answer key, where the contracted form is given, the full form is also correct, and where the full form is given, the contracted form is also correct.

UNIT 1 Simple Present and Present Progressive (pages 2–8)

After You Read 1. T 2. F 3. F 4. F

1

Underlined verbs	Circled verbs
working	are
are traveling	vary
're flying	tend
're e-mailing	is
're doing	gives
making	's
	recommend

2

A. 2. does . . . come
3. means
4. do . . . do
5. sell
6. 'm working
7. owns
8. 're joking
9. guess
10. influence

B. 1. 'm trying
2. Do . . . know
3. mean
4. calls
5. 's always winning OR always wins

C. 1. hear
2. 're expecting
3. 're thinking of
4. do . . . think about
5. sounds
6. do . . . spell

D. 1. smells
2. don't drink
3. 's boiling
4. does . . . boil
5. boils

3

Hi, everybody. ~~I write~~ *I'm writing* this note to introduce myself to you, my classmates in English 047. Our teacher ~~is wanting~~ *wants* a profile from each of us. At first I was confused by this assignment because my English dictionary ~~is defining~~ *defines* profile as a side view of someone's head. I thought, Why does she ~~wants~~ *want* that? She sees my head every day! Then I saw the next definition: a short description of a person's life and character. OK, then. Here is my profile:
    My name is Peter Holzer. Some of my friends ~~are calling~~ *call* me Pay-Ha because that is how my initials ~~sounding~~ *sound* in German. I am ~~study~~ *studying* English here in Miami because I want to attend graduate school in Colorado or Montreal. Maybe ~~are you~~ *you are* asking yourself, "Why ~~he wants~~ *does he want* to leave Miami to go to these places?" The answer is: snow! I ~~am coming~~ *come* from Austria, so I love to ski. In fact, my nickname in my family is Blitz (lightning) because ~~always I am trying~~ *I am always trying* to improve my speed.

4

a. "Sunshine"
b. Alex
c. Red
d. Karl
e. "Bozo"
f. Bertha and Vicki

5–7

Answers will vary.

UNIT 2 Simple Past and Past Progressive

(pages 9–18)

After You Read

1. When Kent proposed, Lois accepted.
2. While they were raising their daughters, they were also doing research on radioactivity.
3. In 1985, millions of people were listening to this hit song. OR By that time she was already showing musical talent. OR They were enjoying their success in the music business when Gloria broke her back in a 1990 traffic accident.
4. Then one day Sergei collapsed while they were practicing.

1

2. T   5. F
3. F   6. T
4. F

2

A. 2. was
   3. doing
   4. were dancing
   5. Did
   6. get
   7. gave
   8. Did
   9. bring
   10. fell
   11. bumped
   12. found

B. 1. were
   2. doing
   3. broke
   4. was skating
   5. were pretending
   6. dropped
   7. was lifting

C. 1. Were
   2. crying
   3. did
   4. know
   5. wasn't crying
   6. came
   7. was watching
   8. was thinking

3

A. 2. were smiling
   3. was watching
   4. looked
   5. did . . . meet
   6. didn't come
   7. was studying
   8. changed

B. 1. found
   2. was surfing
   3. did . . . become
   4. was reading
   5. decided
   6. wanted
   7. was studying
   8. started

C. 1. Did . . . surprise
   2. came
   3. was watching
   4. knocked
   5. ended
   6. had
   7. were eating
   8. asked

4

1. She met Paul when she moved to Australia. OR When she moved to Australia, she met Paul.
2. She got married while she was studying medicine. OR While she was studying medicine, she got married. OR She was studying medicine when she got married. OR When she got married, she was studying medicine.
3. She was living in Australia when she got married. OR She got married when/while she was living in Australia. OR While she was living in Australia, she got married.
4. She got her first job when she received her medical degree.
5. She was practicing medicine at Lenox Hospital when she had a son. OR When she had a son, she was practicing medicine at Lenox Hospital. OR She had a son while she was practicing medicine at Lenox Hospital. OR While she was practicing medicine at Lenox Hospital, she had a son.
6. She wrote a book while she was working at Lenox Hospital. OR While she was working at Lenox Hospital, she wrote a book. OR When she wrote a book, she was working at Lenox Hospital.
7. She did a TV interview when she finished her book. OR When she finished her book, she did a TV interview.
8. She left her job when her book became a success. OR When her book became a success, she left her job.

5

I was writing chapter two of my new book when I ~~was thinking~~ of you. The last time I
thought
saw you, you ~~walked~~ down the aisle to marry
were walking
Dave. That was more than two years ago. How are you? How is married life?

A lot has happened in my life since that time. While I ~~worked~~ at Lenox Hospital, I
was working
began writing. In 2004, I ~~was publishing~~ a
published
book on women's health issues. It was quite successful here in Australia. I even got interviewed on TV. When I ~~was getting~~ a
got
contract to write a second book, I decided to quit my hospital job to write full-time. That's what I'm doing now. Paul, too, has had a career change. While I was writing, he was

attending law school. He ~~was getting~~ *got* his degree last summer.

Oh, the reason I thought of you while I ~~wrote~~ *was writing* was because the chapter was about

rashes. Remember the time you ~~were getting~~ *got*

that terrible rash? We ~~rode~~ *were riding* our bikes when

you ~~were falling~~ *fell* into a patch of poison ivy. And that's how you met Dave! When you

~~were falling~~ *fell* off the bike, he offered to give us a ride home. Life's funny, isn't it?

Well, please write soon, and send my love to Dave. I miss you!

6

C.

7–10

Answers will vary.

UNIT 3 Simple Past, Present Perfect, and Present Perfect Progressive (pages 19–27)

After You Read 1. T   2. F   3. F   4. F

1

A. Circled verbs

flew
started
rode
climbed
ran
was
understood
was
told
wanted
was
left
was

Underlined verbs

has been
has earned

has been climbing
's been dreaming
has been living
has been
has been using

B. 2. F   **5.** T   **8.** T
  3. T   **6.** ?   **9.** T
  4. F   **7.** ?   **10.** T

2

Circled verbs

2. got
3. appeared
4. sold out
5. have been having
6. became
7. have visited
8. paid
9. Have you found

3

A. 2. bought
  3. was
  4. took
  5. changed
  6. has been shooting OR has shot
  7. has competed OR competed
  8. won

B. 1. began
  2. got
  3. hasn't stopped
  4. has become
  5. joined
  6. have been performing OR have performed
  7. have given

C. 1. found
  2. has been working OR has worked
  3. saved
  4. got
  5. began
  6. has been buying OR has bought
  7. has been trading OR (has) traded
  8. has found

4

I ~~am doing~~ *have been doing* adventure sports for about two

years, and this year I've ~~been joining~~ *joined* a

climbing club. All the members ~~followed~~ *have been following* your trip on the *Around-n-Over* website since last January, but I haven't ~~been~~ written to you before. I have a few questions. I know you ~~have been climbing~~ *climbed* Mt. Erciyes in Turkey many years ago. Will you climb it again on this project? Also, ~~you have traveling~~ *you've traveled* to different continents. How have you communicated with people? Did you study other languages before your trip? Last month, I ~~have seen~~ *saw* an article about your project in *Hooked on the Outdoors Magazine*. You've ~~became~~ *become* famous! Have you received many e-mails since you ~~start~~ *started* your project? Thanks for answering my questions, and good luck! Lise Bettmann

5

Items checked

read skydiving guide
stop mail for two weeks

6–9

Answers will vary.

UNIT 4 Past Perfect and Past Perfect Progressive (pages 28–42)

After You Read
1. Lee finished his studies in the United States.
2. Lee started to write scripts.
3. The Lees had their second child.
4. *The Wedding Banquet* won a competition.

1

2. T   4. ?
3. F   5. T

2

2. had already finished
3. had not yet directed
4. had already directed
5. had not yet started
6. had not yet won
7. had already finished
8. had already won

3

2. A. Had she arrived . . .
   B. Yes, she had.
3. A. Had she put on . . .
   B. Yes, she had.
4. A. Had she eaten . . .
   B. No, she hadn't.
5. A. Had she eaten . . .
   B. Yes, she had.
6. A. Had she started . . .
   B. Yes, she had.
7. A. Had they done . . .
   B. No, they hadn't.
8. A. Had the director liked . . .
   B. Yes, he had.
9. A. Had she eaten . . .
   B. No, she hadn't.

4

2. had been practicing
3. had been planning
4. had been dreaming
5. had been traveling
6. had been keeping
7. had been managing
8. had been looking
9. had been hiding
10. had been teaching
11. had been searching
12. had been trying

5

2. Had she been training long before (OR when) she acted in her first kung fu movie?
3. How long had they been filming when (OR before) she had a bad fall?
4. Had newspaper reporters been following her when (OR before) they took pictures of her fall?
5. How long had they been dating before (OR when) she married her director?
6. Where had she and her husband been living before (OR when) they moved to Rome?
7. What kind of work had she been doing before (OR when) she quit her old job to act full-time?
8. Had she been crying before the post-Oscar party?

6

2. had brought
3. had been losing
4. had left
5. had been having
6. had been becoming
7. had hurt
8. had arrested
9. had recommended

2. I had been working with a student director . . . he got a job.

3. . . . I got my next film job, I had been working in a restaurant for five years.

4. I had been selling cars on TV . . . Louis Mille called me.

5. I had almost decided to quit acting . . . I hated that job.

6. . . . he hung up, I had been jumping up and down for 10 minutes.

In 1999, moviegoers gasped at the fighting sequences in *The Matrix* and were amazed to learn that Keanu Reeves ~~has~~ *had* actually performed those scenes himself. Hong Kong director Yuen Wo Ping had trained the actors and ~~designing~~ *designed* the scenes. At that time, Yuen was almost unknown in the United States, but he had already ~~have~~ *had* a long career.

Yuen was born in China in 1945. His father had been a kung fu actor, and he trained Yuen in martial arts. When he was 25, Yuen began to design fight scenes (by then, he had already been ~~acted~~ *acting* for 10 years). In 1978, he directed his first film. *Snake in the Eagle's Shadow,* starring Jackie Chan, was a huge success. Before he worked with Yuen, Chan ~~had struggling~~ *had been struggling* OR *had struggled* to start his career. Yuen's films made him famous.

In the 1980's, kung fu movies became less popular. Yuen turned to modern action films, but with little success. By the end of the '90s, two things ~~have~~ *had* happened: Yuen had almost ~~disappears~~ *disappeared* from the movie business while Hollywood directors ~~have~~ *had* finally discovered high-flying Hong Kong fighting styles. When *The Matrix* exploded on the screen, Western audiences saw something they had never ~~been seeing~~ *seen* before, and Yuen was back in business. In 2001, Yuen repeated his success in *Crouching Tiger, Hidden Dragon,* the first kung fu movie ever to receive multiple Oscars.

9

2. Richard and Molly moved to New York.

3. They talked about returning to Utica.

4. Richard and Molly found an apartment in New York.

5. Lynn Costello called Richard and Molly.

Answers will vary.

Possible answers:

There was a pizza box. They'd been eating pizza.

There was a camera on the TV. Someone had been taking pictures.

There were tissues. Someone had been crying.

Someone had taken off his/her running shoes. Maybe that person had been dancing.

There were cups and bottles on the floor. They'd been drinking soda and they hadn't cleaned up.

There was an Oscar ballot on the floor. They'd been watching the Oscars.

Answers will vary.

PART I From Grammar to Writing (pages 43–45)

1

2. don't know	**16.** had been
3. thought	**17.** was pretending
4. judged	**18.** got
5. spoke	**19.** laughed
6. said	**20.** made
7. seemed	**21.** stopped
8. didn't care	**22.** have carried OR have been carrying
9. wanted	**23.** (have) expressed OR (have been) expressing
10. was	**24.** have prepared OR have been preparing
11. read	**25.** am applying
12. pretended	**26.** feel
13. came	
14. was reading	
15. had . . . seen	

2

2. Since that day

3. Now

Paragraph Section	Information	Form of the Verb
Topic Sentence • what the writer is like now	a serious student	simple present
Body of the Paragraph • habits and feelings during the phase	thought about clothes and makeup; spoke in stereotyped phrases; didn't want people to know she was interested in school; read the newspaper secretly; pretended to be unprepared for tests	simple past
• the event that ended the phase	brother laughed at her	simple past
• behavior since the phase ended	has stopped trying to hide her real interests; has carried news magazines proudly; has expressed opinions in class; has prepared openly for tests	present perfect; present perfect progressive
Conclusion • the results of the change	is applying for college; feels proud of being a good student	present progressive and simple present

4–7

Answers will vary.

UNIT 5 Future and Future Progressive (pages 52–65)

After You Read 1. F   2. T   3. F

1

Circled verbs

starts

'll go

Will you be talking

'm focusing

'm going to visit

leave

're going to be holding

'll see

2

2. it's going to rain
3. I'll see
4. I'll call
5. I'm going
6. I'm sending
7. I'm giving
8. will you be, lands, I'll see

3

3. At 10:05 he'll be (OR he's going to be) vacuuming.
4. At 11:05 he won't be (OR he's not going to be) doing laundry. He'll be (OR he's going to be) dusting.
5. At 12:05 he won't be (OR he's not going to be) making lunch. He'll be (OR he's going to be) doing laundry.
6. At 12:35 he'll be (OR he's going to be) making lunch.
7. At 1:05 he'll be (OR he's going to be) shopping for food.
8. At 2:05 he'll be (OR he's going to be) recycling the garbage.

9. At 3:05 he'll be (OR he's going to be) giving Dr. Eon a massage.

10. At 5:05 he'll be (OR he's going to be) making dinner.

11. At 6:05 he won't be (OR he's not going to be) playing cards with Rocky. He'll be (OR he's going to be) playing chess.

4

1. 'll be going
2. Will . . . be joining
   Yes, I will
3. are . . . going to be leaving
4. will be starting
   're going to be hearing
5. Are . . . going to be making
   No, we're not OR No, we aren't / are not
6. will . . . be getting
7. 'm going to be visiting
   won't be buying

5

2. is
3. 'll be (OR 're going to be) defying
4. 'll be (OR 're going to be) floating
5. offers
6. 'll be (OR 're going to be) reading
7. rocks
8. 'll be (OR 're going to be) getting ready
9. won't be (OR 're not going to be) thinking

6

"Good evening, ladies and gentlemen. This
~~will be~~ *is* Captain Eon speaking. We are
going to be leaving OR *will leave*
OR *will be leaving* OR *are leaving*
~~going to be leave~~ the Earth's gravity field in about five minutes. When you ~~will~~ hear the announcement, you'll be able to unbuckle your seat belts and float around the cabin.
will be taking OR *are going to be taking*
Host robots ~~take~~ orders for dinner soon.
'll be serving / 're serving
They~~'ll serving~~ from 6:30 to 7:30. The shuttle arrives on Mars tomorrow morning at 9:00. Tonight's temperature on the planet is a mild minus 20 degrees Celsius. When you
will be
arrive tomorrow morning, the temperature ~~is~~
feel
18 degrees, but it will ~~be feeling~~ more like 20 degrees. Enjoy your flight."

7

Weeks:	July				August			
	1	2	3	4	1	2	3	4
Jennifer							X	X
Brian		X	X					
Lorna	X	X						
Tranh		X		X		X		X
When they're all available:				*Week 1 in August*				

X = not available

8

Answers will vary.

9

Dr. Eon's Calendar

Feb. 2	meet with Dr. Kato (Student A)
Feb. 3–7	attend World Future Conference (Student B)
Feb. 8	take Bullet Train to Osaka (Student A)
Feb. 9–11	sightseeing (Student A)
Feb. 12	fly to Denver (Student B)
Feb. 13–14	visit Mom and Dad (Student B)
Feb. 15	fly home (Student A)
Feb. 16	give speech at Harvard University (Student B)
Feb. 17	meet with Dr. Rover (Student B)
Feb. 18–20	attend energy seminar (Student A)
Feb. 21	shop with Rocky and Robo (Student A)
Feb. 22	relax (Student B)
Feb. 23–27	work at home (Student B)
Feb. 28	take shuttle to Mars (Student A)

10–12

Answers will vary.

UNIT 6 Future Perfect and Future Perfect Progressive (pages 66–78)

After You Read   **1.** T   **2.** T   **3.** T   **4.** F

1

2. b   **5.** a
3. b   **6.** a
4. a

2

2. By 2015, Debbie won't have gotten married.
3. By 2015, she'll have moved into an apartment.
4. By 2015, she won't have moved to Miami.
5. By 2015, she'll have spent a summer in France.
6. By 2015, she'll have started working at a bank.
7. By 2015, she'll have bought a used car.
8. By 2015, she won't have bought a house.
9. By 2015, she won't have graduated from college.
10. By 2015, she won't have become a parent.

3

2. By the time she moves into an apartment, she won't have gotten married yet.
3. By the time she starts college, she won't have bought a used car yet.
4. By the time she graduates from college, she will have already moved into an apartment.
5. By the time she spends a summer in France, she won't yet have found a job at a bank yet.
6. By the time she graduates from college, she will have already spent a summer in France.
7. By the time she gets married, she will have already graduated from college.
8. By the time she moves to Miami, she won't have bought a house yet.
9. By the time she becomes a parent, she will have already graduated from college.
10. By the time she buys a home, she won't have become a parent yet.

4

(Note: The clause with *by* can go either at the beginning or at the end of the sentence.)

2. Q: By April 19, how much will Valerie have saved?
A: By April 19, she will have saved $35.
3. Q: By June 16, how many books will Sung have read?
A: By June 16, he will have read 15 books.
4. Q: How long will Don have been running by May 29?

A: By May 29, he will have been running for five weeks.
5. Q: How many miles will Tania have run by May 29?
A: By May 29, she will have run 72 miles.
6. Q: Will Rick have saved $100 by March 27?
A: No, he won't.
7. Q: How many apartments will Tim have painted by May 29?
A: By May 29, he will have painted six apartments.
8. Q: Will he have finished by June 19?
A: Yes, he will.
9. Q: Will Talia have lost 20 pounds by May 21?
A: Yes, she will.
10. Q: How long will Erik have been studying by April 26?
A: By April 26, he will have been studying for nine weeks.

5

January 1

By August, I'll ~~be~~ *have been* a word processor for ten years. And I'll ~~earn~~ *have been earning* almost the same salary for three years! That's why I've just made a New Year's resolution to go back to school this year. First I'm going to write for school catalogs and start saving for tuition. By March, I'll have ~~figure~~ *figured* out how much tuition will cost. Then I'll start applying. By summer, I ~~had received~~ *'ll have received* acceptance letters. In August, when I ~~will~~ have my annual review with my boss, I'll have already ~~been~~ decided on a school. I will talk to her about working part-time and going to school part-time. By that time, I'll also have ~~saving~~ *saved* enough to pay for a semester's tuition.

My cousin will ~~had~~ *have* graduated by that time, so he might move in with me and share the rent.

By next New Year's Day, I'll have ~~finish~~ *finished* the first semester!

6

Food: $750, Clothing $800,
Transportation $1,200, Entertainment $540,
Total of all categories: $3,290

Where can they go? 2. Car trip to British Columbia, staying in motels

Answers will vary.

PART II From Grammar to Writing (pages 79–81)

1

    As of today, I'm a working man! ~~By the time~~ *By the time* ~~you get this letter.~~ *you get this letter,* I'll have been taking tickets at Ciné Moderne for more than a week. It's going to be hard to work and go to school full time, but you'll understand why I'm doing it~~When you hear my plans.~~ *when you hear my plans.*

    ~~As soon as school ends. My~~ *As soon as school ends, my* brother Alex and I are going to take a trip to Greece and Turkey. I plan to buy a used car, and we'll camp most of the way. By the end of January, I'll have been saving for more than a year for this trip— and I'll have enough to buy a car.

    Why don't you come with us? I don't finish my finals until June 10. You'll already have finished your exams~~While I'm still taking mine.~~ *while I'm still taking mine.* Maybe you can come early and do some sightseeing until I'm ready to leave. Alex has some business to complete~~Before he goes on~~ *before he goes on* vacation. He won't have finished until July 15, but he can join us then.

    I'm leaving Paris on June 17. I'll drive through Italy and take the ferry from Brindisi to Greece. I'll stay in Greece~~Until Alex joins me.~~ *until Alex joins me.* Just think—while your friends are in summer school you could be swimming in the Aegean!

We'll be leaving Greece~~As soon as Alex arrives~~ *as soon as Alex arrives,* so we'll have a month in Turkey. We'll start back around August 20. Your classes won't have started by then, will they? I hope you will be able to join us for this trip. Alex is looking forward to seeing you again, too.

2

December 10	Philippe starts his new job.
January 31	Philippe will have saved enough for a car.
May 31	Jamie finishes his exams.
June 10	Philippe finishes school.
June 17	Philippe leaves Paris.
July 15	Alex finishes his business and joins Philippe in Greece.
August 20	Alex and Philippe start back.

Answers will vary.

UNIT 7 Negative *Yes/No* Questions and Tag Questions (pages 88–101)

After You Read
1. I think Rio is a great place to live.
2. I think it gets very hot in Cairo.

1

Circled words

do you?

don't you?

is it?

Underlined words

Isn't he going to stay with you?

Can't he rent some?

Isn't it less expensive to buy?

2

2. e	**5.** b	**8.** c	**11.** a
3. h	**6.** g	**9.** j	**12.** d
4. f	**7.** k	**10.** l	

3

2. did you	**5.** aren't you
3. doesn't it	**6.** don't you
4. haven't they	**7.** isn't it

4

2. Haven't you seen; No, I haven't.
3. Didn't you put; Yes, I did.
4. Doesn't it have; No, it doesn't.
5. Aren't you going to paint; Yes, I am.
6. Isn't it; Yes, it is.
7. Isn't it; Yes, it is.
8. Can't you find; Yes, I can.

5

2. Didn't you take piano lessons? OR You took piano lessons, didn't you?
3. Didn't you move to Tokyo? OR You moved to Tokyo, didn't you?
4. Didn't you study music composition? OR You studied music composition, didn't you?
5. Didn't you write traditional music? OR You didn't write traditional music, did you?
6. Didn't you paint on paper? OR You didn't paint on paper, did you?
7. Didn't you continue to miss Korea? OR You continued to miss Korea, didn't you?
8. Didn't you use 1,003 TV monitors? OR You used 1,003 TV monitors, didn't you?
9. Don't you do installations anymore? OR You don't do installations anymore, do you?
10. Didn't you become a U.S. citizen? OR You became a U.S. citizen, didn't you?

6

hasn't
BEN: It's been a long time, Joe, ~~haven't~~ it?

JOE: That depends on what you mean by a
it?
long time, doesn't ~~that?~~

Aren't you
BEN: ~~Are not you~~ afraid to show your face around here?

JOE: I can take care of myself. I'm still alive,
aren't I?
~~amn't I?~~

BEN: Until someone recognizes you. You're
aren't
still wanted by the police, ~~are~~ you?

JOE: I'll be gone by morning. Look, I need a place to stay. Just for one night.

BEN: I have to think about my wife and kid. Don't you have any place else to go?

No, I don't
JOE: ~~Yes, I do~~. There's no one to turn to but you. You have to help me.

BEN: I've already helped you plenty. I went
didn't *keep*
to jail for you, ~~haven't~~ I? And didn't I ~~kept~~ my mouth shut the whole time?

JOE: Yeah, OK, Ben. Don't you remember what happened in Vegas_x~~do you?~~ OR *You remember what happened in Vegas, don't you?*

BEN: Don't ever think I'll forget that! OK, OK. I can make a call.

7

Expect an answer: 2, 3, 7, 10
Don't expect an answer: 1, 4, 5, 6, 8, 9

8

London
2. is, isn't it OR isn't, is it
3. a river OR the ocean, doesn't it
4. two OR thirty-two, doesn't it
5. has, doesn't it OR doesn't have, does it
6. Many, don't they OR Not many, do they
7. is, isn't it OR isn't, is it

Toronto
2. is, isn't it OR isn't, is it
3. has, doesn't it OR doesn't have, does it
4. lake OR river, doesn't it
5. has, doesn't it OR doesn't have, does it
6. can, can't you OR can't, can you
7. is, isn't it OR isn't, is it

9–10

Answers will vary.

UNIT 8 *So, Too, Neither, Not Either, and But* (pages 102–115)

After You Read 1. F 2. F 3. T 4. T 5. F 6. T

1

2. F 5. T 8. T
3. T 6. T 9. T
4. F 7. F 10. F

2

Circled words
2. too 6. didn't
3. neither 7. either
4. did 8. So
5. hadn't 9. but

3

2. did I 6. do I
3. can I 7. do I
4. do too 8. do I
5. do I

4

2. but Bob Phillips isn't.
3. and so does Bob Phillips. OR and Bob Phillips does too.
4. and so does Bob Phillips. OR and Bob Phillips does too.
5. and Bob Phillips doesn't either. OR and Neither does Bob Phillips.
6. and so does Bob Phillips. OR and Bob Phillips does too.
7. and so does Bob Phillips. OR and Bob Phillips does too.
8. but Bob Phillips didn't.
9. and so has Bob Phillips. OR and Bob Phillips has too.
10. but Bob Phillips does.
11. but Bob Phillips didn't.
12. and neither does Bob Phillips. OR and Bob Phillips doesn't either.

5

My brother is just a year older than I am (I'm 18). We have a lot of things in common. We look alike. I am 5'10", and so *is he* ~~he is~~. I have straight black hair and dark brown eyes, and so does he. We share some of the same interests too. I love to play soccer, and he *does* too. Both of us swim everyday, but I can't dive and *neither* ~~either~~ can he.

Although there are a lot of similarities between us, there are also many differences. For example, he likes eating all kinds of food, but I don't. Give me hamburgers and fries every day! My brother doesn't want to go to college, but I *do* ~~don't~~. I believe it's important to get as much education as possible, but he wants to get real-life experience. Our personalities are quite different. I am quiet and easygoing, but *he's not* OR *he isn't* ~~he not~~. He has lots of energy and talks a lot. When I think about it, we really are more different than similar.

6

	Ryan	Ryan's Brother
2. is 5'10" tall	☑	☑
3. has black hair	☑	☑
4. has dark brown eyes	☑	☑
5. loves soccer	☑	☑
6. swims	☑	☑
7. dives	☐	☐
8. prefers hamburgers and fries	☑	☐
9. wants to go to college	☑	☐
10. prefers real-life experience	☐	☑
11. is quiet	☑	☐
12. is easygoing	☑	☐

7

	Man	Woman
2. cooks	☐	☑
3. eats out a lot	☑	☑
4. enjoys old movies	☑	☑
5. reads biographies	☑	☑
6. enjoys fiction	☐	☐
7. plays sports	☐	☑
8. watches sports on TV	☐	☐
9. watches news programs	☑	☑
10. wants to see the documentary	☑	☑

8–10

Answers will vary.

11

Possible answers:

Michael wears glasses, and so does Matthew.
Michael reads French, but Matthew doesn't.
Michael is married, but Matthew isn't.
Michael doesn't have a beard, but Matthew does.
Michael plays sports, and so does Matthew.

12–14

Answers will vary.

PART III From Grammar to Writing
(pages 116–117)

1

Citizens of Brasília and citizens of Washington, D.C., live on different continents, but their cities still have a lot in common. Brasília is its nation's capital, and so is Washington. Brasília did not exist before it was planned and built as the national capital. Neither did Washington. Both cities were designed by a single person, and both have a definite shape. However, twentieth-century Brasília's shape is modern—that of an airplane— but eighteenth-century Washington's isn't. Its streets form a wheel.

The cities reflect their differences in location and age. Brasília is located in a dry area in the highlands, while Washington was built on wet swampy land. As a result, Brasília has moderate temperatures all year, but Washington doesn't. Washington is famous for its cold winters and hot, humid summers. Brasília was built 600 miles from the Atlantic coast in order to attract people to an unpopulated area. Washington, near the Atlantic coast, includes old towns that had already existed. Brasília is home to many famous theaters and museums, and so is Washington. However, as a new city, Brasília has not yet become its nation's real cultural center. Washington hasn't either. Washington is its country's capital, but it is not its country's most popular city. Neither is Brasília. Many people still prefer the excitement of Rio and New York.

2

Possible answers:

Brasilia: in South America, twentieth century, shape of an airplane, located in a high and dry area, moderate temperatures all year, 600 miles from the coast, built in an unpopulated area

Both cities: national capital, didn't exist before, planned as a city, designed by one person, definite shape, national theater, famous museums, not the favorite city of its country's residents

Washington, D.C.: in North America, eighteenth century, shape of a wheel, located in a swamp, hot summers and cold winters, near the coast, includes older towns

3–6

Answers will vary.

UNIT 9 Gerunds and Infinitives: Review and Expansion (pages 124–137)

After You Read 1. T   2. T   3. F   4. T

1

Underlined words (gerunds)
2. eating
4. selecting
6. going
7. seeing

Circled words (infinitives)
3. to eat
5. to eat
8. to include

2

2. Having, 200 (exact number: 170)
3. to lose, eating, 250 (exact number: 280)
4. to gain, 650 (exact number: 670)
5. eating, 350 (exact number: 340)
6. choosing, 200 (exact number: 210)
7. to stay away, 660 (exact number: 650)

3

2. recommended ordering
3. volunteered to throw out
4. has stopped (OR stopped) eating
5. deserved (OR deserves) to receive
6. is trying to decide
7. admits (OR admitted) stopping
8. remember playing

4

2. Andre's (OR Andre) wanting to go
3. stopped using
4. finding
5. to see
6. switching
7. to go
8. support their (OR them) offering
9. appreciate my friend's (OR my friend) persuading
10. to express

11. having
12. expected us to find
13. didn't count (OR hadn't counted) on seeing
14. to bring
15. need to have
16. attempt to stay away
17. urge the administration to set up
18. keep on buying

5

Re: love those tacos

I love ~~eat~~ *eating* OR *to eat* tacos for my lunch. I think they are delicious, convenient, nutritious, and inexpensive. I don't even mind ~~to have~~ *having* the same thing every day. What do you think?

Re: vegetarian travel

I'm a vegetarian. I stopped ~~to eat~~ *eating* meat two years ago. I feel a little nervous about traveling to other countries. I'm going to Ghana in September. Is it easy ~~finding~~ *to find* meatless dishes there?

Re: takoyaki

Hi! I am Paulo and I come from Brazil. I enjoy trying different foods. I really want ^*to* try takoyaki (fish balls made with octopus) when I go to Japan. Is there a takoyaki shop you can recommend my going to? I look forward to ~~hear~~ *hearing* from you.

Re: recipe exchange

My name is Natasha. I'm interested in ~~exchange~~ *exchanging* recipes with people from other countries. If you want to know about Russian food, I'd be glad ~~sending~~ *to send* you some information.

Re: calamari

Hi! I was in Italy last month. I don't usually like eating seafood, so I was not eager ~~trying~~ *to try* calamari (squid). I was surprised ~~finding~~ *to find* that

I liked it! I expected it ~~being~~ *to be* tough, but it's actually quite tender if prepared well.

Re: cheap and delicious in Taiwan

Are you going to Taiwan? If so, I suggest ~~to try~~ *trying* the little restaurants around the National University in Taipei. ~~Eat~~ *Eating* there is cheap and it's easy ~~finding~~ *to find* the neighborhood. The dumpling shops are great—once you eat one dumpling there, you won't want ~~stopping~~ *to stop.*

6

Items checked
Lily: 2, 3, 5, 6, 7
Victor: 1, 3, 5, 6

7–8

Answers will vary.

9

Answers will vary.

Name: _____Jennifer Johnson_____
1. I enjoy _____working with others_____.
2. I expect _____to make a lot of money_____.
3. I'm good at _____talking to people_____.
4. I dislike _____working inside_____.
5. I don't mind _____working nights_____.
6. I'm willing _____to learn new skills_____.
7. I never complain about _____following orders_____.
8. I'm eager _____to meet new people_____.
9. I plan _____to major in business_____ next year.
10. I dream about _____owning my own business_____ one day.
11. I can't stand _____rushing_____.
12. I expect people _____to be friendly_____.

10–12

Answers will vary.

UNIT 10 *Make, Have, Let, Help,* and *Get* (pages 138–148)

After You Read 1. b. **2.** a **3.** b

1

2. b **5.** a **7.** b
3. a **6.** b **8.** a
4. a

2

2. h, made **6.** b, had
3. e, made **7.** i, had
4. a, got **8.** d, let
5. g, let **9.** f, made

3

A. 2. made Ana (OR her) work
  3. had Fernando (OR him) clean
  4. got Uri (OR him) to teach
  5. helped Greta (OR her) find
  6. had Hector (OR him) ask

B. 2. made (OR had) her (OR María) drive
  OR got her (OR María) to drive
  3. let him (OR John) borrow
  4. didn't let him (OR John) use
  5. helped them (OR the class) choose
  (OR to choose)
  6. didn't get him (OR John) to read

4

Orcas are beautiful and intelligent, so
aquariums easily get audiences ~~buy~~ *to buy* tickets for
orca shows. What does this mean for the orca?
In the wild, an orca may swim up to 100 miles
a day and dive hundreds of feet below the
water. In captivity, we have this animal ~~lives~~ *live* in
a small pool where it may get sick and die of
an infection. Some people argue that captive
orcas have helped us ~~learned~~ *learn* OR *to learn* about these
animals. However, orcas cannot behave
naturally in an aquarium. In captivity, trainers
make them ~~to~~ perform embarrassing tricks for
a "treat." In the wild, these animals have rich
social lives in families. How can watching
tricks help ~~we~~ *us* learn about their lives? Orcas
don't belong in aquariums!

Don't let these beautiful animals ~~suffering~~ *suffer* in
order to entertain us! First, help us stop
aquarium shows. Stop going to these shows
and get your friends and family ~~stop~~ *to stop* also. Next,
we must make aquariums stop buying orcas.
Write to your mayor and tell him or her how
you feel. Finally, aquariums must ~~let~~ *have* others
~~retrained~~ *retrain* these animals and release them to
the wild.
  Help us help the orcas! Sign this e-letter and
send it to your friends.

5

2. F **5.** T **7.** T
3. F **6.** F **8.** T
4. T

6–10

Answers will vary.

PART IV From Grammar to Writing (pages 149–151)

1

  It's October 1957, and the Soviet Union has
just launched Sputnik. Homer, a teenage boy
(played by Jake Gyllenhaal), watches the
satellite fly over his poor coal-mining town in
West Virginia and dreams of building and
~~to launch~~ *launching* his own rocket. He teams up with
three friends, and "The Rocket Boys" start
to put together and ~~firing~~ *fire* their homemade
missiles. The boys' goal is to win the regional
science fair. First prize will bring college
scholarships and a way out of Coalwood. The
school science teacher, Miss Riley, encourages
him, but Homer's father (played by Chris
Cooper) is angry about the boys' project. He
wants Homer to follow in his footsteps and
~~working~~ *work* at the mine. Nevertheless, the boys
continue launching rockets, failing in different
ways, and ~~to learn~~ *learning* with each failure. People
begin changing their minds and ~~to admire~~ *admiring* the

MOVIE TITLE: _October Sky_

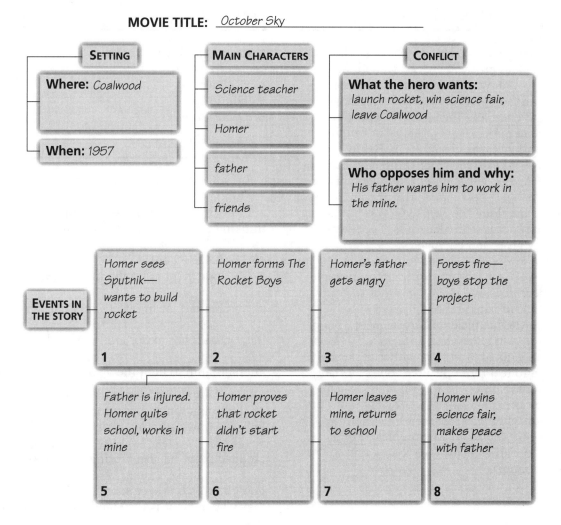

SETTING	MAIN CHARACTERS	CONFLICT
Where: _Coalwood_	_Science teacher_	**What the hero wants:** _launch rocket, win science fair, leave Coalwood_
When: _1957_	_Homer_	
	father	**Who opposes him and why:** _His father wants him to work in the mine._
	friends	

EVENTS IN THE STORY

1. _Homer sees Sputnik—wants to build rocket_
2. _Homer forms The Rocket Boys_
3. _Homer's father gets angry_
4. _Forest fire—boys stop the project_
5. _Father is injured. Homer quits school, works in mine_
6. _Homer proves that rocket didn't start fire_
7. _Homer leaves mine, returns to school_
8. _Homer wins science fair, makes peace with father_

Rocket Boys. Some even help them. However, success does not come easily in Coalwood. When a forest fire starts nearby, a rocket is blamed, and the boys must give up their project. Then Homer's father is injured, and Homer quits school to support his family as a miner. His father is proud of him, but Homer can't stand giving up his dream and ~~to work~~ _working_ in the mine. He uses mathematics to prove a rocket did not start the fire. Then he tells his father he plans to leave the mine and ~~returning~~ _return_ to school.

The Rocket Boys win first prize at the science fair, and all four of them receive scholarships. The whole town celebrates, and Homer wins another very valuable prize—his father attends the science fair and launches the rocket. It's clear that the father and son will try to make peace and ~~respecting~~ _respect_ each other.

2 |

Answers may vary. See diagram above.

3–6 |

Answers will vary.

UNIT 11 Phrasal Verbs: Review
(pages 158–168)

After You Read
1. came back
2. picked up
3. cut off
4. pick out

1

A. Have you noticed that some spaces cheer (you) up and give you energy, while others bring (you) down? This feng shui diagram uses mythological animals to explain why. Look (it) over, and then imagine yourself in the center. A phoenix takes off in front of you and gives you inspiration. Behind you, a tortoise guards you from things you cannot see. On your left and right, a dragon and a tiger balance each other. The dragon floats above the floor and helps you take in (the big picture), not just small details. The tiger's energy gives you courage.

These symbols can be important in setting up (a work environment). Dana, for example, needed ideas and energy in order to get ahead. Unfortunately, her undecorated, windowless cubicle took away (most of her powers). After she hung up (a scenic poster) in the phoenix area in front of her desk, she began to feel more inspired. She gave her tiger some power by picking out (plants) to put on the file cabinet to her right. For her dragon, she hung a cheerful mobile from the top of the left wall of her cubicle. Try (these ideas) out in your own work area and see what happens!

B. **2.** F   **4.** T   **6.** F
    3. T   **5.** F   **7.** T

2

2. down	**9.** up
3. up	**10.** down
4. out	**11.** out
5. out	**12.** out
6. over	**13.** out
7. out	**14.** up
8. together	

3

2. put up	**8.** went up
3. settle on	**9.** letting in
4. turned out	**10.** kept on
5. tear down	**11.** set up
6. figure out	**12.** go back
7. put on	**13.** give up

4

2. took them down
3. cheer him up
4. try them out
5. light it up
6. touch it up

5

I just read an article about feng shui. The
                    down
author suggests sitting ~~up~~ in your home and thinking about how your environment makes
                    it out
you feel. I tried ~~out it~~.

My apartment is bright and sunny. This
                up
cheers me ~~out~~. At night, it's very dark, but I've
            out
figured ~~up~~ what to do. I'm going to buy
                        up   OR   *up at night.*
another lamp to light ˄ the apartment ~~at night up.~~ I'll leave it on when I go out at night, so I can see light as soon as I come in. I also like the light green walls in my bedroom, but the
                        me down
chipped paint has been bringing ~~down me~~. I'm
                up
going to touch it ~~over~~ soon.

My apartment is too small, but I can't tear
down
~~up~~ the walls. I think it will look more spacious if I just straighten it up. I'll try to put books back after I take them off the shelves and
hang up OR *put away*
~~hang away~~ my clothes at night. With just a few small changes, I'll end up feeling happier in my
                    out.
home. It's worth trying ~~on~~.

6

T	**2.** up	F	**5.** down
T	**3.** out	F	**6.** around
T	**4.** back	T	**7.** back

7

Answers will vary.

8

Possible answers:

She turned the light off.
She cleaned up the table.
She turned the bed around.
She took off the bedspread.
She took the curtains down.
The weather cleared up.
She hung up a mirror.
She put away the clothes.
She turned on the TV.
She threw away the flowers.
She touched up the paint.
One of the dresser handles fell off.
The cat woke up.
She straightened out the picture.

9–10

Answers will vary.

UNIT 12 Phrasal Verbs: Separable and Inseparable (pages 169–180)

After You Read
1. got back
2. talk into
3. turn down
4. sign up
5. shows up
6. take off

1

A. Underlined verbs
keep on
leave . . . out
acting up
figure out
call . . . back
hold on
Put . . . down
writing . . . down
hangs up
laid . . . off

B.
1. acting up
2. keep on
3. hangs up
4. laid off
5. hold on
6. leave out
7. call back
8. put down
9. figure out
10. writing down

2
2. end up with
3. let . . . down
4. hang up
5. got to
6. help out
7. fall for
8. Watch out for
9. give . . . back
10. go along with
11. find out
12. turn . . . down
13. lay out
14. put on
15. pick out
16. turned up
17. fill out
18. count on

3
2. turn it down
3. filled it out
4. leave them out
5. called her back
6. wrote them down
7. take it off
8. turn it off

4
2. give them up
3. fill you up
4. Try our plan out
5. Find them out
6. sign up for our plan
7. Fill it out
8. stick to our plan
9. take you off
10. Turn your hobby into
11. takes in $2,000
12. turn work down
13. take employees on
14. go after those jobs
15. set it up
16. send the materials out
17. Check them out
18. send them back
19. put it off
20. pass it up
21. cash in on this great opportunity

5
TM: Hello. Ms. Linder?

JL: Yes. Who's this?

TM: This is Bob Watson from *Motorcycle Mama*. I'm calling to offer you a 12-month subscription for the low price of just $15 a year. Can I sign ~~up you~~ *you up*?

JL: No, thanks. I'm not interested in signing
up
~~in~~ for any more magazine subscriptions.
                    down
Besides, I just sat ~~up~~ for dinner.
                                it out
TM: Why don't you at least try ~~out it~~ for six
months? Don't pass this great opportunity
   up
~~down~~! It's a once in a lifetime chance!

JL: Sorry, I'm really not interested. I don't
even have a motorcycle.

TM: Well then, this is a great opportunity to
            out all about them
find ~~all about them out~~! We'll send you a free
                        it over
copy and you can look ~~over it~~.

                                into
JL: You're not going to talk me ~~in~~ it! In fact,
                            up
I'm going to hang the phone ~~down~~ right now.
                        off
And please take my name ~~out~~ your list.

                on
TM: No, hold ~~out~~! Don't go away! Don't turn
this great offer down! You'll be sorry if you do.
Chances like this don't come around every day!
                out on it
Don't miss ~~it out on~~!

JL: OK. I have an idea. Why don't you give
                                call you back
me your phone number, and I'll ~~call back you~~
during YOUR dinner?
                            up OR *up*
[click as the telemarketer hangs ^the phone^.]

JL: Hello? Hello?

6

A. **2.** $49.95   **8.** $50
   3. set up   **9.** sign up
   4. show up   **10.** give
   5. $30   **11.** back
   6. turn   **12.** one day
   7. on

B. **2.** T   **4.** F   **6.** F
   3. F   **5.** T   **7.** F

7–11

Answers will vary.

PART V From Grammar to Writing
(pages 181–183)

1

2. get on   **7.** using up
3. stick with OR   **8.** lie down
     keep on with   **9.** turn off/out
4. picking up   **10.** left out
5. put together   **11.** come along
6. fix up   **12.** threw out/away

2

Time	To Do
7:30	take shower
8:15	take bus to school
9:00	English class
12:00	lunch
1:00–5:00	McDonald's
5:30–6:00	pick up things for apartment
7:00–10:30	homework
11:00	go to bed

3–6

Answers will vary.

UNIT 13 Adjective Clauses with Subject Relative Pronouns
(pages 190–204)

After You Read 1. c   **2.** d   **3.** a   **4.** b

1

Most of us have very few "best friends"
throughout our lives. These are friends (who) are
loyal to us through good times and bad. They
are people (who) accept us completely (warts and
all) and (who) know our most secret thoughts.
But we have contact with many others (whose)
relationships with us may be less deep but are
still important. What would our lives be
without these acquaintances, buddies, and dear
old friends?

ACQUAINTANCES. These are people whose paths often cross ours. We attend the same school committee meetings or share a car pool with them. Acquaintances may exchange favors easily. The neighbor who borrows your chairs for a big party or the colleague who waters your plants while you're on vacation fits this category. But we usually don't get too intimate with them. One woman commented, "Our next-door neighbor, who carpools with us, is very nice. But we don't have anything in common. We never get together for anything but car pool."

BUDDIES. A lot of people have a friend who shares a particular activity or interest. These usually aren't close relationships, but they're important ones that keep us connected to our interests and hobbies. Because they're based on activities rather than feelings, it's relatively easy to make a new buddy. One foreign-exchange student reported, "For the first two months I was here, I didn't have any real friends. My table-tennis partner, who's from Beijing, was my only social contact. We couldn't communicate in English very well, but we had a good time anyway. Without him, I would have been completely isolated."

OLD FRIENDS. "Delores knew me when I worked in the mailroom," recalls an advertising executive. "I'll never forget this day. The vice president who promoted me called me for an interview. I didn't have the right clothes, and Delores was the one who came with me to buy my first business suit." We all have old friends who knew us "back when." They keep us in touch with parts of ourselves which are easy to lose as we move through life. "Whenever I go home, I always

visit Delores," recalls the executive. "We look through old photo albums and talk about experiences that have helped form us. She always reminds me how shy I used to be. I agree with George Herbert, who said that the best mirror is an old friend."

2

A. 2. h 5. i 8. d
3. g 6. f 9. b
4. j 7. c 10. a

B. 2. An album is a book which (OR that) has pages for saving photos.
3. A soul mate is a person who (OR that) is very similar to you in thought and feeling.
4. A colleague is a person who (OR that) has the same job or profession as you.
5. A confidant is a person who (OR that) listens to your private feelings and thoughts.
6. Empathy is a feeling which (OR that) lets you experience another person's feelings.
7. Friendship is a relationship which (OR that) exists between friends.
8. An in-law is a person who (OR that) is your husband's or wife's relative.
9. A reunion is an event which (OR that) brings people together after a long separation.
10. A spouse is the person who (OR that) is married to you.

3

1. who (OR that) has
2. who (OR that) have
3. which (OR that) are
4. who (OR that) face
5. which (OR that) is
6. who (OR that) have
7. whose . . . are
8. whose . . . include
9. which appeared
10. who (OR that) doesn't read (OR hasn't read)
11. who (OR that) share
12. who (OR that) stays

4

2. They'll meet us at the restaurant which is (OR that's) across the street from the library.
3. The navy blue suit which (OR that) was on sale looked the best.

4. Bill and Sue aren't close friends with the Swabodas, whose interests are very different from theirs.
5. I loaned some chairs to the new neighbors, who are having a party tonight.
6. I was just laughing at an old picture of Jason which (OR that) shows him holding hands with Amy.
7. My boyfriend, who went to Venezuela for two weeks, left me a lot of plants to water.

5

A writer once said that friends are born, not made. I think he meant that friendship is like love at first sight—we become friends immediately with people who ~~they~~ are compatible with us. I don't agree with this writer. Last summer I made friends with some
who are OR *who were*
people ~~who's~~ completely different from me.

In July, I went to Mexico City to study Spanish for a month. In our group, there were
who
five adults, ~~which~~ were all language teachers from our school. Two teachers stayed with friends in Mexico City, and we only saw those teachers during the day. But we saw the teachers who stayed with us in the dormitory both day and night. They were the ones who ~~they~~ helped us when we had problems. Bob Taylor, who is much older than I am, became a really good friend. In my first week, I had a problem that was getting me down. Mexico
which
City, ~~that~~ is a very exciting place, was too distracting. I went out all the time, and I
has
stopped going to my classes. Bob, who ~~have~~ studied abroad a lot, helped me get back into my studies. After the trip I kept writing to Bob,
whose
~~who's~~ letters are always interesting and encouraging. Next summer, he's leading
that OR *which*
another trip ~~what~~ sounds interesting. It's a three-week trip to Spain, which is a place he knows a lot about. I hope I can go.

6

Ann—wearing scarf

Kado—lower right, talking to Ann

Pat—wearing glasses, sitting next to Bob

Asha—wearing jewelry

Pete—not talking to anyone, sitting next to Asha

Answers will vary.

UNIT 14 Adjective Clauses with Object Relative Pronouns or *When* and *Where*   (pages 205–218)

After You Read
1. Hoffman
2. Fong-Torres
3. Hoffman
4. Hoffman
5. Fong-Torres

1

The kitchen is usually steamy with large pots of soup cooking on the wood stove for hours, or laundry being boiled in vats for greater whiteness; behind the kitchen, there's a tiny balcony, barely big enough to hold two people, on which we sometimes go out to exchange neighborly gossip with people peeling vegetables, beating carpets, or just standing around on adjoining balconies. Looking down, you see a paved courtyard, in which I spend many hours bouncing a ball against the wall with other kids, and a bit of garden, where I go to smell the few violets that come up each spring and climb the apple tree, and where my sister gathers the snails that live under the boysenberry bushes, to bring them proudly into the house by the bucketful. . . .

Across the hall from us are the Twardowskis, who come to our apartment regularly. . . . I particularly like the Twardowskis' daughter, Basia, who is several years older than I and who has the prettiest long braids, which she sometimes coils around her head. . . .

• • • • •

Pani Konek teaches at the Cracow Music School, which I've been attending for two years—ever since it has been decided that I should be trained as a professional pianist. I've always liked going to school. At the beginning of the year, I like buying smooth navy blue fabric from which our dressmaker will make my school uniform—an anonymous overdress <u>we are required to wear</u> over our regular clothes in order to erase economic and class distinctions; I like the feel of the crisp, untouched notebook . . . and dipping my pen into the deep inkwell in my desk, and learning how to make oblique letters. It's fun to make up stories about the eccentric characters <u>I know</u>, or about the shapes <u>icicles make on the winter windows</u>, and try to outwit the teacher when I don't know something, and to give dramatic recitations of poems <u>we've memorized</u>. . . .

2

2. who(m) . . . stayed
3. when . . . was
4. which . . . had
5. that (OR which) . . . wanted
6. where (OR in which) . . . were
7. who(m) . . . take care of
8. that (OR which) . . . put
9. that (OR which) . . . have
10. that (OR which) . . . find

3

2. I lived with my parents and my siblings, who (OR that, OR whom) you've met.
3. I had two sisters, who (OR whom) I got along well with (OR with whom I got along well), and an older brother.
4. My sisters and I shared a room, where we spent nights talking.
5. My brother, who (OR whom) I hardly ever saw, slept on the living room couch.
6. It was a large old couch, which my father had made himself.
7. My best friend, who (OR whom) I saw every day, lived across the hall.
8. We went to the same school, where we both studied English.
9. Mr. Robinson, who (OR whom) everyone was a little afraid of (OR of whom everyone was a little afraid), was our English teacher.

10. After school I worked in a bakery that (OR which) my aunt and uncle owned.
11. They sold delicious bread and cake, which people stood in line for hours to buy.
12. I took piano lessons from a woman whose sister worked in the bakery.
13. I remember one summer when the whole family went to the lake.
14. It was a great summer, which I'll never forget.
15. My brother and sisters, who (OR whom) I miss, live far away now.
16. When we get together we like to talk about the old days when we all lived at home.

4

Tai Dong, where I grew up, is a small city on the southeast coast of Taiwan. My family moved there from Taipei the summer ~~when~~ I was born. I don't remember our first house, which we rented from a relative, but when I was two, we moved to the house ~~that~~ I grew up in. This house, where my parents still live, is on a main street in Tai Dong. To me, this was the best place in the world. My mother had a food stand in our front courtyard, where she sold omelettes early in the morning. All her customers, whom I always chatted with, were very friendly to me. On the first floor, my father conducted his tea business in the front room. After school, I always went straight to the corner where he sat drinking tea with his customers. In the back was our huge kitchen with its stone floor and brick oven. I loved dinnertime because the kitchen was always full of relatives and the customers ~~that~~ my father had invited to dinner. It was a fun and noisy place to be. Next to the kitchen, there was one small bedroom. My oldest cousin, whose father wanted him to learn the tea business, slept there. Our living room and bedrooms were upstairs. My two sisters slept in one bedroom, and my older brother and I slept in the other. My youngest sister shared a room with my grandmother, who took care of her a lot of the time.

5

The correct picture is B.
The description is in formal English.

Student A's answers are underlined once.
Student B's answers are underlined twice.

Ben Fong-Torres was born in Alameda, California, in 1945. He was the son of first-generation Chinese parents. His father had immigrated to the United States <u>in 1929</u>, when the Exclusion Act, which limited the number of Chinese entering the country, was still in effect. To avoid this obstacle, his father first went to <u>the Philippines</u>, where he obtained a birth certificate and added *Torres* to his name. Ben's mother came to the United States <u>ten years later</u>, when their marriage was arranged by relatives.

Ben, along with his brother and sister, grew up in <u>Oakland, California</u>, where there was a large Chinese community. His family owned <u>a Chinese restaurant</u>, where all the children worked when they were not in school. Ben's parents, whose views were quite traditional, were a little surprised and concerned about their children's love for U.S. culture. Ben was an enthusiastic reader of cartoons and a fan of <u>popular music</u>, which he heard on the radio.

At the age of twelve, Ben went with his father to <u>Texas</u>, where they opened another Chinese restaurant. It was a difficult time for Ben because he was among people who had had no previous contact with Asians. Back in Oakland, after the failure of the Texas restaurant, Ben got jobs writing for various magazines and newspapers. After graduation from college in 1966, he wrote for <u>*Rolling Stone* magazine</u>, which covered stories about contemporary U.S. political and cultural life. His interviews with hundreds of famous musicians included the Beatles, the Rolling Stones, Grace Slick, and an interview with <u>Ray Charles</u>, for which he won an award for music journalism. Fong-Torres was also a DJ for San Francisco radio station KSAN, which plays rock music, and in 1976 he won an award for broadcasting excellence. Fong-Torres and <u>Diane Sweet</u>, who he married in 1976, still live in San Francisco. He hosts many events for the Chinese community in that city, and continues to write about music for the e-zine (Internet magazine) *Asia Currents* and other publications.

7–10

Answers will vary.

PART VI From Grammar to Writing (pages 219–220)

1

Octavio Paz is considered one of the greatest writers <u>that the Spanish-speaking world has produced</u>. He was born in Mexico in 1914. As a child, he was exposed to writing by his grandfather and father. His childhood was hard because of his father's political activities, <u>which forced his family into exile and poverty</u>.

Paz began writing <u>when he was very young</u>. He published his first poem at age 16. He attended law school in Mexico City, <u>where he joined a Marxist student group</u>. Around the same time, he married his first wife, Elena Garro. Paz's literary career received a boost in his early twenties, <u>when he sent a manuscript to the Chilean poet Pablo Neruda</u>. Neruda was impressed, and he encouraged Paz to go to Spain to attend a writing conference. Paz remained there and joined the forces <u>that were fighting against General Franco in the Spanish Civil War</u>. Later, he went on to become a diplomat, representing his country in France, Japan, the United States, and India.

Paz wrote both poetry and prose. He is most famous for *The Labyrinth of Solitude*, a collection of essays <u>that deal with the character of the Mexican people</u>. He also founded *Vuelta*. In 1990 he received the Nobel Prize for Literature. He died eight years later.

2

2. Around the same time, he married his first wife, Elena Garro, who was also a writer.
3. Paz's literary career received a boost in his early twenties, when he sent a manuscript to the Chilean poet Pablo Neruda, who was already famous in Spain and Latin America.
4. He also founded *Vuelta*, which was one of Latin America's most famous literary magazines.

3–6

Answers will vary.

UNIT 15 Modals and Similar Expressions: Review (pages 226–238)

After You Read 1. T   2. T   3. F   4. F   5. T

1

A. Underlined words

2. might apply, Should . . . submit, will . . . be able to use, could use, ought to send, might have
3. must get
4. do . . . have to send, must be, can't last, should tell
5. can't send
6. had to be, could take place
7. must need, have to be

B. Ability: will . . . be able to use, can't send

Advice: should . . . submit, ought to send, should tell

Necessity: do . . . have to send, must be, can't last, have to be

Future Possibility: might apply, could use, might have, could take place

Assumptions: must get, had to be, must need

2

2. must
3. 've got to, can
4. be able to, could
5. couldn't
6. can't, 'd better not
7. must, had to
8. have got to
9. can, couldn't
10. must, 'll be able to
11. can, 've got to
12. don't have to

3

2. can tell OR 'm able to tell
3. don't have to hire
4. can make OR are able to make
5. can't be OR couldn't be
6. might never know OR may never know
7. must love OR have to love OR have got to love
8. might look OR may look OR could look
9. might be OR may be OR could be
10. don't have to love
11. 'd better feel OR 've got to feel
12. must be OR has to be OR has got to be
13. shouldn't have
14. can cry OR 're able to cry
15. should talk OR ought to talk
16. might do OR may do OR could do
17. 'd better start

4

Did anyone watch "Pop Idols" last night? I couldn't ~~not~~ believe Jennifer Tasco didn't win!
had OR *has*
She ~~have~~ to be the best singer on the show.

Tonight on "Get a Job," Ronald Trunk interviewed Lateesha and Sam. Trunk can only
fire
keep one of them—who should he ~~fires~~? I think
might
he ~~mights~~ get rid of Lateesha, but I really believe Sam ought to go. Last week, he said he
wasn't able to OR *couldn't*
~~didn't able to~~ work because he had a headache. Ha! He's just lazy.

Everybody knows that Sam was really sick last week. He had to go to the doctor! If you don't
must not
know that, then you ~~don't have to~~ know very much about the show. That's my guess.

I just read an interesting article about "Be
could OR *might* OR *may*
Afraid." Watching this show ~~should~~ be dangerous for people with an extreme fear of things like snakes or insects. So if you
shouldn't OR *'d better not*
have that problem, you ~~ought to~~ watch "Be Afraid."

"Amazing Journey" will start next summer. That's great, because I won't be in school, so
have
I won't ~~having~~ to worry about missing classes
could OR *might* OR *may*
to watch. They ~~will~~ go to Vietnam this year, but it's not certain yet.

couldn't
I cried after "Housemates" on Monday. I ~~can't~~ even sleep that night. They were so mean to
might not OR *may not*
Sharifa! I ~~not might~~ watch this show anymore— it depends on what happens next week.

I just watched "Lose to Win." All these people are competing to lose the most weight. This
can't OR *must not* OR *couldn't*
~~doesn't have to~~ be healthy! I think they exercise too hard and they have too much stress. Some people might not lose weight in a week even when they don't cheat. That's normal.

A. 2. should
   3. 'd better not
   4. must
   5. have to
   6. couldn't
   7. might not
   8. ought to
   9. must not

   10. 'll be able to
   11. 've got to
   12. 's got to be
   13. shouldn't
   14. can
   15. 's got to
   16. can

B. 2. F   **4.** F
   3. T   **5.** F

6–10

Answers will vary.

UNIT 16 Advisability in the Past
(pages 239–248)

After You Read **1.** F   **2.** F   **3.** F   **4.** T

1

2. b   **4.** b   **6.** b
3. a   **5.** a   **7.** a

2

   4. shouldn't have taken
   5. should . . . have done
   6. might have asked
   7. could have paid
   8. ought to have worn
   9. should . . . have fired
10. shouldn't have
11. should . . . have handled
12. ought to have warned
13. shouldn't have . . . fired

3

Answers may vary slightly. Possible answers:
   2. I might have warned him.
   3. I shouldn't have eaten all the chocolate.
   4. She might have called.
   5. He could have offered to lend me some money.
   6. I shouldn't have jogged five miles.
   7. They shouldn't have charged me for the plastic bag.

   8. I ought to have done the laundry.
   9. I should have invited her to the party.
10. He might have sent me a card.

4

About a week ago, Jennifer was late for work again, and Doug, our boss, told me he wanted to fire her. I was really upset. Of course, Jennifer shouldn't ~~had~~ *have* been late so often, but he might ~~has~~ *have* talked to her about the problem before he decided to let her go. Then he told me to make her job difficult for her so that she would quit. I just pretended I didn't hear him. What a mistake! I ought ~~a~~ *to* have confronted him right away. Or I could at least have warned Jennifer. Anyway, Jennifer is still here, but now I'm worried about my own job. Should I ~~of~~ *have* told Doug's boss? I wonder. Maybe I should ~~handle~~ *have handled* things differently last week. The company should never ~~has~~ *have* hired this guy.

5

Checked items
Walk to work
Buy coat
Call Ron

6

Answers will vary. Possible answers:
She shouldn't have left the window open.
She should have cleaned up her room.
She should have washed the dishes.
She should have fed the cat.
She should have studied for her test.
She should have watered her plant.
She shouldn't have left the stove on.

7–10

Answers will vary.

UNIT 17 Speculations and Conclusions about the Past

(pages 249–261)

After You Read

1. Possible
2. Certain
3. Impossible

1

2. d	5. f	7. a
3. h	6. b	8. g
4. c		

2

2. carved	7. have drawn
3. have	8. could
4. must	9. Could
5. could	10. have
6. have	

3

2. must not have had
3. couldn't have supported
4. could have developed
5. must have made
6. must have fished
7. must have eaten
8. may have lived
9. could have made
10. had to have come
11. could . . . have called
12. must have had
13. might have moved
14. couldn't have created

4

2. Dinosaurs must not have survived the cold.
3. A huge meteor might have hit the Earth.
4. A Bigfoot couldn't have kidnapped Ostman.
5. Ostman must have seen a bear.
6. Ostman could have dreamed (OR dreamt) about a Bigfoot.
7. The man had to have changed the photo.
8. The man might have seen a large fish.
9. The man may have seen a dead tree trunk.
10. A dinosaur couldn't have been in the lake.

5

2. They couldn't have been.
3. They might have.
4. They could have.
5. They must have.
6. They may have.
7. He might not have been.
8. He must have.

6

Rapa Nui (Easter Island) is a tiny island in the middle of the Pacific. To get there, the first settlers had to ~~had~~ *have* traveled more than 1,000 miles in open boats. Some scientists believed only the Polynesians of the Pacific islands could have ~~make~~ *made* the journey. Others thought that Polynesians couldn't have carved the huge stone statues on Rapa Nui. They believed Mayans or Egyptians ~~maybe~~ *might* OR *may* OR *could* have traveled there. (Some people even said that space aliens might *have* helped!) Finally, a University of Oslo scientist was able to study the DNA from ancient skeletons. Professor Erika Halberg announced, "These people ~~has~~ *had* to have been the descendants of Polynesians."

We now know that the islanders built the statues, but we have also learned that they must ~~had~~ *have* solved even more difficult problems. The first settlers came some time between A.D. 400 and 700. At first, Rapa Nui must ~~be~~ *have been* a paradise with its fishing, forests, and good soil. Their society may have grown too fast for the small island, however. Botanical studies show that by the 1600s they had cut down the last tree. The soil must ~~not~~ have washed away, so they couldn't farm. And with no wood for boats, they couldn't have *been* able to fish. For a period of time, people starved and fought violently, but when the Dutch discovered Rapa Nui in 1722, they found a peaceful, healthy population growing fields of vegetables. How ~~the islanders could~~ *could the islanders* have learned in this short period of time to live peacefully with so few resources? For our troubled world today, this might be the most important "mystery of Easter Island."

1. b **3.** e **5.** d
2. f **4.** c **6.** a

8

Possible answers:
1. a ceramic pillow to rest the head on
2. a safety pin to close clothing
3. a razor and mirror made of bronze and wood
4. snow goggles to protect the eyes from glare
5. a stick chart to show sailors islands and currents

9–11

Answers will vary.

PART VII From Grammar to Writing (pages 262–264)

1

Underlined sentences

He might have even decided that I couldn't afford to send a gift.
He couldn't have been angry with me!

Bracketed sentences

[He could've sent me an invitation and let me decide for myself.]
[I should have called him to discuss it.]
[He shouldn't have decided for me.]

2

2. 1 **3.** 4 **4.** 2

3

Possible answers:

Paragraph 2

You might have even decided that I couldn't afford to send a gift.

You couldn't have been angry with me!

Paragraph 3

You could've sent me an invitation and let me decide for myself.

You shouldn't have decided for me.

On the other hand, I should have called you to discuss it.

4–7

Answers will vary.

UNIT 18 The Passive: Overview (pages 270–284)

After You Read
1. students
2. Reza Deghati
3. a group of professionals OR geographers, explorers, teachers, and mapmakers
4. people in over 160 million homes OR people in 145 countries

1

2. A	**5.** P	**8.** P	**11.** P	**14.** P
3. P	**6.** P	**9.** P	**12.** A	**15.** A
4. A	**7.** P	**10.** P	**13.** P	

2

2. speak Russian
3. Korean is spoken
4. is spoken by 341 million people
5. 1,070 million (1.07 billion) people speak
6. Arabic is spoken by
7. speak English
8. Turkish is spoken by

3

2. No, it wasn't.
3. was created
4. Is . . . grown
5. No, it isn't
6. is . . . spelled
7. 's been eaten OR has been eaten
8. are . . . used
9. aren't OR 're not raised
10. is . . . mined
11. are found
12. 's produced OR is produced
13. is found
14. are spoken
15. Are . . . seen
16. Yes, they are

4

2. is . . . sent
3. is put
4. is used
5. is numbered

6. was shot OR is shot
7. Have . . . been lost OR Have . . . been damaged
8. damaged OR lost
9. are . . . divided
10. are packed
11. are saved
12. are . . . taken
13. is notified
14. is shipped
15. is traced
16. are found
17. is started

5

2. Quinoa isn't spelled with a *k*. It's spelled with a *q*.
3. Llamas aren't raised only for transportation. They're raised for many uses.
4. Llamas aren't raised for meat in the lowlands. Cattle are raised for meat in the lowlands.
5. Rubber isn't found in that region. Oil is found in that region.
6. The parrot isn't seen in the highest mountains. The condor is seen in the highest mountains.
7. A great civilization wasn't created on the shores of the Pacific. It was created on the shores of Lake Titicaca.
8. Portuguese isn't spoken in the government. Spanish is spoken in the government.
9. Traditional textiles aren't woven by machine. They're woven by hand.

6

3. are not allowed
4. is controlled by the feet, the head, and the body
5. wasn't played
6. has been made popular by Pelé, Beckham, and other international stars
7. have been played (by different cultures)
8. was enjoyed
9. was banned by King Edward III of England
10. were played
11. are held (by the World Cup Association)

7

Reza Deghati ~~is~~ *was* born in Tabriz, Iran, in 1952. When he was only 14 years old, he began teaching himself photography. At first, he took pictures of his own country—its people and its architecture. When he was 25, he ~~was~~ decided to become a professional photographer. During a demonstration he was asked by a French news agency to take photos. He only shot one and a half rolls of film (instead of the usual 20 to 40), but his photos ~~was~~ *were* published in *Paris Match* (France), *Stern* (Germany), and *Newsweek,* (U.S.A).

Reza, as he is ~~knew~~ *known* professionally, has covered several wars, and he has ~~be~~ *been* wounded on assignment. Among all his assignments, the project dearest to his heart is photographing children, who he calls "the real victims of war." He has donated these photos to humanitarian organizations.

When he was interviewed ~~by an interviewer~~, he was asked to give advice to wannabe photojournalists. Reza replied, "There is a curtain between the photographer and the subject unless the photographer is able to break through it. . . . Open your heart, to them, so they know you care."

Today Reza Deghati lives in Paris. His photos ~~is~~ *are* widely distributed in more than 50 countries around the world, and his work is published in *National Geographic* as well as many other internationally famous magazines and newspapers.

8

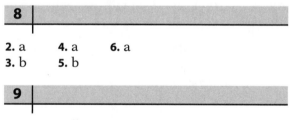

2. a   4. a   6. a
3. b   5. b

9

Answers will vary.

		Mindanao	Luzon
G R O W	tobacco	N	Y
	corn	Y	N
	bananas	Y	N
	coffee	N	Y
	pineapples	N	Y
	sugar	Y	Y
R A I S E	cattle	Y	Y
	pigs	Y	Y
M I N E	gold	Y	Y
	manganese	N	Y
P R O D U C E	cotton	N	Y
	rubber	Y	N
	lumber	Y	N

11–13

Answers will vary.

UNIT 19 The Passive with Modals and Similar Expressions (pages 285–295)

After You Read **1.** T   **2.** ?   **3.** T   **4.** ?   **5.** F

1

Underlined words
will . . . be completed, could be finished,
might be speeded up, has to be done, must be
completed, 's finished, can be increased, will . . .
be provided, should be given, ought to be added,
will be, is going to be placed, will be done, have
got to be understood, might be discovered

2

2. can be protected
3. can't be considered
4. can be compared
5. must be attached
6. can't be used
7. might be damaged
8. has to be sucked
9. could be washed

10. don't have to be concerned
11. can be sent
12. burned up OR burnt up
13. should be taken
14. doesn't have to be squeezed
15. can be prepared
16. eaten
17. must be attached
18. has got to be provided
19. are going to be given
20. will be used
21. must be allowed
22. could be lost

3

2. should be kept
3. ought to be made
4. might be accepted
5. had better be required
6. can't be simulated
7. should be sent
8. have to be approved
9. can't be changed
10. could be done
11. are going to be surprised

4

6:15 A.M. I used the sleeping restraints last
night, so my feet and hands didn't float around
as much. I slept a lot better. I'm going to
suggest some changes in the restraints
though—I think they ought to be ~~make~~ *made* more
comfortable. I felt really trapped. And maybe
these sleeping quarters could ˄ designed *be*
differently. They're too small.
10:45 A.M. My face is all puffy, and my eyes are
red. Exercise helps a little—I'd better ~~be gotten~~ *get*
on the exercise bike right away. I can be
~~misunderstanding~~ *misunderstood* very easily when I look like
this. Sometimes people think I've been crying.
And yesterday Max thought I was angry
when he turned on *Star Trek*. Actually, I love
that show.
1:00 P.M. Lunch was pretty good. Chicken
teriyaki. It's nice and spicy, and the sauce can
actually ~~been~~ *be* tasted, even at zero gravity.
They'd better fly in some more of it for us
pretty soon. It's the most popular dish in the
freezer.

4:40 P.M. I'm worried about my daughter. Just before I left on this mission, she said she was planning to quit school at the end of the semester. That's only a month away. I want to call her and discuss it. But I worry that I might

get angry and yell. I might ~~be~~ overheard by the

be ^

others. They really should figure out some way to give us more privacy.

10:30 P.M. The view of Earth is unbelievably breathtaking! My favorite time is spent looking out the window—watching Earth pass below. At night a halo of light surrounds the horizon.

be seen

It's so bright that the tops of the clouds can ~~see~~.

has

It can't be described. It simply ~~have~~ to be experienced.

5

2. could	**5.** can't
3. must	**6.** have to be helped
4. be picked up by	

6–10

Answers will vary.

UNIT 20 The Passive
Causative
(pages 296–305)

After You Read Items checked: 1, 2, 4, 7, 8

1

2. F	**4.** T	**6.** T	**8.** T
3. T	**5.** F	**7.** F	

2

2. Debra got her hair permed on the 7th.
3. Amber had the dog groomed on the 14th.
4. They're going to get the windows washed on the 16th.
5. They had the carpets cleaned on the 13th.
6. Amber is going to have (OR is having) her ears pierced on the 25th.
7. Jake got his hair cut on the 12th.
8. They're going to have food and drinks delivered on the 20th.

3

2. have/get it dry cleaned
3. 're going to have/get them washed OR 're having/getting them washed
4. 'm going to have/get it cut OR 'm having/getting it cut
5. have/get it colored
6. 've . . . had/gotten it repaired
7. Did . . . have/get it painted OR Have . . . had/gotten it painted
8. have/get them developed

4

The party was tonight. It went really well! The house looked great. Mom and Dad had the

cleaned

floors waxed and all the windows ~~clean~~ professionally so everything sparkled. And of

painted OR *had painted*

course we ~~had~~ the whole house ~~painted~~ ourselves last summer. (I'll never forget *that.* It took us two weeks!) I wore my new black

had

dress that I ~~have~~ shortened by Bo, and I got

my hair cut

~~cut my hair~~ by André. He did a great job. There

invited

were a lot of guests at the party. We had ^ almost

50 people ~~invited~~, and they almost all showed up! The food was great too. Mom made most of the main dishes herself, but she had the rest

prepared

of the food ~~prepare~~ by a caterer. Mom and Dad hired a professional photographer, so at the

had   *taken*

end of the party we ~~took~~ our pictures ^. I can't

wait to see them.

5

Amber did the job herself: 3, 5, 7
Amber hired someone to do the job: 2, 4, 6, 8

6

Answers will vary.

7

Answers may vary. Possible answers:
She had her nose shortened. She had her chin lengthened. She had her lips enlarged. She had her tattoo and mole removed. She had her

teeth straightened. She had her hair cut, permed, and colored. She had the lines around her mouth and eyes removed (OR filled in). She had her left ear pierced.

8–11

Answers will vary.

PART VIII From Grammar to Writing
(pages 306–307)

1

Two Buddhist monks built Haeinsa Temple in 802 A.D. The king gave them the money to build the temple after the two monks saved his queen's life. Haeinsa burned down in 1817, but <u>the Main Hall was rebuilt</u> in 1818 on its original foundations. Today, <u>Haeinsa is composed</u> of several large, beautiful buildings. It contains many paintings and statues. Someone carved three of the statues from a single ancient tree. Behind the Main Hall is a steep flight of stone stairs that leads to the Storage Buildings. <u>These buildings</u>, which escaped the fire, <u>were constructed</u> in 1488 in order to store wooden printing blocks of Buddhist texts. <u>It was believed</u> that these printing blocks could protect the country against invaders. Monks carved the 81,258 wooden blocks in the 13th century. A century later, nuns carried them to Haesina for safekeeping. Architects designed the Storage Buildings to preserve the wooden blocks. For more than five hundred years, <u>the blocks have been kept</u> in perfect condition because of the design of these buildings. <u>Haeinsa</u>, which means *reflection on a smooth sea*, <u>is also known</u> as the Temple of Teaching because it houses the ancient printing blocks.

2

2. Three of the statues were carved from a single ancient tree.
3. The 81,258 wooden blocks were carved (by monks) in the 13th century.
4. A century later, they were carried (by nuns) to Haeinsa for safekeeping.
5. The Storage Buildings were designed to preserve the wooden blocks.

3

1. 802 A.D.
2. Two monks.
3. *Possible answers:* To store wooden printing blocks of Buddhist teachings. OR Because the king gave money to two monks who had saved the queen's life.
4. *Possible answers:* Beautiful buildings, stone stairs, many paintings and statues, special storage buildings
5. Ancient printing blocks of Buddhist texts

4–6

Answers will vary.

UNIT 21 Present Real Conditionals
(pages 314–325)

After You Read 1. F 2. T 3. T 4. F 5. T

1

You're shopping in a foreign city. Should you pay full price, or should you bargain? <u>If you don't know the answer</u>, you can pay too much or miss a fun experience. <u>Bargaining is one of the greatest shopping pleasures if you know how to do it</u>. The strategies are different in different places. Check out these tips before you go.

Hong Kong
Hong Kong is one of the world's greatest shopping cities. <u>If you like to bargain</u>, you can do it anywhere except the larger department stores. The trick is not to look too interested. <u>If you see something you want</u>, pick it up along with some other items and ask the prices. Then make an offer below what you are willing to pay. <u>If the seller's offer is close to the price you want</u>, then you should be able to reach an agreement quickly.

Italy
Bargaining in Italy is appropriate in outdoor markets with street vendors. In stores, <u>you can politely ask for a discount if you want to bargain</u>. Take your time. <u>Make conversation if you speak Italian</u>. Show your admiration for the object by picking it up and pointing out its wonderful features. When you hear the price, look sad. Make your own offer. <u>End the bargaining politely if you can't agree</u>.

Mexico

In Mexico, people truly enjoy bargaining. There are some clear rules, though. <u>You should bargain</u> <u>only if you really are interested in buying the object.</u> <u>If the vendor's price is far more than you want to pay,</u> <u>then politely stop the negotiation.</u> <u>If you know your price is reasonable,</u> <u>walking away will often bring a lower offer.</u>

Remember, bargaining is always a social interaction, not an argument. <u>And it can still be fun</u> <u>even if you don't get the item you want at the price you want to pay.</u>

2

2. If you'd like to buy some nice but inexpensive clothes, take the train to open air markets in towns *outside* of the city. OR Take the train to open air markets in towns *outside* of the city if you'd like to buy some nice but inexpensive clothes.
3. If you're looking for a shopping mall, you need to go away from the city center. OR You need to go away from the city center if you're looking for a shopping mall.
4. If you want to go shopping in the Grand Bazaar, you have to go during the week. OR You have to go during the week if you want to go shopping in the Grand Bazaar.
5. If you want to buy some unusual gifts, shop in Soho. OR Shop in Soho if you want to buy some unusual gifts.
6. If your son wants to buy computer games, he should try the Panthip Plaza. OR Your son should try the Panthip Plaza if he wants to buy computer games.
7. If you plan to buy some silver jewelry in Mexico, you should be able to get something nice at a very good price. OR You should be able to get something nice at a very good price if you plan to buy some silver jewelry in Mexico. OR If you plan to buy some silver jewelry in Mexico, try bargaining. OR Try bargaining if you plan to buy some silver jewelry in Mexico.
8. If you'd like to find some nice secondhand clothing shops, try the Portobello market on the weekend. OR Try the Portobello market on the weekend if you'd like to find some nice secondhand clothing shops.

3

2. You can make better business decisions if you have good business skills.

3. A buyer needs great interpersonal skills if she's negotiating prices.
4. If there's a big international fashion fair, I'm usually there.
5. If I go to a fair, I can see hundreds of products in a few days.
6. I usually stay two weeks if I travel to Europe.
7. If my husband can come, he and our son, Pietro, do things together.
8. Pietro comes to the fair with me if my husband can't get away.
9. I always go shopping if I have free time.

4

Answers will vary. Possible answers:

3. When people are watching the sun rise in Honolulu (OR Wellington), people are watching the sun set in Johannesburg (OR Madrid).
4. When it's midnight in Jakarta, it's 6:00 P.M. in Madrid.
5. When people are eating lunch in Montreal, people are eating dinner in Johannesburg (OR Madrid).
6. When people are getting up in Honolulu, people are going to bed in Bombay (OR Jakarta).
7. When it's 7:00 A.M. in Honolulu, it's 7:00 P.M. in Johannesburg.
8. When it's 5:00 A.M. in Wellington, it's 9:00 A.M. in Los Angeles.

5

Tomorrow I'm flying to Hong Kong for a fashion show! My son, Pietro, is flying with me, and my husband is already there. Whenever Pietro's off from school, I ~~liked~~ *like* to take him on trips with me. If my husband comes too, they ~~are going~~ *go* sightseeing during the day.

Our plane leaves Los Angeles around midnight. If we ~~flew~~ *fly* at night, we can sleep on the plane. (At least that's the plan!)

I love Hong Kong. We always have a great time when we ~~will~~ go there. The shopping is fantastic. When I'm not working, I'm shopping.

I'll call you when I arrive at the hotel (around
7:00 A.M.). When it ~~will be~~ 's 7:00 A.M. in Hong
Kong, it's midnight in London. Is that too late
to call? If you want to talk, just ~~calling~~ call. And, of
course you can always e-mail me.

2. F   **4.** F   **6.** F
3. T   **5.** T

7

Answers will vary.

8

See figure below.

9–12

Answers will vary.

UNIT 22 Future Real Conditionals
(pages 326–335)

After You Read **1.** b   **2.** a   **3.** d   **4.** c

1

2. e   **4.** a   **6.** b
3. f   **5.** c

2. If I give my boyfriend a new pair of shoes,
he'll walk out of the relationship.
3. If I use my lucky pen, I'll get a good grade
on the test.

2

1. unless, If   **4.** Unless, If
2. If, if, If   **5.** if, If
3. If, unless   **6.** if, if, unless

3

3. washes   **11.** itches
4. 'll rain   **12.** 'll give
5. walk   **13.** throws
6. 'll have   **14.** 'll start
7. sweep   **15.** sit
8. 'll sweep   **16.** 'll not (OR won't) get
9. is   **17.** throw
10. 'll get   **18.** 'll have

4

2. If you take the job, you won't have the chance
to travel a lot. You'll never leave the office.
3. If you stay at Eastward, you won't get a raise
every year. You'll get one (OR a raise) every
two years.
4. If you join Eastward, you're not going to
have wonderful health care benefits. You'll
have terrible health care benefits.
5. If you go to Eastward, you won't have
helpful co-workers. You'll have uncooperative
co-workers.

	Best Time to Go	Currency	Time: When it's noon in New York . . .
Caracas, Venezuela	*December–April*	**bolívar**	*1:00 P.M.*
Istanbul, Turkey	*April–October*	*Turkish lira*	**8:00 P.M.**
Rio de Janeiro, Brazil	**April–October**	*real*	**2:00 P.M.**
Seoul, South Korea	*October–March*	**won**	**2:00 A.M.***
Vancouver, Canada	**July–September**	*Canadian dollar*	**9:00 A.M.**
Moscow, Russia	*May–September*	**ruble**	*8:00 P.M.*

*the next day

6. If you accept Eastward's offer, it won't be the best career move of your life. It will be the worst.

5

Answers will vary. Possible answers:

3. If I take out student loans, I'll have to depend on my family. OR I'll have to depend on my family if I take out student loans.

4. If I go to law school, I'll earn more money. OR I'll earn more money if I go to law school.

5. If I earn more money, I'll pay back my loans quickly. OR I'll pay back my loans quickly if I earn more money.

6. If I pay back my loans quickly, I'll put my sister through college. OR I'll put my sister through college if I pay back my loans quickly.

7. If I go to law school, I may (OR might OR could) go into politics. OR I may (OR might OR could) go into politics if I go to law school.

8. If I go into politics, I'll be able to improve life for others. OR I'll be able to improve life for others if I go into politics.

9. If I go into politics, I might (OR may OR could) get elected to city council. OR I might (OR may OR could) get elected to city council if I go into politics.

10. If I get elected to city council, I might (OR may OR could) run for mayor. OR I might (OR may OR could) run for mayor if I get elected to city council.

6

Should I campaign for student council
                              want
president? I'll have to decide soon if I ~~wanted~~
       I'm
to run. If ~~I'll be~~ busy campaigning, I won't have much time to study. That's a problem because
                    unless I get OR *if I don't get*
I'm not going to get into law school ~~if I get~~ good grades this year. On the other hand, there's so
                  will get OR *is going to get*
much to do in this school, and nothing ~~is getting~~ done if Todd Laker becomes president again. A lot of people know that. But will I know what
       I
to do if ~~I'll~~ get the job? Never mind. I'll deal with that problem~~,~~ if I win. If I become
       I'll OR *I'm going to*
president, ~~I~~ cut my hair. That always brings me good luck.

7

Issues checked: 1, 3, 4

8–11

Answers will vary.

UNIT 23 Present and Future Unreal Conditionals (pages 336–347)

After You Read   **1.** F   **2.** T   **3.** T   **4.** F   **5.** T

1

2. a. T	**5. a.** T	**8. a.** T
b. F	**b.** T	**b.** T
3. a. F	**6. a.** F	**9. a.** F
b. F	**b.** T	**b.** T
4. a. F	**7. a.** F	**10. a.** T
b. T	**b.** F	**b.** T

2

2. wouldn't be
3. were
4. would moan
5. were
6. could wish
7. had
8. wouldn't have to deal
9. were
10. thought
11. could find
12. realized
13. would understand
14. insisted
15. might have to wait
16. were
17. could ride

3

2. If my husband were ambitious, he would ask for a raise. OR My husband would ask for a raise if he were ambitious.

3. If I were in shape, I'd play sports. OR I'd play sports if I were in shape.

4. If I had enough time, I would (plan to) study for the exam. OR I would (plan to) study for the exam if I had enough time.

5. If I weren't too old, I would go back to school. OR I would go back to school if I weren't too old.

6. If my boss explained things properly, I could (OR would be able to) do my job. OR I could (OR would be able to) do my job if my boss explained things properly.

7. If I were good at math, I would balance my checkbook. OR I would balance my checkbook if I were good at math.

8. If I didn't feel nervous all the time, I could (OR would be able to) stop smoking. OR I could (OR would be able to) stop smoking if I didn't feel nervous all the time.

9. If I weren't so tired, I wouldn't get up so late. OR I wouldn't get up so late if I weren't so tired.

4

2. I wish I were a handsome prince.
3. I wish I didn't live in the sea.
4. I wish I lived in a castle.
5. I wish I didn't have to swim all day long.
6. I wish I were married to a princess.
7. I wish the fisherman didn't come here every day.
8. I wish his wife didn't always want more.
9. I wish she were satisfied.
10. I wish they left (OR would leave) me alone.

5

2. What would you do if you were the leader of this country?
3. How would you feel if you never needed to sleep?
4. What would you do if you had more free time?
5. What would you ask for if you had three wishes?
6. What would you do if you didn't have to work?
7. Where would you travel if you had a ticket for anywhere in the world?
8. If you could build anything, what would it be?
9. If you could meet a famous person, who would you want to meet?
10. Who would you have dinner with if you could invite three famous people?

6

What would happen to the women if all the men

disappeared
in the world ~~would disappear~~? What would

if
happen to the men ~~when~~ there were no women? Philip Wiley's 1951 science-fiction novel, *The Disappearance*, addresses these intriguing questions. The answers show us how society has changed since the 1950s.

lived
According to Wiley, if men and women ~~live~~ in different worlds, the results would be catastrophic. In Wiley's vision, men are too

aggressive to survive on their own, and women are too helpless. If women didn't control them,

would
men ~~will~~ start more wars. If men ~~aren't~~ there
                                              weren't
to pump gas and run the businesses, women wouldn't be able to manage.

were
If Wiley ~~is~~ alive today, would he write the same novel? Today, a lot of men take care of their children, and a lot of women run businesses. If
                                          would learn
Wiley were here to see these changes, he ~~learns~~ that men are not more warlike than women, and women are not more helpless than men.

I think if all people, both men and women,

                                        would
learned to cooperate more, the world ~~will~~ be a much better place.

7

2. T	4. F	6. T	8. F
3. T	5. F	7. T	

8–12

Answers will vary.

UNIT 24 Past Unreal Conditionals (pages 348–358)

After You Read Items checked: 1, 4, 5, 6, 7

1

2. a. F	6. a. T
b. T	b. F
3. a. F	7. a. T
b. T	b. F
4. a. T	8. a. T
b. T	b. F
5. a. F	
b. T	

2

2. would have gone . . . hadn't lost
3. could have gone . . . hadn't gotten
4. wouldn't have felt . . . had found
5. had . . . been
6. wouldn't have known . . . hadn't shown
7. hadn't rescued . . . wouldn't have saved

8. hadn't helped . . . might have gone
9. wouldn't have been . . . hadn't met
10. couldn't have bought . . . hadn't stayed
11. would have been . . . hadn't been

3

2. I wish I hadn't hit little George when he was trying to help me. I wish I had been nice to him.
3. I wish my father hadn't had a heart attack. I wish I hadn't had to stay and run the business.
4. I wish we had been able to go on a honeymoon. I wish we hadn't needed the money to save the business.
5. I wish I had been able to trick George out of his business. I wish he had accepted my offer to buy his business.
6. I wish I hadn't lost $8,000. I wish George hadn't gotten into trouble with the law because of me.
7. I wish Daddy hadn't been upset about the business. I wish he hadn't yelled at us last night.
8. We wish we had known about George's troubles earlier. We wish we had helped him immediately.

4

2. If Fox hadn't quit high school in order to act, he would have graduated.
3. If Fox hadn't moved to Los Angeles, he might not have gotten several roles on TV.
4. If he hadn't met Tracey Pollan on the TV show *Family Ties*, they might not have gotten married.
5. If Fox hadn't been very successful on TV, he wouldn't have gotten the leading role in *Back to the Future*.
6. If actor Eric Stolz had remained in *Back to the Future*, Fox couldn't have played the lead.
7. If Fox had had free time, he could have watched old movies and sports on TV.
8. If he hadn't become ill, he would have stayed in his TV series *Spin City*.
9. If Fox hadn't stopped working, he might not have written a book called *Lucky Man* about his life and illness.
10. If he hadn't developed Parkinson's disease, he wouldn't have started an organization to search for a cure.

5

Tonight we rented the movie <u>Back to the Future</u>. I thought it was great, and I usually don't like science fiction movies. I might never *have* ~~had~~ seen it if I hadn't read Fox's autobiography, <u>Lucky Man</u>. His book was so good that I wanted to see his most famous movie. Now I wish I *had seen* ~~saw~~ it in the theater when it first came out. It would have been better if we ~~would have~~ *had* watched it on a big screen. Michael J. Fox was very good. He looked really young—just like a teenager. Of course, he still looks very young—I would have recognized him even *if* ~~when~~ I hadn't known he was in the film.

In the movie, Marty McFly goes back in time. He wants to change the past in order to improve his present life as a teenager. It's a funny idea, but it's very different from Fox's real philosophy. He's had a lot of problems in his life, but he still calls himself "Lucky Man." As a teenager, he was too small to become a professional hockey player—but if he hadn't looked so young, he *couldn't* ~~can't~~ have gotten his role in the TV hit series <u>Family Ties</u>. In Hollywood, he had to sell his furniture to pay his bills, but he kept trying to find acting jobs. If he *hadn't* ~~wouldn't have~~, he might never have become a star. Getting Parkinson's disease was a terrible blow, but he has even turned that into something good. If Fox *hadn't* ~~hasn't~~ become sick, he might never ~~had~~ *have* become so close to his family. And he wouldn't have started the Michael J. Fox Foundation to help find a cure.

6

2. a	**5.** a	**7.** b
3. b	**6.** a	**8.** b
4. b		

7–10

Answers will vary.

PART IX From Grammar to Writing

1

My biggest problem in school is my fear of talking in class. <u>My hands always shake</u>(if)I <u>answer a question or present a paper.</u>(If)<u>it is a big assignment, I even feel sick to my stomach</u>.

There are several reasons for my problem, but my family's attitude is the most important. My family motto is, "Children should be seen, but not heard."(Because)<u>my parents never ask for our opinions, we never give them</u>. <u>I can feel my mother's disapproval</u>(if)<u>a talkative friend visits</u>. In addition, my parents classify their children. My older brother is the "Smart One." I am the "Creative One." I think <u>I would do better in school</u>(if)<u>they expected more</u>, but <u>they don't expect much.</u>(Therefore)<u>, I have not tried very hard</u>.

Recently I decided to do something about my problem. I discovered that <u>I feel less nervous about giving a speech in class</u>(if)<u>I role-play my presentation with a friend</u>. I have also joined a discussion club.(As a result)<u>, I get a lot of practice talking</u>. <u>My problem has causes,</u>(so)<u>it must have solutions</u>!

2

2. I became more courageous because he believed in me. OR Because he believed in me, I became more courageous.
3. We worked in groups, so I got used to talking about ideas with classmates.
4. I have gotten a lot of practice. As a result, I feel more confident.
5. Sena didn't understand the question. Therefore, she didn't raise her hand.

3–6

Answers will vary.

UNIT 25 Direct and Indirect Speech

After You Read
Items checked
1. "Your credit card payment is late."
2. "Traffic was bad."
3. "I run a mile every day."
4. "People were more honest ten years ago."

1

"<u>Lying during a job interview is risky business</u>,"(says)Martha Toledo, director of the management consulting firm Maxwell. "<u>The truth has a funny way of coming out</u>." Toledo (tells)the story of one woman applying for a job as an office manager. The woman(told)the interviewer <u>that she had a B.A. degree</u>. Actually, she was eight credits short. She also (said)<u>that she had made $50,000 at her last job</u>. The truth was $10,000 less. "<u>Many firms really do check facts</u>,"(warns)Toledo. In this case, a call to the applicant's company revealed the discrepancies.

Toledo relates a story about another job applicant, George. During an interview, George (reported)<u>that he had quit his last job</u>. George landed the new job and was doing well until the company hired another employee, Pete. George and Pete had worked at the same company. Pete eventually(told)his boss <u>that his old company had fired George</u>.

2

2. wanted	6. said	10. told
3. her	7. her	11. her
4. said	8. told	12. she
5. had	9. wasn't	

3

2. He said (that) his car had broken down (OR broke down).
3. He said (that) he had to drive his aunt to the airport.
4. She said (that) she exercised (OR exercises) every day.
5. He said (that) he had just mailed (OR he just mailed) the check.
6. He said (that) he was (OR he's) 35.

4

3. Lisa said (that) the starting salary was (OR is) good.
4. Ben said (that) he needed (OR needs) more money.

152 FOCUS ON GRAMMAR TEACHER'S MANUAL

5. She said (that) they wanted (OR want) someone with some experience as a programmer.

6. He told her (that) he worked (OR works) as a programmer for Data Systems.

7. Lisa said (that) they needed (OR need) a college graduate.

8. He told her (that) he had graduated (OR graduated) from Florida State.

9. She said (that) they didn't (OR don't) want a recent graduate.

10. He told her (that) he had gotten (OR got) his degree four years ago.

11. She told him (that) it sounded like the right job for him.

12. He said (that) he thought so too.

5

Everyone gets urgent e-mail messages. They

tell you that Bill Gates now ~~wanted~~ *wants* to give

away his money—to YOU! They ~~say~~ *tell* you that a popular floor cleaner kills family pets. They

report that your computer monitor ~~had~~ *has* taken photographs of you. Since I'm a good-hearted person, I used to forward these e-mails to all my friends. Not long ago, a very annoyed friend

~~explains~~ *explained* that the story about killer bananas was a hoax (an untrue story). He told me about these common telltale signs of hoaxes:

! The e-mail always says that it ~~was~~ *is* very urgent. It has lots of exclamation points.

you
! It tells ^that it is not a hoax and quotes

important people. (The quotations are false.)
! It urges you to send the e-mail to everyone you know.

He also ~~told~~ *said* that *Hoaxbusters* (http://hoaxbusters.org) had lists of Internet hoaxes. You can avoid the embarrassment of forwarding all your friends a false warning. So,

before *you* announce that sunscreen ~~had~~ *has* made people blind, check out the story on *Hoaxbusters*!

6

Answers may vary slightly.
2. She said (that) she never missed (OR misses) an aerobics class, but she's going to sleep late on Sunday.

3. She said (that) the weekly staff meeting was on Monday, but it's on Tuesday.

4. She said (that) she loved the meat sauce, but she's a vegetarian.

7–12

Answers will vary.

UNIT 26 Indirect Speech: Tense Changes   (pages 379–390)

After You Read
Items checked
1. "It has been raining for more than 24 hours."
2. "I'm back in my hometown this summer to help."
3. "With another few feet of water, nothing will be safe."
4. "Governments have to do something about climate change."

1

2. c	**5.** a	**8.** b
3. c	**6.** c	**9.** a
4. a	**7.** b	**10.** a

2

2. They said (that) it was going to pass (OR is going to pass) north of here (OR there).
3. They said (that) the gas station had run out of gasoline that afternoon (OR yesterday afternoon).
4. They said (that) it wasn't (OR isn't) really a hurricane, just a big storm.
5. They said (that) they had closed (OR have closed) the bridge because of rising water.
6. They said (that) they wouldn't (OR won't) restore the electricity until today.
7. They said (that) they couldn't (OR can't) reopen the schools for at least a week.
8. They said (that) we ought to use bottled water for a few days.

3

Answers may vary slightly.
2. That's right. He said (that) floods were (OR are) the most widespread of all natural disasters.
3. That's wrong. He said (that) floods were (OR are) usually caused by intense, heavy rainfall.

4. That's wrong. He said (that) a flash flood was (OR is) a flood that comes with little or no warning.
5. That's right. He said (that) a flash flood was (OR is) the most dangerous type of flood.
6. That's wrong. He said (that) flash floods caused (OR cause) 75 percent of all flood-related deaths.
7. That's right. He said (that) we had (OR have) made progress in predicting floods.
8. That's wrong. He said (that) people had to (OR must) improve their protection of the Earth and the environment.
9. That's right. He said (that) replacing grass and dirt with roads and buildings could (OR can) lead to flooding.
10. That's right. He said (that) many scientists believe (OR believed) that global warming was (OR is) causing an increase in the number of floods.
11. That's wrong. He said (that) we couldn't (OR can't) completely stop floods from happening.

4

2. I'm worried about you and Eva.
3. If you weren't so stubborn, you'd pack up and leave right now.
4. I've had some experience with floods.
5. You have to put sandbags in front of your doors.
6. You ought to fill the sinks and bathtubs with clean water.
7. You should buy a lot of batteries.
8. We (OR Uta and I) are worried. We can't stay here.
9. We want to stay with you (OR you and Eva).
10. We're leaving tonight.
11. We should have called you (OR you and Eva) sooner.
12. The storm will hit tonight.
13. The rainfall is going to be very heavy.
14. The storm may (OR might) last for several hours.

5

What is it like to live through a flood? For my report, I interviewed the Nemec family, who experienced last month's floods in our city.
                          they
They reported that ~~we~~ had experienced fear and sadness. On September 14, the family went to a movie. Jerzy, a high school student, said
        couldn't
they ~~can't~~ drive the car home because their

                    said OR *told me*
street was flooded. He ~~told~~ it had happened in only three hours. Mrs. Nemec said that all their
                                      had
belongings were ruined, but that their cat ~~has~~ gone to an upstairs bedroom. They were sad about losing so many things, but she said she
would
~~will~~ have been much sadder to lose the family pet. Jerzy's father also said it had been a
                there
complete mess ~~here~~, and the family had
            that
worked all ~~this~~ week to clean out the house. Anna, who is in junior high school, wanted to keep her old dollhouse. It had belonged to her mother and her mother's mother. At first, her
                    couldn't
father told her that she ~~can't~~ keep it because seeing it would just make her sad. Anna replied that she saw memories in that dollhouse—not just broken wood. In the end, they kept it. Mrs. Nemec said that Anna had taught them
                that day
something important ~~today~~.

6

Items checked
2. should go home immediately
3. may stay closed
4. are dangerous
5. drive slowly
6. avoid driving
7. will close at 1:00
8. will stay open until 5:00
9. will be closed tomorrow
10. will close at noon
11. will stay open until evening
12. are open now

7–10

Answers will vary.

UNIT 27 Indirect Instructions, Commands, Requests, and Invitations (pages 391–400)

After You Read Items checked: 1, 3, 5, 6

1

| 11:00 A.M. | (told. . .)to bring my nightshirt . . . |
| 8:30 P.M. | (told. . .)to relax and watch . . . |

9:30 P.M.	(asked . . .) to explain
11:30 P.M.	(asked . . .) to get . . .
	(instructed . . .) not to leave . . .
7:00 A.M.	(invited . . .) to join him . . .
	(told . . .) not to worry
8:00 A.M.	(told . . .) to get more exercise

2

3. She said to sip some hot herbal tea with honey.
4. She told her not to drink black tea.
5. She said to pinch the place between her upper lip and her nose.
6. She told him to make a toothpaste of one tablespoon of baking soda and a little water.
7. She said to brush his teeth as usual.
8. She told him to spread cool, cooked oatmeal over the rash.
9. She said to try soaking the rash in a cool bath with a quarter cup baking soda.
10. She told him not to scratch the rash.
11. She said to eat onions or garlic every day.
12. She told him to ask his doctor about a vitamin B supplement.

3

Words underlined

to follow him

to show me the ship

to come aboard

to pilot the ship

not to leave the controls

to slow down

to point the ship toward the Earth

not to panic

to wake up

Answers may vary slightly.

2. Follow me.
3. (Please) show me the ship. OR Could you please show me the ship?
4. Come aboard! OR Why don't you come aboard? OR Please come aboard!
5. Pilot the ship.
6. Don't leave the controls.
7. Slow down.
8. Point the ship toward the Earth.
9. Don't panic.
10. Wake up.

4

In writing class today, the teacher asked Juan ^to^ read one of his stories. It was wonderful and everyone in class enjoyed it a lot. After class, the teacher invited me ^to^ read a story in class next week. I don't feel ready to do this. I asked her ~~no~~ ^not^ to call on me next week because I'm having trouble getting ideas. She told me ~~that~~ not to worry, and she said to wait for two weeks. I still was worried about coming up with an idea, so I decided to talk to Juan after class. I asked him ^to^ tell me the source for his ideas. He was really helpful. He said that they came from his dreams! I was very surprised. He ~~said~~ ^told^ me to keep a dream journal for ideas. Then he invited me ×to read some of his journal.× It was very interesting, so I asked him to give me some tips on remembering dreams. (Juan says that everyone dreams, but I usually don't remember my dreams in the morning.) Again, Juan was very helpful. He said ~~getting~~ ^to get^ a good night's sleep because the longer dreams come after a long period of sleep. He also ~~tell~~ ^told^ me to keep my journal by the bed and to write as soon as I wake up. He said ~~to no~~ ^not to^ move from the sleeping position. He also told me not ^to^ think about the day at first. (If you think about your day, you might forget your dreams.) Most important—every night he tells himself ~~that~~ to remember his dreams. These all sound like great ideas, and I want to try them out right away. The only problem is—I'm so excited about this, I'm not sure I'll be able to fall asleep!

5

Items checked

1.	Do	5.	Not Mentioned
2.	Do	6.	Don't Do
3.	Don't Do	7.	Don't Do
4.	Do	8.	Not Mentioned

6

Answers will vary.

7

Answers may vary slightly.

His parents told him (OR said) to take the garbage out, but he didn't.

His parents told him (OR said) to wash the dishes, and he did.

His parents told him (OR said) to do his homework, but he didn't.

His parents told him (OR said) to let the cat in, and he did.

His parents told him (OR said) not to watch any horror movies, but he did.

His parents told him (OR said) not to invite his friends over that night, and he didn't.

8–9

Answers will vary.

UNIT 28 Indirect Questions
(pages 401–412)

After You Read Items checked: 1, 2

1

Underlined items

what I would change about my current job

what my greatest success had been

how much money I was making

if I had cleaned out my car recently

why my employer didn't want me to stay

if I was good enough to work for his company

if I really want this job

Direct questions checked

1, 2, 4, 5, 7, 9

2

2. He asked (her) when the interview was.
3. He asked (her) where the company was.
4. He asked (her) if she needed directions.
5. He asked (her) how long it takes (OR took) to get there.
6. He asked (her) if she was going to drive.
7. He asked (her) who was going to interview her.
8. He asked (her) when they would let her know.

3

Answers may vary slightly.

2. Mr. Stollins asked (Claire OR her) what kind of experience she had.
3. Claire asked (him OR Mr. Stollins) if (OR whether) there was opportunity for promotion.
4. Mr. Stollins asked (her OR Claire) if (OR whether) she was interviewing with other companies.
5. Claire asked (him OR Mr. Stollins) what her responsibilities would be.
6. Claire asked (him OR Mr. Stollins) how job performance was rewarded.
7. Mr. Stollins asked (her OR Claire) what her starting salary at her last job had been.
8. Mr. Stollins asked (her OR Claire) if (OR whether) she had gotten along well with her last employer.
9. Claire asked (him OR Mr. Stollins) if (OR whether) they hired many women.
10. Mr. Stollins asked (her OR Claire) why she had applied for this position.
11. Claire asked (him OR Mr. Stollins) if (OR whether) they had had any major layoffs in the past few years.

4

This morning I interviewed Carlos Lopez for the administrative assistant position. Since this job requires a lot of contact with the public, I did some stress questioning. I asked Mr. Lopez why ~~couldn't he~~ *he couldn't* work under pressure. I also asked him why his supervisor disliked him. Finally, I inquired when he would quit the job

with our company~~?~~ .

Mr. Lopez kept his poise throughout the interview. He answered all my questions calmly, and he had some excellent questions of his own. He asked ˣif we expected changes in the job.ˣ He also wanted to know how often ~~do we evaluate~~ *we evaluate/we evaluated* employees. I was quite impressed when he asked why ~~did I decide~~ *I decided* to join this company.

Mr. Lopez is an excellent candidate for the job, and I believe he will handle the responsibilities well. At the end of the interview, Mr. Lopez inquired when we could let him know our decision~~?~~**.** I asked him ~~if whether~~ *if OR whether* he was considering another job, and he said he was. I think we should act quickly to hire Mr. Lopez.

5

Items checked
OK to Ask
Reason for leaving job
Reason for seeking position that is open
Skills
Job performance

Not OK to Ask
Age
National origin
Height or weight
Marital status
Information about spouse
Arrest record
Financial situation

Illegal questions
2. What nationality are you?
3. Are you married?
4. What does your husband do?
5. Do you owe anyone any money?
6. Have you ever been arrested?
7. How tall are you?

Reported illegal questions
2. He asked her what nationality she was.
3. He asked her if she was married.
4. He asked her what her husband did.
5. He asked her if she (OR they) owed anyone any money.
6. He asked her if she had ever been arrested.
7. He asked her how tall she was.

6–10

Answers will vary.

UNIT 29 Embedded Questions (pages 413–426)

After You Read
Words circled **2.** not   **3.** to do   **4.** we tip
5. I can

1

Underlined phrases
if a tip was necessary at all
how to calculate the right tip instantly
who you should tip here
how tipping properly can get you the best service for your money
how I got along without it
how to tip everyone
who to tip
when to tip
how much to tip

2

2. how I can tell if (OR whether) the tip is included in the bill?
3. if (OR whether) restaurant servers accept tips now?
4. why this happened?
5. if (OR whether) I should tip her instructor.
6. how much I should tip the airport and train porters?
7. who expects a tip and who doesn't.

3

A. 2. how much we are supposed to tip the taxi driver?
B. 1. how we are going to choose.
   2. how much a bus tour costs?
C. 1. what they put in the sauce.
D. 1. where the Forum is?
E. 1. how much the subway costs?
   2. how far you're going.
   3. where they sell them.
F. 1. if (OR whether) they have tour buses that go there.
   2. we could rent a car and drive there?

4

2. how to get
3. when (OR what time) to leave

4. where to go
5. how to figure out
6. who to invite

I wonder ˄*if* you can help me out with this tipping

dilemma. I never know what ~~doing~~ *to do* at the hairdresser's. I don't know if I should tip the

person who washes my hair~~?~~. What about the person who cuts it, and the person who colors it? And what happens if the person is the

owner˄~~?~~ *if* OR *whether* Do you know ~~do~~ I still need to tip him or her? (Although often I'm not even sure who

✗ *is* the owner˄!) Then I never know how much to

tip or where ~~should I~~ *I should* leave the tip~~?~~. Do I leave it on the counter or in the person's hands? What if somebody's hands are wet or have hair color on them? Can I just put the tip in his or her pocket? It all seems so complicated! I can't

imagine how ✗do people figure all this out~~?~~. OR ! But I really need to find out what to do—and FAST! My hair is getting very long and dirty. Please help!

2. a	**5.** b	**7.** a
3. b	**6.** b	**8.** a
4. a		

Answers will vary.

PART X From Grammar to Writing
(pages 427–429)

1

In September 2004, I purchased a computer from your company. After the one-year warranty expired, I bought an extended service contract every year. I always received a renewal notice in the mail that told me <u>that my policy was going to expire in a few weeks</u>. This year, however, I did not receive the notice, and, as a result, I missed the deadline.

Upon realizing this mistake, I immediately called your company and asked <u>if I could renew the service contract</u>. The representative said, "<u>It's too late, Miss</u>." He said that <u>if I wanted to extend my contract, they would have to send someone to my home to inspect my computer</u>. He also told me <u>I would have to pay $160 for this visit</u>. He said <u>that my only other option was to ship my computer back to the company for inspection</u>. I told him <u>that neither of these options was acceptable</u>.

When I asked him <u>why I hadn't been notified that my contract was going to</u> expire, he said, "<u>We don't send notices out anymore</u>." I said <u>that I wanted to make a complaint</u>. He said, "<u>Don't complain to me. I don't even park the cars of the people who make these decisions</u>."

I think <u>that your representatives should be more polite when speaking to customers</u>. I also think <u>that your customers should have been told that they would no longer receive renewal notices in the mail</u>. That way, I would not have missed the deadline. I would, therefore, greatly appreciate it if I could have my service contract renewed without having to go through the inconvenience and expense of having my computer inspected.

Thank you for your attention.

(Examples given after the answers will vary.)

2. direct
3. inside
4. indirect
5. direct
6. word *that* . . . statement
7. direct

Answers will vary.

Notes

Notes

Notes

Using the PowerPoint® presentations

The PowerPoint presentations are saved as .PPS files, which means that they open in Slide Show view and cannot be edited. The instructions in this section explain the basic steps of opening and using the PowerPoint presentations.

2.1. Start a Presentation

2.1.1. Windows

- Insert the PowerPoint® presentations CD-ROM into the CD-ROM drive. On most computers, a Contents page will open automatically.
- If the Contents page does not open automatically, open **My Computer**, double-click on the CD-ROM drive, and then double-click on the "**Start.html**" file.
- On the Contents page, click the link for "**PowerPoint presentations.**"
- Click the link for the presentation you wish to view.

2.1.2. Macintosh

- Insert the PowerPoint® presentations CD-ROM into the CD-ROM drive.
- Double-click on the CD-ROM drive icon, the symbol that looks like a CD.
- Double-click on the "**Start.html**" file.
- On the Contents page, click the link for "**PowerPoint presentations.**"
- Click the link for the presentation you wish to view.

2.2. Advance Through Slides

To advance from one slide to the next or from one animation to the next, click the left mouse button, the **Down Arrow** button (⬇) or the **Right Arrow** button (➡) on the keyboard.

2.3. Go Back Through Slides

To go back to previous slides, or to go back through the animations on a slide, click the **Up Arrow** button (⬆) or the **Left Arrow** button (⬅) on the keyboard.

2.4. Exit a Presentation

Press the "**Esc**" (escape) button on the keyboard.

Technical Support

For Technical Support, email
EPSupport@pearsoned.com

License Agreement